CompTIA Network+

All in One Complete Training Guide

www.ipspecialist.net

Document Control

Proposal Name	:	CompTIA Network+ Workbook
Document Version	:	1.0
Document Release Date	:	March 2018
Reference	:	CompTIA

Feedback:

If you have any comments regarding the quality of this book, or otherwise alter it to suit your needs better, you can contact us by email at info@ipspecialist.net

Please make sure to include the book title and ISBN in your message

About IPSpecialist

IPSPECIALIST LTD. IS COMMITTED TO EXCELLENCE AND DEDICATED TO YOUR SUCCESS.

Our philosophy is to treat our customers like family. We want you to succeed, and we are willing to do anything possible to help you make it happen. We have the proof to back up our claims. We strive to accelerate billions of careers with great courses, accessibility, and affordability. We believe that continuous learning and knowledge evolution are most important things to keep re-skilling and up-skilling the world.

Planning and creating a specific goal is where IPSpecialist helps. We can create a career track that suits your visions as well as develop the competencies you need to become a professional Network Engineer. We can also assist you with the execution and evaluation of proficiency level based on the career track you choose, as they are customized to fit your specific goals.

We help you STAND OUT from the crowd through our detailed IP training content packages.

Course Features:

- *Self-Paced learning*
  - O Learn at your own pace and in your own time
- *Covers Complete Exam Blueprint*
  - O Prep-up for the exam with confidence
- *Case Study Based Learning*
  - O Relate the content to real-life scenarios
- *Subscriptions that suit you*
  - O Get more pay less with IPS Subscriptions
- *Career Advisory Services*
  - O Let industry experts plan your career journey
- *Virtual Labs to test your skills*
  - O With IPS vRacks, you can testify your exam preparations
- *Practice Questions*
  - O Practice Questions to measure your preparation standards
- *On Request Digital Certification*
  - O On digital request certification from IPSpecialist LTD.

About the Authors:

This book has been compiled with the help of multiple professional engineers. These engineers specialize in different fields like Networking, Security, Cloud, Big Data, IoT, etc. Each engineer develops content in its specialized field that is compiled to form a comprehensive certification guide.

About the Technical Reviewers:

Nouman Ahmed Khan

AWS-Architect, CCDE, CCIEX5 (R&S, SP, Security, DC, Wireless), CISSP, CISA, CISM is a Solution Architect working with a major telecommunication provider in Qatar. He works with enterprises, mega-projects, and service providers to help them select the best-fit technology solutions. He also works closely with a consultant to understand customer business processes and helps select an appropriate technology strategy to support business goals. He has more than 14 years of experience working in Pakistan/Middle-East and UK. He holds a Bachelor of Engineering Degree from NED University, Pakistan, and M.Sc. in Computer Networks from the UK.

Abubakar Saeed

Abubakar Saeed has more than twenty-five years of experience, Managing, Consulting, Designing, and implementing large-scale technology projects, extensive experience heading ISP operations, solutions integration, heading Product Development, Presales, and Solution Design. Emphasizing on adhering to Project timelines and delivering as per customer expectations, he always leads the project in the right direction with his innovative ideas and excellent management.

Muhammad Yousuf

Muhammad Yousuf is a professional technical content writer. He is Cisco Certified Network Associate in Routing and Switching, holding bachelor's degree in Telecommunication Engineering from Sir Syed University of Engineering and Technology. He has both technical knowledge and industry sounding information, which he uses perfectly in his career.

Afreen Moin

Afreen Moin is a professional Technical Content Developer. She holds a degree in Bachelor of Engineering in Telecommunications from Dawood University of Engineering and Technology. She has a great knowledge of computer networking and attends several training programs. She possesses a keen interest in research and design related to computers which reflect in her career.

Free Resources:

With each workbook bought from Amazon, IPSpecialist offers free resources to our valuable customers. Once you buy this book you will have to contact us at support@ipspecialist.net or tweet @ipspecialistnet to get this limited time offer without any extra charges.

Free Resources Include:

Exam Practice Questions in Quiz Simulation: IP Specialists' Practice Questions have been developed keeping in mind the certification exam perspective. The collection of these questions from our technology workbooks is prepared keeping the exam blueprint in mind, covering not only important but necessary topics as well. It is an ideal document to practice and revise your certification.

Career Report: This report is a step by step guide for a novice who wants to develop his/her career in the field of computer networks. It answers the following queries:

- Current scenarios and future prospects.
- Is this industry moving towards saturation or are new opportunities knocking at the door?
- What will the monetary benefits be?
- Why to get certified?
- How to plan and when will I complete the certifications if I start today?
- Is there any career track that I can follow to accomplish specialization level?

Furthermore, this guide provides a comprehensive career path towards being a specialist in the field of networking and also highlights the tracks needed to obtain certification.

IPS Personalized Technical Support for Customers: Good customer service means helping customers efficiently, in a friendly manner. It is essential to be able to handle issues for customers and do your best to ensure they are satisfied. Providing good service is one of the most important things that can set our business apart from the others of its kind.

Great customer service will result in attracting more customers and attain maximum customer retention.

IPS is offering personalized TECH support to its customers to provide better value for money. If you have any queries related to technology and labs you can simply ask our technical team for assistance via Live Chat or Email.

Become an Author & Earn with Us

If you are interested in becoming an author and start earning passive income, IPSpecialist offers "Earn with us" program. We all consume, develop and create content during our learning process, certification exam preparations, and during searching, developing and refining our professional careers. That content, notes, guides, worksheets and flip cards among other material is normally for our own reference without any defined structure or special considerations required for formal publishing.

IPSpecialist can help you craft this 'draft' content into a fine product with the help of our global team of experts. We sell your content via different channels as:

1. Amazon – Kindle
2. eBay
3. LuLu
4. Kobo
5. Google Books
6. Udemy and many 3rd party publishers and resellers

Table of Contents

About this Workbook

This workbook covers all the information you need to pass the CompTIA Network+ No1-007 exam. The workbook is designed to take a practical approach to learning with real-life examples and case studies.

- ➢ Covers complete CompTIA Network+ No1-006blueprint
- ➢ Summarized content
- ➢ Case Study based approach
- ➢ Ready to practice labs on VM
- ➢ 100% pass guarantee
- ➢ Mind maps

CompTIA Certifications

CompTIA is a performance-based certification that helps you develop a career in IT fundament by approving the hands-on skills required to troubleshoot, configure, and manage both wired and wireless networks.

CompTIA certifications help individuals build exceptional in Information Technology and enable organizations to form a skilled and confident staff. CompTIA certifications have four IT certification series that different test knowledge standards-from entry level to expert level. CompTIA offers certification programs at the core level to professional level, which begins with the core IT fundamentals, infrastructure, cybersecurity leads to the professional level.

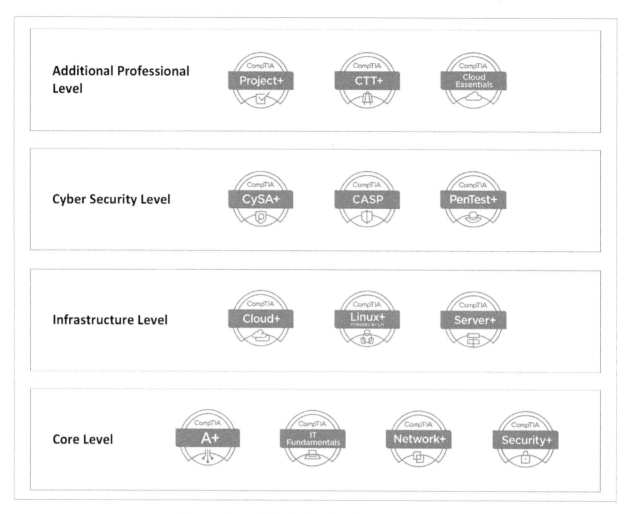

Figure 1. CompTIA offering Certification Programs

How does CompTIA Certifications help?

CompTIA certifications are a de facto standard in the networking industry, which helps you boost your career in the following ways:

1. Gets your foot in the door by launching your IT career
2. Boosts your confidence level
3. Proves knowledge which helps improve employment opportunities

As for companies, CompTIA certifications is a way to:

1. Screen job applicants
2. Validate the technical skills of the candidate
3. Ensure quality, competency, and relevancy
4. Improve organization credibility and customer loyalty
5. Meet the requirement in maintaining organization partnership level with OEMs
6. Helps in Job retention and promotion

CompTIA Network & Cloud Certification Tracks

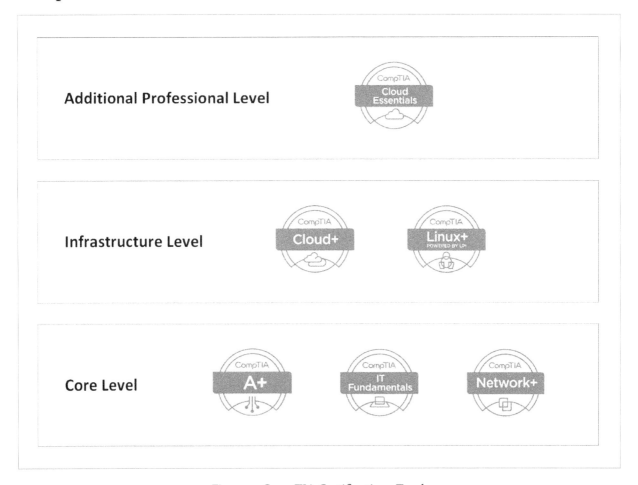

Figure 2. CompTIA Certifications Track

About the CompTIA Network+ Certification Exam

Candidates are encouraged to use this document to help prepare for the CompTIA Network+ N10-006 exam. This exam will certify that the successful candidate has the knowledge and skills required to troubleshoot, configure and manage common network wireless and wired devices.

Knowledge and skills include:

- Establishing basic network design and connectivity
- Understanding and maintaining network documentation
- Identifying network limitations and weaknesses
- Implementing network security, standards, and protocols

The successful candidate will have a basic understanding of emerging technologies including unified communications, mobile, cloud and virtualization technologies.

Exam details

Required exam:	N10-006 JK0-023 (for CompTIA Academy Partners only)
Number of questions:	Maximum of 90
Types of questions:	Multiple choice and performance-based
Length of test:	90 minutes
Recommended Experience:	• CompTIA A+ Certified, or equivalent
	• Minimum of 9 months of experience in network support or administration; or academic training
Passing score:	720 (on a scale of 100—900)

Exam objectives (domains)

The table below lists the domains measured by this examination and the extent to which they are represented:

Domain	% of Examination
Network Architecture	22%
Network Operations	20%
Network Security	18%
Troubleshooting	24%
Industrial Standards, Practices & Network Theory	16%
Total	100%

Chapter 1: Network Architecture

Functions and Applications of Networking Devices

The integrant of a network architecture is consists of numerous devices that perform a definite function or set of functions in a network. It is essential to understand the purpose of each device so that the individual would be familiar with the functionalities of the devices that are used in the network. In this section, we will cover these requirements.

Router

Routers are the main networking devices designed to route traffic towards the destination. Router functions at layer 3 (Internet layer of OSI Model). Routers are the devices that link up the with the internet and make the World Wide Web conceivable. They also split and combines the network. Routers are more intelligent than switches.

Functions

- Routers work on Internet Protocol ((IP) specifically on the logical address also known as IP address.
- Router Perform actions on the layer 3, i.e., Network Layer of the OSI model.
- They route traffic from one network to the desired destination network.
- As described, a Router is an intelligent device that either first finds out the network or the traffic that relates to their network.
- After deciding, the router forwards the traffic the to the required destination.

Applications

- Routers provide interfaces for different physical network connections such as copper cables, optic fiber, or wireless transmission.
- The Network Administrator can configure the routing table manually as well as dynamically.
- Routers learn its routing table by using static and dynamic routing protocols.
- Multiple routers are used in interconnected networks.
- Dynamic exchange of information about the destination is possible by the dynamic routing protocol; the administrator will have to advertise routing path manually for static networks.

Switch

Switches are the network devices that optimize traffic flow on the network. Switches connect the network devices by providing physical interfaces in a network. Switches are smarter than the hub; it learns the Media Access Control Address (MAC Address) also known as the physical address of the device.

Functions

- Switches filter the MAC addresses of all the connected devices.
- Switches perform functioning on Data link layer (Layer 2) of OSI model.
- It learns the physical address of all the devices that are connected to it and then uses the MAC address to control traffic flow.
- Switches forward the data frames only to the destination address rather than forward the data to all the connected ports.
- Switches reduce the traffic by spontaneous segmentation of network.

Applications

- It connects the departments of one company to the other without involving in their communication.
- Switches can transfer large files within the local area network without affecting the upper layer traffic flow of the network.
- Switches can be used to create virtual local area networks(VLANs) to improve the flexibility of the network.
- It is very efficient as it does not forward the data that have errors.
- It avoids collision domains.

Multilayer Switch:

Although a basic switch works entirely on Data-Link layer (layer 2) of the OSI model, a multilayer switch can perform its function on both layer 2 and layer 3. Multilayer switches are also called layer 3 switches and intelligent switch.

Functions

- Multilayer switches have an advance functioning, a switch with some router characteristics.
- Multilayer switches can be connected to other multilayer switches to provide scalability to the network.
- It can be logically segmented into multiple broadcast domains.
- Layer 3 switch must be capable enough to make a forwarding decision.
- Switches must store network flows so that forwarding can occur in hardware.

Applications

- Multilayer switches efficiently used in VLANs networks.
- Multilayer switches can create VLANs and decide VLANs route.
- Multilayer switches can connect to other multilayer switches and basic switch to extend the VLANs throughout the organization

Firewall

Firewalls are physical devices and software that defend an internal network or system from unauthorized access by performing as a filter. Firewalls are an essential mechanism to fight against the malicious activities on the internet.

Functions

- Firewalls filter the flow of traffic that either be inbound traffic or outbound traffic of a network.
- Itinspects each packet by certain rules and policies.
- By functioning, the firewall has two types of network-based firewall and host-based firewall.
- Network-based firewall is mostly implemented on hardware appliances such as they protect the whole network, but they cannot fight against the traffic generating from inside the network itself.
- Host-based firewall installed on the 'host' that provides the firewall services, it will come across a network technology in future.

Applications

- The firewall provides the platform for IPSec to implement virtual private networks.
- Monitoring security-related actions.
- Protects from several sorts of IP spoofing and routing attacks.
- Provides a suitable platform for various internet activity that does not require security such as NAT, internet usage audits or Logs.

Host-based Intrusion Detection System

Host-based Intrusion Detection System (HIDS) is a system of sensors that are installed on various servers within the organization and maintained by some central manager. HIDS can protect only the events associated with the servers on which they are installed.

Functions

Based upon the functionalities HIDS can be divided into five basic types.

- *Log Analyzer:* Find out log entities that may predict a security incident.
- *Signature-based Sensors:* Analyses inbound traffic and contrast them with a set of built-in security actions signatures.
- *System Call Analyzer:* inspect an application's system calls, analyse the action and contrast it to a database of signatures.
- *Application Behavior Analyzer:* inspect an application's system calls to see if it allows doing such action.
- *File integrity Reviewer:* a review for changes in files

Applications

- Protect specific system activities.
- Certify success or failure of an attack
- Appropriate for encrypted and switched domain.
- Used along with the IDS/IPS and firewalls to provide an extra layer of protection from anything that penetrates the previous layer.

Intrusion Detection System /Intrusion Prevention System

An Intrusion Detection System (IDS) is much greater than a firewall. Effectively, an IDS is an intelligent proctor of network traffic it looks after the normal traffic and points out the odd traffic as a threat but not to prevent them.

An Intrusion Prevention System (IPS) is quite similar to an IDS but can acquire more actions in response to a threat than an IDS. IPS point out the attacks from inside and outside intruders as well as prevent them being successful.

Functions

- IDS is designed to detect security violations.
- IDS aids in reducing damage caused by hacking.
- IPS gather the prevent the action of a firewall with the in-depth packet analysis function of an IDS.
- IDS/IPS can be configured to notify the network administrator when the threat has been detected.
- IPS can address the detected threat by adjusting connections or even shut down a port.

Applications

- Easy deployment as one sensor can protect hundreds of systems.
- A single control point for traffic can protect thousands of systems placed below the device, not concerned about the operating system or application.
- Protect against network Dos, DDoS attacks, and SYN flood, etc.
- IPSs are reconfigurable to each application that required protection.

Access Point(Wired/Wireless)

An access point is consists of a wireless switch with a router module. Furthermore, access points are both wireless and wired. An access point is a device that connects a Wireless Local Area Network (WLAN), mostly in buildings, offices or homes. An access point connects to a wired router, switch, or hub through Ethernet cable, and designs a Wi-Fi signal to the specified area.

Functions

- An AP is responsible for connecting the number of wired/wireless network host.
- An AP allows the communication between the connected wired/wireless networks.
- WAP have antennas to provide signal wirelessly and an Ethernet port to connect to wired networks.

Applications

- AP can be used as a wireless bridge between the two wired networks.
- APs with a router module possess the ability to connect wired/wireless clients to the Internet.
- QoS is achieved by the access points on wired networks that access the information confidentially.

Content Filter:

A content filter is an extraordinary device that can be configured to block some documents based on their content that might be objectionable. The content filter helps decide which content is suitable for screening and access through a given system.

Functions

- Different types of the content filter based on the type of content they filter e.g, Application-layer content filtering configured to be more sensitive than the Network filtering.
- Application layer content filters can be configuring in such a way that the user disallowed the website that contains inappropriate data or graphics.
- Control filter controls by the software commonly known as web-filtering programs or censorware.

Applications

- Control filter usually used in public Wi-Fi access points and places that promotes BYOD policy.
- It is often used in schools, colleges, and libraries to protect from offensive websites or harmful images.
- It can be used in employer's wireless networks to protect from illegal activities.
- Control filtering on wireless networks can also help in providing sustainability and increase productivity in many organizations by blocking time-wasting websites such as Twitter, Facebook, etc.

Load Balancer

A load balancer is a device that acts as a reverse proxy and divides network or application traffic across some servers. A load balancer acts as the traffic police sitting in front of the servers and routing client requests across the servers that execute it in a way that the speed and capacity will not be compromised and also assure that not any server is overloaded, might be caused degradation in performance.

Functions

A load balancer performs the following functions:

- It distributes a load of a network and client requests efficiently.
- Assures great accessibility and stability by sending client request only to the active servers
- Provides flexibility by increasing or decreasing the servers on demand.

Applications

- Load balancer acts upon layer 4 and layer 7 of the OSI model.
- Layer 4 load balancer manages data found in networks and transport layer protocols such as IP, TCP, FTP, and UDP.
- Layer 7 load balancers divide request based upon data found in application layer protocols such as HTTP.
- The load balancer can handle changeable workloads and rank up to millions of requests per seconds.
- Assist routing requests to multiple applications on a single EC2 instance.

Hub

A hub is a device that possesses many ports into which connection can be built. Hub connects all the nodes of the network in a star topology network. All the devices in the network connect directly through a single cable via Ethernet cable.

Functions

- Hub performs its function at the physical layer (Layer 1) of the OSI model.
- The basic function of a hub is to transmit data from one device and send to all the connected ports including the transmitting device.
- It broadcasts the data but the further procedure is handled by the intended receiver that addressing in the frame.
- To avoid a broadcasting collision, the hub applies Carrier Sense Multiple Access with Collision Detection (CSMA/CD) techniques on the transmitter.

Applications

- Active Hubs regenerate a signal before forwarding it to all the nodes and needs a power supply.
- Small hubs with four to five hubs with necessity cables are enough to create a small network at low cost.
- Hubs with more ports are also available for the networks that demand a higher capacity.

Analog Modem

Analog Modem, an acronym for MOdulator and DEModulator. The modulator modulates an analog carrier signal to encode digital information whereas demodulator demodulates the signal to decode the transmitted information.

Functions

- The main objective of an analog modem is to generate a signal that can be transmitted easily and decoded to regenerate the original data.
- These signals are transmitted through telephone lines and demodulated by another modem at the receiver end to understand the digital data.

Applications

- A modem permits entirely non-digital way to provide connectivity between network areas.
- Enable devices to discuss existing infrastructure, as phone-lines or coax.

Packet Shaper

A packet shaper is mainly a hardware device that can investigate traffic at a granular level. Initially, it analyses the traffic flow pass through it and classifies all traffic with minimum assistance from a network administrator.

Functions

- The shaping functionality is usually built-in routers and some switches to deal with times when network require outpaces the ability of a device or its port.
- Packet shaper controls the inbound and outbound traffic flows when congestion occurs.

Applications

- Packet shaper provides bandwidth management solution that efficiently works on applications running over Wide Area Networks and on the Internet.
- Packet shaper provides management and to the web-connected application such as cloud applications, social media, audio/video communication.

- It provides smart QoS tools for safe, superior application and web content varieties while containing the influence of unacceptable traffic.

VPN Concentrator

A virtual private network is a network connection that is designed to secure, although it flows through an unsecured network, usually the Internet. Tunneling between two private networks over the public internet make VPN network secure. VPN concentrators create tunneling in VPN networks that receive multiple VPN connections from the remote access site.

Functions

- VPN concentrators perform the following functions:

  1. Settlement of tunnels

  2. Managing tunneling parameters

  3. Authenticating users and assigning users addresses

  4. Encoding and decoding data

  5. Managing security keys

  6. Managing data transfer over the tunnel

- The VPN concentrators perform this functions by using standard protocols such as Point-to-Point Tunnelling Protocol (PPTP) or Layer 2 Tunnelling Protocol (L2TP)

Applications

- VPN concentrators provide high availability, high-performance scalability components.
- VPN concentrators are capable of supporting 100 to 10,000 remote-access users simultaneously.

Usage and Applications of Networking Services

After getting familiar with the networking devices and its functional characteristic, now you are able to create your network infrastructure. For this purpose, you should able to correlate the functions of various networking devices with their services used in your network.

This section will describe a remote access network and their related protocols.

Virtual Private Network (VPN)

A Virtual Private Network (VPN) can be best described as an encrypted tunnel between two computer devices across an insecure network such as the Internet. Although, a VPN

is designed to create virtual private, and secure network using encapsulation protocol, also called tunneling protocol.

VPNs provide impressive flexibility in network infrastructure and a reduced total amount of ownership in the WAN topology. It provides cost-effective and secure encrypted communication upon the leased lines.

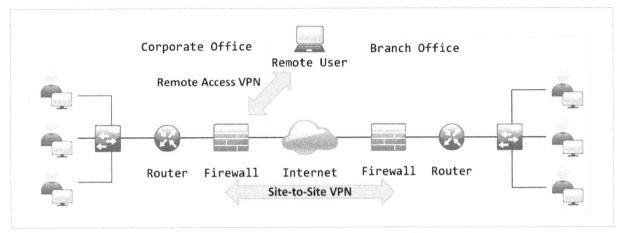

Figure 1-01: Virtual Private Network

Types of VPNs

There are two basic types of VPNs:

1) Remote Access VPN
2) Site-to-Site VPN

1) *Remote access VPN*

Remote access VPN allows the user to connect to a private network and access its services remotely. The connection is secure and private between the user and the private network although it built on the Internet. It is useful for business and home users.

2) *Site-to-Site VPN*

A site to site VPN is also called as Server-to-Server VPN and is mainly used incorporates. Enterprises with branch offices in different geographical locations use site-to-site VPN to connect the network of one branch office to another branch office. Site-to-site VPN practically provide a virtual bridge between the Enterprises and their geographically distant site offices.

VPN Protocols

The types mentioned above of VPNs are based on different security protocols. Each of these has individual features and security levels.

IPSec

Internet Protocol Security (IPSec) provides secure Internet communication over an IP network. Practically IPSec can be used to provide secure communication on all TCP/IP related communications.

IPSec provides three main security services:

- **Data Verification**: Verify the data received is surely from the intended receiver
- **Protection from data manipulating**: protects the data from being changeable during the transmission
- **Privacy of Transactions:** Ensures the transmitted data is readable only by the intended receiver

IPSec has two main modes:

1) **Transport Mode:** used to send and receive encrypted data packets among the same networks.
2) **Tunneling mode**: used to send and receive encrypted data among the different networks.

GRE

Generic Routing Encapsulation (GRE) is a protocol used to encapsulate many network layer protocols that have to be sent on point-to-point links in IP network.

It encapsulates the original payload into an outer packet that sent through the tunnel. GRE is a flexible tool that can be used to send multicast and IPV6 packets.

SSL VPN

Secure Socket Layer (SSL) protocol used to provide secure authentication and communication privacy over the Internet. SSL protocol uses cryptography technique and is usually used in e-commerce for online shopping websites and service providers. SSL connections appear with https instead of http in the URL.

PTP/PPTP

Point-to-Point Tunneling Protocol (PPTP) is used to create a secure tunnel between the two points on a network implement on other protocol specifically on Point-to-Point Protocol (PPP).

PPTP cannot authenticate some tunnels, but Layer 2 Tunnelling Point (L2TP) can do. That's why it has been highly replaced by L2TP.

Remote Authenticate Dial-In User Service (RADIUS)

Remote Authenticate Dial-In User Service (RADIUS) offers a centralized system for AAA that describes Authentication, Authorization, and Accounting. RADIUS server referred to the remote access server become the clients of another remote access server.

RADIUS server's performance based on certificates, Kerberos, and other authentication types. RADIUS used UDP protocol between the servers to broadcast their communication.

Remote Access Service (RAS)

Remote Access Service (RAS) is a remote access solution that is compatible with MS windows server products. RAS provides users to access the same at the same time from remote locations, yet sometimes access is very slow.

RAS is implemented in Windows NT server as RAS server but in Windows server 2000,03,08 as Routing and Remote Access Server (RRAS). It can provide dial-up connections using the modem as well as VPN connections using WAN mini ports.

Terminal Access Controller Access Control System (TACACS/TACACS+)

Terminal Access Controller Access Control System (TACACS) primarily represents two evolutions of the protocol. TACACS developed in the early ARPANet days, possessed limited functions and used UDP (connectionless protocol). Its architecture is based on Authentication, Authorization, and Accounting (AAA).

TACACS+ is a service that is similar to RADIUS but uses TCP (connection-oriented protocol) between the RAS and TACACS+ server for their communication because TCP has several advantages over UDP. TACACS + also follows AAA architecture, but it separates their functions and adds encryption function.

Web Services

Web services use universal standard web technologies to communicate between two electronic devices over the Internet. Web services are designed to be accessible by other applications. There are two participants to make web services system.

A service provider is providing the information and the service requester that is requesting for the information. Web services software usually written in markup languages such as HTTP, XML, etc.

Unified Voice Services

Unified communication is a set of integrated applications that have been designed to support a single communications platform as one entity. Unified communications usually enable the organization to use integrated voice, data, and video in the unified supported platform.

Unified voice services provide integrated real-time or near real-time unified messaging, emails and voice calls.

Network Controllers

In early stages, computers are controlled by Network Interface Cards (NICs) that were used to convert the parallel digital stream into serial digital stream delivered from the computer and could be sent over the wire. As the time passes, network controller becomes intelligent by adding software and services. Now network controller supports many services like broadband cable systems, wireless, voice, satellite and so on.

Network Services

This section describes installation and configuration of some important network services. It also discusses the purpose and influence of this network services in your network.

Dynamic Host Configuration Protocol (DHCP)

Dynamic Host Configuration Protocol (DHCP) provides administrators with a methodology to dynamically assign IP address rather than manually.

DHCP can provide the following parameters:

- IP addresses
- Subnet Masks
- Default gateways
- DNS server and much more

There are four processes to complete DHCP operation

1. **DHCPDiscover:** when a DHCP client boots up, it broadcast a DHCP discover message, looking for a DHCP server.

2. **DHCPOffer:** If a DHCP server exists on the local site, it will reply with a DHCP offer, containing the offered IP address, subnet mask, etc.

3. **DHCPRequest:** marking that it will accept the offered protocol information.

4. **DHCPAck:** At last, the server acknowledging the client's approval of offered protocol information

Static Vs. Dynamic IP Addressing

There are two possible ways to configure IP addressing on a host device. Network Administrator can either manually approach each and every network device and assign an IP address to each device. This technique is called Static IP Addressing. Static IP addressing can be easy to deploy on a small-scale network, but it is very difficult to deploy on a large-scale network having hundreds or thousands of networking devices. Another

limitation of static IP addressing is; an administrator has to remove IP address from the network device when it is not used to assign it to any other device.

Another approach is Dynamic IP addressing. Dynamic IP addressing is an automated procedure of assigning IP address and other network related parameters such as DNS information to the client. Using Dynamic Host Configuration Protocol (DHCP), the network administrator can configure a DHCP server and assign a pool of addresses. DHCP automatically listens for DHCP request packets and bind the IP addresses from the pool with a lease. When a lease expires, the address is sent back to the pool.

DHCP Relay and Server:

DHCP Relay agent forwards the DHCP packets from server to client and Client to server. Relay agent helps the communication like forwarding request and replies between client and servers. Relay agent, when receiving a DHCP message, it generates a new DHCP request to send it out from another interface with including default gateway information as well as Relay-Agent information option (Option-82). When the Relay Agent gets the reply from the server, it removes the Option 82 and forwards it back to the client.

Determining the Packet Forwarding Address

By using UDP broadcast, DHCP client sends an initial DHCP-Discover packet because it initially doesn't have network information to which they are connected. As we know, the router does not forward the broadcast request, by configuring the router interface that is receiving the DHCP-Discover broadcast packets to forward it to a helper address. More than one helper address can also configure on an interface. This is what DHCP relay agent is. In a Cisco Router, by using "ip helper-address" command in interface configuration mode, DHCP relay agent can be configured.

Relay Agent Information Option

When a DHCP relay agent added the information in the DHCP-Discover broadcast packet, it added Remote ID and Circuit ID as a relay agent information (Option 82) and Unicast it to the DHCP Server. The server uses this information to assign IP addresses, security policies, Quality of Service and Access Control. When the Server sends the packet back to the relay agent, Option 82 information will be stripped from the packet and send it back to the client who initiates the request

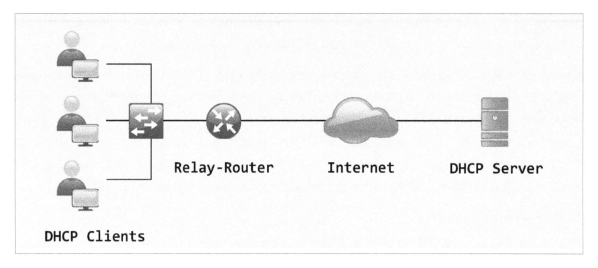

Figure 1-02: DHCP Relay Agent

DHCP Protocol Operations:

DHCP is the process of allocating the IP address dynamically so that these addresses are assigned automatically and also that they can be reused when hosts don't need them. *Round Trip time* is the measurement of time from discovery of DHCP server until obtaining the leased IP address. RTT can be used to determine the performance of DHCP.

IP SLAs DHCP Relay Agent Options

IP SLA (Service Level Agreement) DHCP option uses relay agent option 82 information and is used for releasing the IP address when it is not in use, or the DHCP operation ends.

Reserved/Excluded addresses: Reserved addresses are those addresses configured on the DHCP server for internal servers, printers, routers, workstations, etc. These addresses will not be assigned to any hosts.

DHCP Lease

DHCP Lease can be defined as time configured on a DHCP server to allow a host to use assigned IP address. When this lease expires, the client has to renew the lease.

Lab 1-1: DHCP Configuration

Case Study: In this case, in a small network configure Dynamic Host Configuration Protocol (DHCP) to obtain ip address automatically by creating a DHCP pool on Router.

Note: In this Lab, we use Cisco IOS Software Release 15.4(2) T to configure DHCP

Topology Diagram:

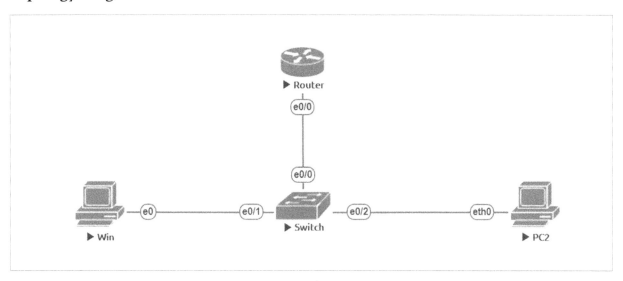

Router Configuration:

Router>

Router>en

Router#config t

Enter configuration commands, one per line. End with CNTL/Z.

Router(config)#host R1

R1(config)#int e0/0

R1(config-if)#ip address 192.168.10.1 255.255.255.0

`// Assigning IP address to Ethernet interface of Router`

R1(config-if)#no shutdown

R1(config-if)#

`*May  9 01:10:57.996: %LINK-3-UPDOWN: Interface Ethernet0/0, changed state to up`

`*May  9 01:10:59.000: %LINEPROTO-5-UPDOWN: Line protocol on Interface Ethernet0/0, changed state to up`

R1(config-if)#exit

R1(config)#ip dhcp pool IP10

R1(dhcp-config)#network 192.168.10.0 255.255.255.0

R1(dhcp-config)#default 192.168.10.1

R1(dhcp-config)#exit

```
// Configuring DHCP pool
```

R1(config)#ip dhcp exc 192.168.10.1 192.168.10.10

```
// Configuring DHCP excluded addresses
```

R1(config)#exit

R1#

```
*May  9 01:20:11.810: %SYS-5-CONFIG_I: Configured from console by console
```

R1#show ip dhcp pool

```
Router                                                    —    □    ×

*May 14 20:59:07.322: %LINK-3-UPDOWN: Interface Ethernet0/0, changed state to up
*May 14 20:59:08.330: %LINEPROTO-5-UPDOWN: Line protocol on Interface Ethernet0/
0, changed state to up
R1#show ip dhcp ?
  binding   DHCP address bindings
  conflict  DHCP address conflicts
  database  DHCP database agents
  import    Show Imported Parameters
  pool      DHCP pools information
  relay     Miscellaneous DHCP relay information
  server    Miscellaneous DHCP server information

R1#show ip dhcp pool

Pool IP10 :
 Utilization mark (high/low)    : 100 / 0
 Subnet size (first/next)       : 0 / 0
 Total addresses                : 254
 Leased addresses               : 0
 Pending event                  : none
 1 subnet is currently in the pool :
 Current index        IP address range                    Leased addresses
 192.168.10.1         192.168.10.1    - 192.168.10.254     0
R1#
```

As shown in the output, no DHCP address is leased yet.

Windows PC (PC1) Configuration:

Go to Windows PC and Login with password "**ipspecialist.**"

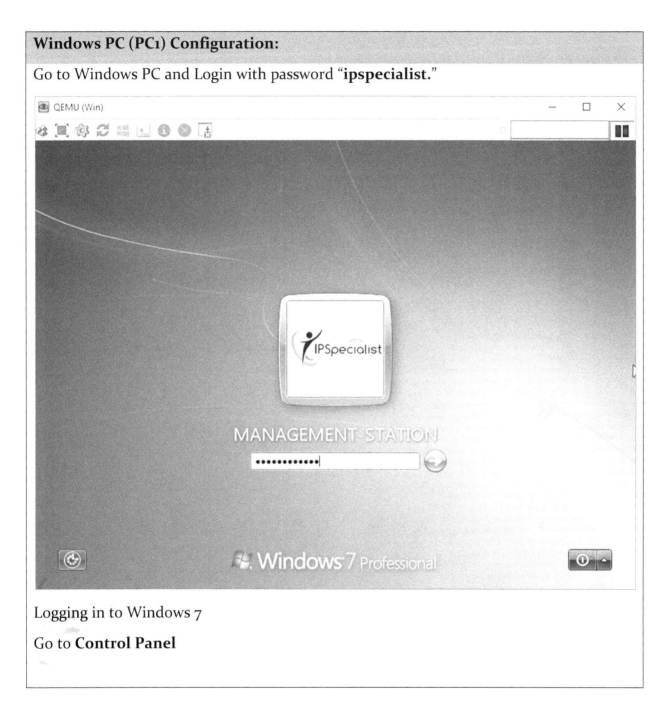

Logging in to Windows 7

Go to **Control Panel**

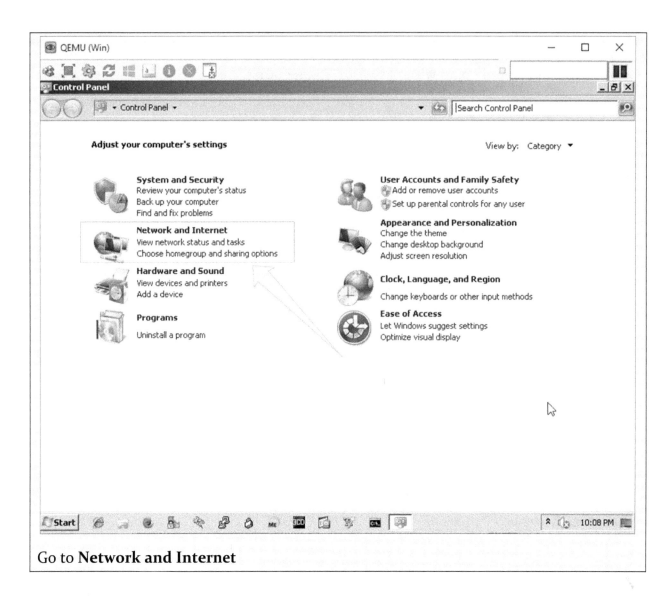

Go to **Network and Internet**

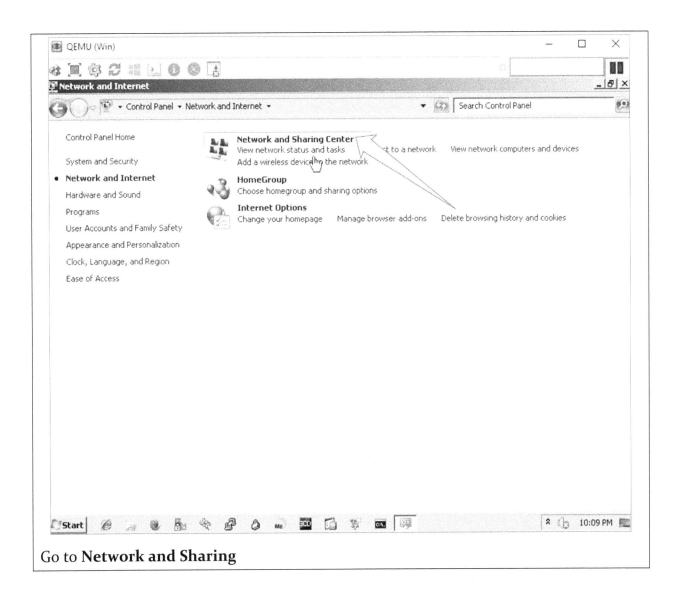

Go to **Network and Sharing**

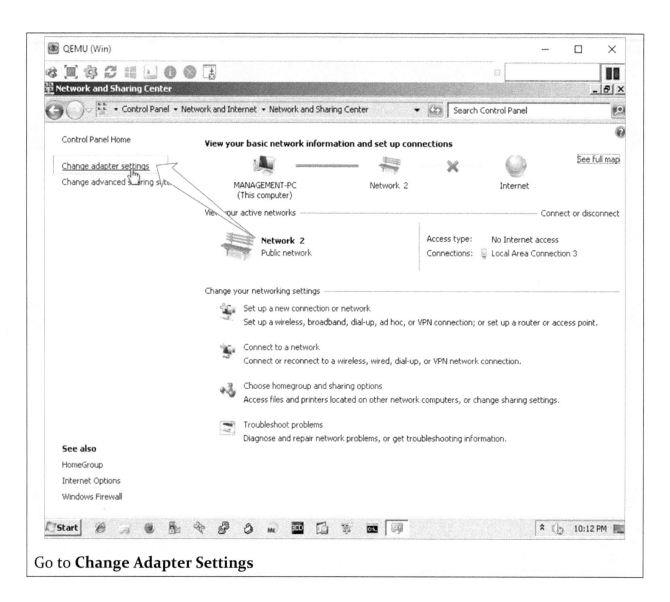

Go to **Change Adapter Settings**

Select the **LAN Adapter** and go to **properties**

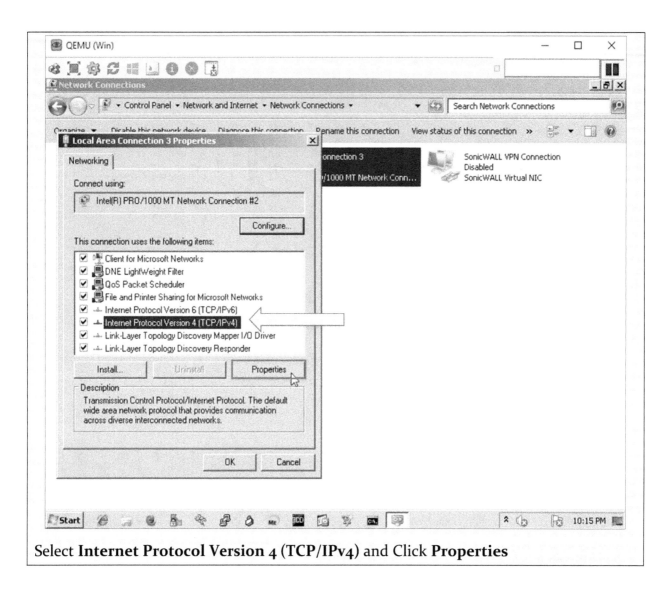

Select **Internet Protocol Version 4 (TCP/IPv4)** and Click **Properties**

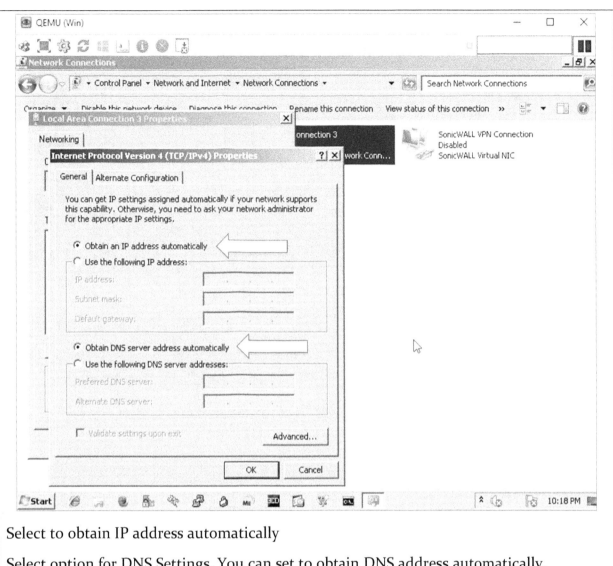

Select to obtain IP address automatically

Select option for DNS Settings. You can set to obtain DNS address automatically.

Virtual PC (PC2) Configuration:

Go to VPC and type "**IP DHCP**" to configure VPC to obtain IP address via DHCP.

```
PC2                                                    —    □    ×

Welcome to Virtual PC Simulator, version 1.0 (0.8c)
Dedicated to Daling.
Build time: Dec 31 2016 01:22:17
Copyright (c) 2007-2015, Paul Meng (mirnshi@gmail.com)
All rights reserved.

VPCS is free software, distributed under the terms of the "BSD" licence.
Source code and license can be found at vpcs.sf.net.
For more information, please visit wiki.freecode.com.cn.
Modified version supporting unetlab by unetlab team

Press '?' to get help.

VPCS> ip dhcp
DDORA IP 192.168.10.12/24 GW 192.168.10.1

VPCS>
```

As shown in the output, VPC obtain IP address of 192.168.10.12/24

Verification:

Go to command prompt of Windows PC and type "**ipconfig**"

Output showing the IPv4 address 192.168.10.11 has been assigned to the PC, Subnet of 255.255.255.0 and default gateway 192.168.10.1.

Ping 192.168.10.1 (gateway) and 192.168.10.12 (PC2)

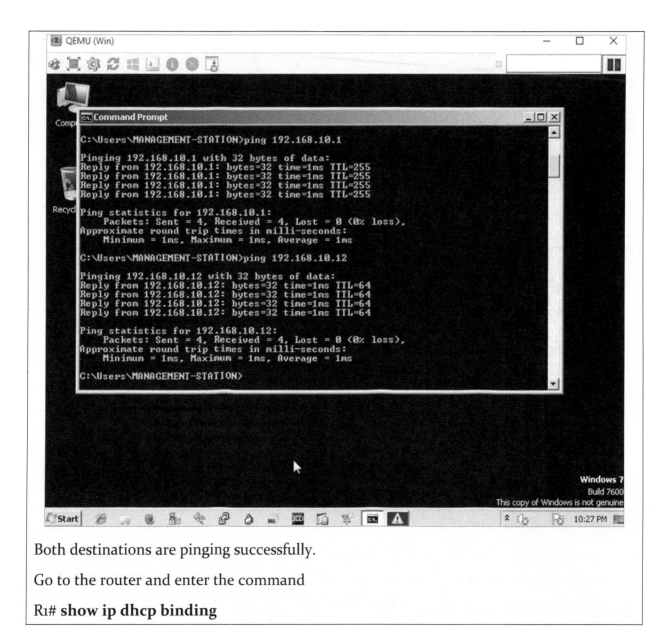

Both destinations are pinging successfully.

Go to the router and enter the command

R1# **show ip dhcp binding**

```
Router                                                    —    □    ×
 terminal   Write to terminal
  <cr>

R1#wr me
Building configuration...
[OK]
R1#show ip dhcp ?
  binding   DHCP address bindings
  conflict  DHCP address conflicts
  database  DHCP database agents
  import    Show Imported Parameters
  pool      DHCP pools information
  relay     Miscellaneous DHCP relay information
  server    Miscellaneous DHCP server information

R1#show ip dhcp binding
Bindings from all pools not associated with VRF:
IP address         Client-ID/              Lease expiration      Type
                   Hardware address/
                   User name
192.168.10.11      0150.0000.0300.00       May 15 2018 11:20 PM  Automatic
192.168.10.12      0100.5079.6668.04       May 15 2018 11:24 PM  Automatic
R1#
R1#
```

The result is showing DHCP bindings.

R1#**show ip dhcp pool**

```
Router                                                    —    □    ×
R1#show ip dhcp pool

Pool IP10 :
 Utilization mark (high/low)    : 100 / 0
 Subnet size (first/next)       : 0 / 0
 Total addresses                : 254
 Leased addresses               : 2
 Pending event                  : none
 1 subnet is currently in the pool :
 Current index      IP address range                  Leased addresses
 192.168.10.13      192.168.10.1    - 192.168.10.254    2
R1#
```

DHCP pool information

R1#**show ip dhcp server statistics**

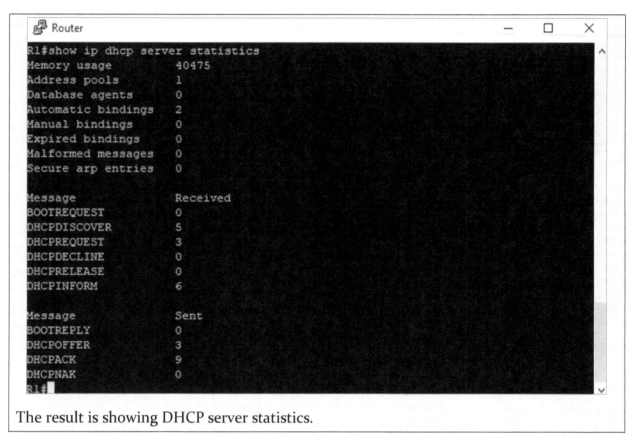

The result is showing DHCP server statistics.

Static Vs. Dynamic IP Addressing

In DHCP devices such as servers, network printers, plotters, and router interfaces are statistically configured that cannot be changed. Then, the client computers get their IP addresses from a DHCP server when required.

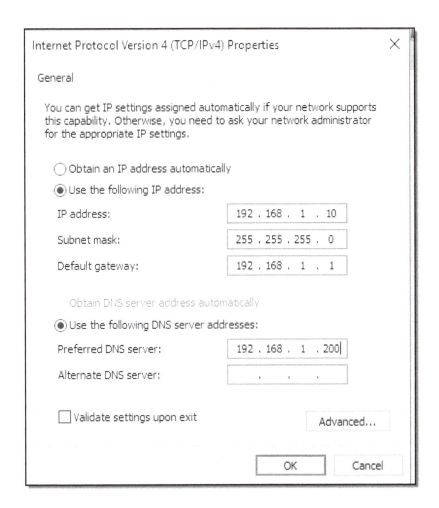

Figure 1-03: Static configuration on Windows 10

Reservations

DHCP reservation is a process of assigning a permanent IP address. This IP address uses the DHCP scope that is reserved for leased use to a particular DHCP client.

Scopes

A scope is a range of IP addresses that can be assigned to clients. The scope can be set by IP subnet that is using the organization. But be careful that scopes do not overlap with other scopes as it occurs conflict.

Leases

Automatically, DHCP leases an address for 8 days. When 50% of the lease expires, the client will have to renew the lease with the same DHCP server.

DHCP Options

DHCP can be configured to provide additional parameters that entirely configures TCP/IP on a client. Some common DHCP optional types configured by the DHCP server including gateway, router, DNS, and WINS.

DHCP Relay

If the client and server are on different subnets, IP helper shifts a router into a relay agent where it will take a broadcast from one domain and forward as a unicast to the client address listed from the original broadcast domain. The receiving device will send the relevant data to the relay agent who will relay to the client.

Domain Name Systems (DNS)

Domain Name Systems (DNS) translates between the human-readable domain names and IP addresses and is supported by all operating systems on the network. DNS is designed in a hierarchical structure. DNS comprises specific servers that manage records.

DNS Server

A DNS server is a special type of server that directs, holds and processes Internet domain names and their related records. DNS server involves software and configuration that allows resolving hostnames to IP addresses for an IP network. It performs its functions individually and can communicate with other DNS server to exchange their databases and records.

DNS Records

DNS servers use different types of records, some of them are described below with their specifications.

Address (A) record: used to resolve a simple hostname to an IPV4 address.

Mail Exchange (MX) record: directs the mail server about the routing of mail.

AAAA record: deals to resolve IPV6 addresses

CNAME record: aliases on other records.

PTR record: recall a resolution for a service or host.

Dynamic DNS

Dynamic DNS commonly known as DDNS is a service that converts domain names to IP address. DDNS has similar functions like DNS, but it deals with dynamic IP addresses. It can solve the problem of changing domestic IP addresses by combining with a stable

domain name without purchasing f static IP. It can update the server if any changes occur in the databases.

Proxy/Reverse Proxy Server

A proxy server is a server that builds a connection on behalf of the other user-operated in another location, specifically a website.

A reverse proxy server that builds a connection back to the user on behalf of the intended server that possesses information.

Network Address Translation (NAT)

Network Address Translation (NAT) is a technology used for the mapping of IP addresses. It allows private IP networks that use unlisted IP addresses to connect to the public network.

NAT usually operates on router and firewall to connect at least two networks and translates the private addresses inside the network into authorized addresses, before packets are delivered to another network.

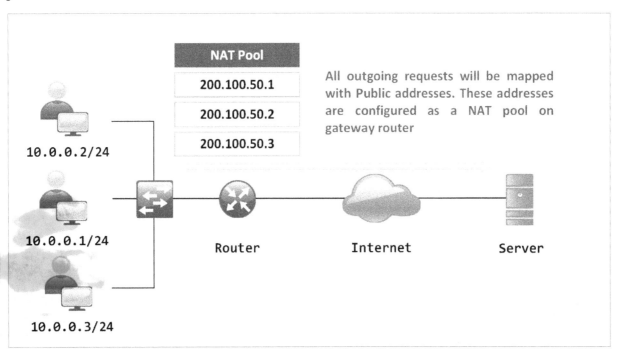

Fig 1-04: Network Address Translation (NAT)

NAT has three forms that are described below.

Port Address Translation (PAT)

Port Address Translation (PAT) is an advanced form of NAT that allows multiple computers on inside network to be mapped over the single public address by assigning a separate port number to ongoing transmission.

Lab 1-2: Port Address Translation

Case Study: In this Case, we are troubleshooting the process of Port Address Translation in which a number of IP address of an internal network i.e. 192.168.10.0/24 will be translated By PAT (Port Address Translation) into 192.168.30.0/24 network along with Port numbers.

Note: In this Lab, we use Cisco IOS Software Release 15.4(2)T to configure NAT

Topology Diagram:

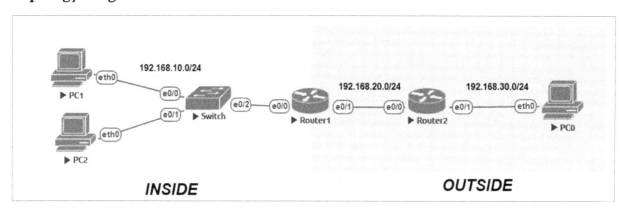

Router1 Configuration:

Router>

Router>en

Router#config t

Enter configuration commands, one per line. End with CNTL/Z.

Router(config)#hostname Router1

Router1(config)#int eth 0/0

Router1(config-if)#ip add 192.168.10.1 255.255.255.0

Router1(config-if)#no sh

Router1(config-if)#ip nat inside

```
*May 14 22:02:26.652: %LINK-3-UPDOWN: Interface Ethernet0/0, changed state to up

*May 14 22:02:27.657: %LINEPROTO-5-UPDOWN: Line protocol on Interface Ethernet0/0,
changed state to up

*May 14 22:02:28.836: %LINEPROTO-5-UPDOWN: Line protocol on Interface NVI0, changed
state to up
```

```
Router1(config-if)#ex

Router1(config)#int eth 0/1

Router1(config-if)#ip add 192.168.20.1 255.255.255.0

Router1(config-if)#ip nat outside

Router1(config-if)#no sh

Router1(config-if)#ex

*May 14 22:03:11.057: %LINK-3-UPDOWN: Interface Ethernet0/1, changed state to up

*May 14 22:03:12.061: %LINEPROTO-5-UPDOWN: Line protocol on Interface Ethernet0/1,
changed state to up


Router1(config)#access-list 10 permit 192.168.10.0 0.0.0.255

Router1(config)#ip nat pool PAT-POOL 1.1.1.1 1.1.1.2 netmask  255.255.255.252

Router1(config)#ip nat inside source list 10 pool PAT-POOL overload

Router1(config)#ip route 0.0.0.0 0.0.0.0 192.168.20.2

Router1(config)#
```

Router12Configuration:

```
Router>

Router>en

Router#config t

Enter configuration commands, one per line.  End with CNTL/Z.

Router(config)#hostname Router2

Router2(config)#int eth 0/0

Router2(config-if)#ip add 192.168.20.2 255.255.255.0

Router2(config-if)#no sh

Router2(config-if)#ex

Router2(config)#

*May 14 22:07:37.049: %LINK-3-UPDOWN: Interface Ethernet0/0, changed state to up
```

```
*May 14 22:07:38.053: %LINEPROTO-5-UPDOWN: Line protocol on Interface Ethernet0/0,
changed state to up
```

Router2(config)#int eth 0/1

Router2(config-if)#ip add 192.168.30.1 255.255.255.0

Router2(config-if)#no sh

```
*May 14 22:07:59.682: %LINK-3-UPDOWN: Interface Ethernet0/1, changed state to up
```

```
*May 14 22:08:00.686: %LINEPROTO-5-UPDOWN: Line protocol on Interface Ethernet0/1,
changed state to up
```

Router2(config-if)#ex

Router2(config)#ip route 0.0.0.0 0.0.0.0 192.168.20.1

VPC Configuration

Go to PC0 and Enter the following command

VPC> **IP 192.168.30.2/24 192.168.30.1**

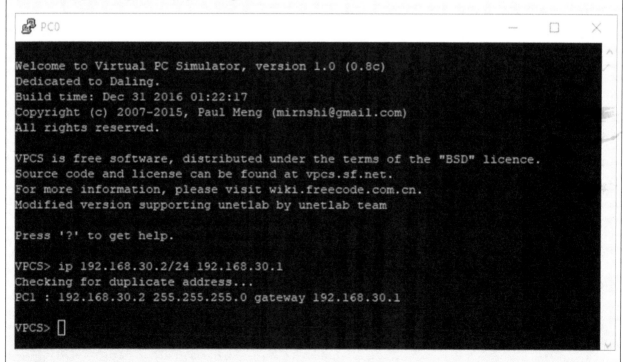

Go to PC1 and Enter the following command

VPC> **IP 192.168.10.10/24 192.168.10.1**

Generate some traffic to verify the connectivity

VPC> **Ping 192.168.30.2**

```
PC1                                              —    □    ✕

Build time: Dec 31 2016 01:22:17
Copyright (c) 2007-2015, Paul Meng (mirnshi@gmail.com)
All rights reserved.

VPCS is free software, distributed under the terms of the "BSD" licence.
Source code and license can be found at vpcs.sf.net.
For more information, please visit wiki.freecode.com.cn.
Modified version supporting unetlab by unetlab team

Press '?' to get help.

VPCS> ip 192.168.10.10/24 192.168.10.1
Checking for duplicate address...
PC1 : 192.168.10.10 255.255.255.0 gateway 192.168.10.1

VPCS> ping 192.168.30.2

84 bytes from 192.168.30.2 icmp_seq=1 ttl=62 time=0.730 ms
84 bytes from 192.168.30.2 icmp_seq=2 ttl=62 time=1.339 ms
84 bytes from 192.168.30.2 icmp_seq=3 ttl=62 time=1.394 ms
84 bytes from 192.168.30.2 icmp_seq=4 ttl=62 time=1.507 ms
84 bytes from 192.168.30.2 icmp_seq=5 ttl=62 time=1.673 ms

VPCS> ▮
```

Ping Successful.

Go to PC2 and Enter the following command

VPC> **IP 192.168.10.20/24 192.168.10.1**

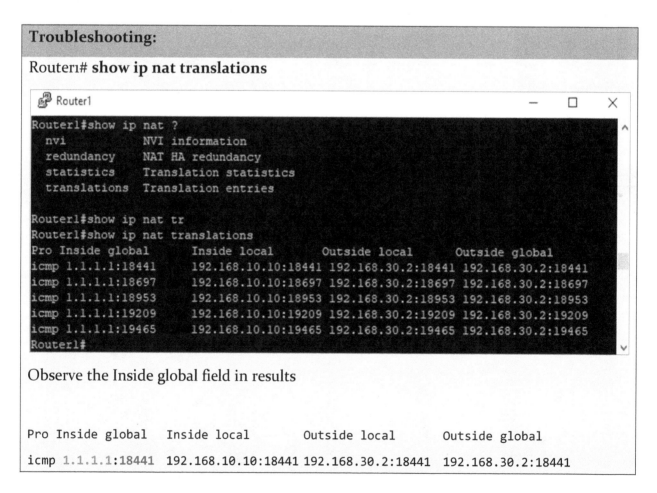

```
icmp 1.1.1.1:18697   192.168.10.10:18697 192.168.30.2:18697   192.168.30.2:18697

icmp 1.1.1.1:18953   192.168.10.10:18953 192.168.30.2:18953   192.168.30.2:18953

icmp 1.1.1.1:19209   192.168.10.10:19209 192.168.30.2:19209   192.168.30.2:19209

icmp 1.1.1.1:19465   192.168.10.10:19465 192.168.30.2:19465   192.168.30.2:19465
```

Router# **show ip nat statistics**

```
Router1                                                    —   □   ×

Router1#show ip nat statistics
Total active translations: 5 (0 static, 5 dynamic; 5 extended)
Peak translations: 5, occurred 00:00:51 ago
Outside interfaces:
  Ethernet0/1
Inside interfaces:
  Ethernet0/0
Hits: 10  Misses: 0
CEF Translated packets: 10, CEF Punted packets: 0
Expired translations: 0
Dynamic mappings:
-- Inside Source
[Id: 1] access-list 10 pool PAT-POOL refcount 5
 pool PAT-POOL: netmask 255.255.255.252
       start 1.1.1.1 end 1.1.1.2
       type generic, total addresses 2, allocated 1 (50%), misses 0

Total doors: 0
Appl doors: 0
Normal doors: 0
Queued Packets: 0
Router1#
```

Static NAT

Static Network Address Translation allows the translation of IP addresses when the source IP address is altered but the destination IP address remains same. Static NAT permits a host on the inside of the NAT to begins connection to a host on the outside of the NAT. Static NAT facilitates many hosts on the inside to get any host on the outside of the NAT.

Lab 1-3: Static Network Address Translation

Case Study: In this Case, Static (One to One mapping) is performed in the shown network topology. The Source IP address 192.168.10.10 is translated into 192.168.30.2 IP address.

Topology:

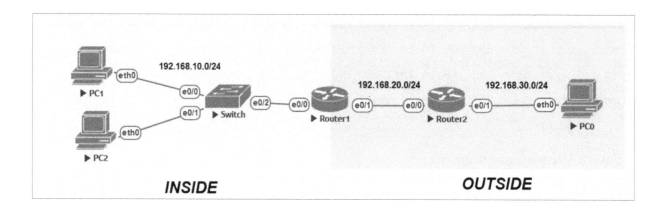

Router 1 Configuration for Static Network Address Translation
Router>
Router>en
Router#config t
Router(config)#int e0/0
Router(config-if)#ip address 192.168.10.1 255.255.255.0
Router(config-if)#ip nat inside
Router(config-if)#no shutdown
Router(config-if)#ex
Router(config)#int e0/1
Router(config-if)#ip address 192.168.20.1 255.255.255.0
Router(config-if)#ip nat outside
Router(config-if)#no shutdown
Router(config-if)#ex
Router(config)#ip route 0.0.0.0 0.0.0.0 192.168.20.2
Router(config)#ip nat inside source static 192.168.10.10 100.100.100.100

Router 2 Configuration

```
Router>en

Router#config t

Enter configuration commands, one per line.  End with CNTL/Z.

Router(config)#int eth 0/0

Router(config-if)#ip add 192.168.20.2  255.255.255.0

Router(config-if)#no sh

Router(config-if)#ex

*May 14 22:56:28.437: %LINK-3-UPDOWN: Interface Ethernet0/0, changed state to up

*May 14 22:56:29.441: %LINEPROTO-5-UPDOWN: Line protocol on Interface Ethernet0/0,
changed state to up


Router(config)#int eth 0/1

Router(config-if)#ip add 192.168.30.1 255.255.255.0

Router(config-if)#no sh

Router(config-if)#ex

*May 14 22:56:37.670: %LINK-3-UPDOWN: Interface Ethernet0/1, changed state to up

*May 14 22:56:38.670: %LINEPROTO-5-UPDOWN: Line protocol on Interface Ethernet0/1,
changed state to up


Router(config)#ip route 0.0.0.0 0.0.0.0 192.168.20.1
```

VPC Configuration

Go to PCo and Enter the following command

VPC> **IP 192.168.30.2/24 192.168.30.1**

```
PC0                                                        —    □    ×

Welcome to Virtual PC Simulator, version 1.0 (0.8c)
Dedicated to Daling.
Build time: Dec 31 2016 01:22:17
Copyright (c) 2007-2015, Paul Meng (mirnshi@gmail.com)
All rights reserved.

VPCS is free software, distributed under the terms of the "BSD" licence.
Source code and license can be found at vpcs.sf.net.
For more information, please visit wiki.freecode.com.cn.
Modified version supporting unetlab by unetlab team

Press '?' to get help.

VPCS> ip 192.168.30.2/24 192.168.30.1
Checking for duplicate address...
PC1 : 192.168.30.2 255.255.255.0 gateway 192.168.30.1

VPCS> []
```

Go to PC1 and Enter the following command

VPC> **IP 192.168.10.10/24 192.168.10.1**

Generate some traffic to verify the connectivity

VPC> **Ping 192.168.30.2**

PC1

```
Build time: Dec 31 2016 01:22:17
Copyright (c) 2007-2015, Paul Meng (mirnshi@gmail.com)
All rights reserved.

VPCS is free software, distributed under the terms of the "BSD" licence.
Source code and license can be found at vpcs.sf.net.
For more information, please visit wiki.freecode.com.cn.
Modified version supporting unetlab by unetlab team

Press '?' to get help.

VPCS> ip 192.168.10.10/24 192.168.10.1
Checking for duplicate address...
PC1 : 192.168.10.10 255.255.255.0 gateway 192.168.10.1

VPCS> ping 192.168.30.2

84 bytes from 192.168.30.2 icmp_seq=1 ttl=62 time=0.730 ms
84 bytes from 192.168.30.2 icmp_seq=2 ttl=62 time=1.339 ms
84 bytes from 192.168.30.2 icmp_seq=3 ttl=62 time=1.394 ms
84 bytes from 192.168.30.2 icmp_seq=4 ttl=62 time=1.507 ms
84 bytes from 192.168.30.2 icmp_seq=5 ttl=62 time=1.673 ms

VPCS>
```

Ping Successful.

Go to PC2 and Enter the following command

VPC> **IP 192.168.10.20/24 192.168.10.1**

PC2

```
Welcome to Virtual PC Simulator, version 1.0 (0.8c)
Dedicated to Daling.
Build time: Dec 31 2016 01:22:17
Copyright (c) 2007-2015, Paul Meng (mirnshi@gmail.com)
All rights reserved.

VPCS is free software, distributed under the terms of the "BSD" licence.
Source code and license can be found at vpcs.sf.net.
For more information, please visit wiki.freecode.com.cn.
Modified version supporting unetlab by unetlab team

Press '?' to get help.

VPCS> ip 192.168.10.20/24 192.168.10.1
Checking for duplicate address...
PC1 : 192.168.10.20 255.255.255.0 gateway 192.168.10.1

VPCS>
```

Verification:

Ping from PC1 to PC0

VPC> **ping 192.168.30.2**

```
PC1                                              —    □    ×
84 bytes from 192.168.30.2 icmp_seq=5 ttl=62 time=1.452 ms

VPCS>
VPCS> ping 192.168.30.2

84 bytes from 192.168.30.2 icmp_seq=1 ttl=62 time=2.330 ms
84 bytes from 192.168.30.2 icmp_seq=2 ttl=62 time=1.384 ms
84 bytes from 192.168.30.2 icmp_seq=3 ttl=62 time=1.529 ms
84 bytes from 192.168.30.2 icmp_seq=4 ttl=62 time=1.476 ms
84 bytes from 192.168.30.2 icmp_seq=5 ttl=62 time=1.357 ms

VPCS>
```

Generating some traffic for network address translation.

Go to router 1 and enter the following command;

Router# **show ip nat statistics**

```
Router1                                          —    □    ×
Router#
Router#show ip nat st
Router#show ip nat statistics
Total active translations: 6 (1 static, 5 dynamic; 5 extended)
Peak translations: 6, occurred 00:00:22 ago
Outside interfaces:
  Ethernet0/1
Inside interfaces:
  Ethernet0/0
Hits: 10  Misses: 0
CEF Translated packets: 10, CEF Punted packets: 0
Expired translations: 0
Dynamic mappings:

Total doors: 0
Appl doors: 0
Normal doors: 0
Queued Packets: 0
Router#
```

Translation statistics shown in the results.

Now enter the command

Router# **show ip nat translation**

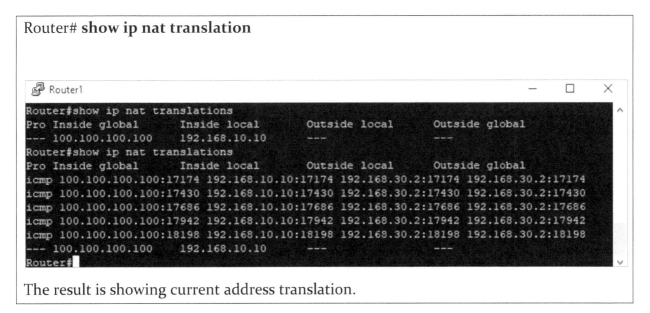

The result is showing current address translation.

Dynamic Network Address Translation

Dynamic Network Address Translation allows the translation of IP addresses when the destination IP address is altered but the source IP address remains same. Dynamic NAT permits a host on the outside of the NAT to begins connection to a host on the inside of the NAT. Dynamic NAT facilitates any host on the inside to get many hosts on the outside of the NAT.

Lab 1-4: Dynamic Network Address Translation

Case Study: In this Case, we are troubleshooting the process of Dynamic Network Address Translation in which the internal network 192.168.10.0/24 is dynamically translated into the pool of network 200.200.200.1 to 200.200.200.200.

Topology:

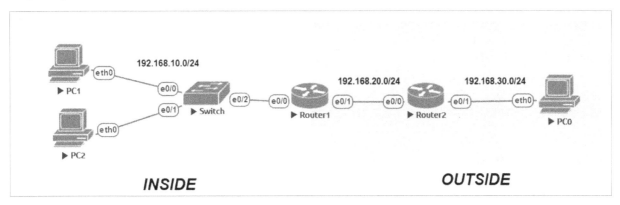

Router 1 Configuration: Dynamic Network Address Translation
Router>
Router>en

```
Router#config t

Router(config)#int eo/o

Router(config-if)#ip nat inside

Router(config-if)#int eo/1

Router(config-if)#ip nat outside

Router(config-if)#exit

Router(config)#access-list 10 permit 192.168.10.0 0.0.0.255

Router(config)#ip    nat    pool    CompTIA    200.200.200.1    200.200.200.200    netmask
255.255.255.0

Router(config)#ip nat inside source list 10 pool CompTIA

Router(config)#ip route 0.0.0.0 0.0.0.0 192.168.20.2

Router#debug ip nat

IP NAT debugging is on
```

Router 2 Configuration

```
Router>en

Router#config t

Enter configuration commands, one per line.  End with CNTL/Z.

Router(config)#int eth o/o

Router(config-if)#ip add 192.168.20.2  255.255.255.0

Router(config-if)#no sh

Router(config-if)#ex

*May 14 22:56:28.437: %LINK-3-UPDOWN: Interface Ethernet0/0, changed state to up

*May 14 22:56:29.441: %LINEPROTO-5-UPDOWN: Line protocol on Interface Ethernet0/0,
changed state to up


Router(config)#int eth o/1

Router(config-if)#ip add 192.168.30.1 255.255.255.0

Router(config-if)#no sh
```

Router(config-if)#ex

*May 14 22:56:37.670: %LINK-3-UPDOWN: Interface Ethernet0/1, changed state to up

*May 14 22:56:38.670: %LINEPROTO-5-UPDOWN: Line protocol on Interface Ethernet0/1, changed state to up

Router(config)#ip route 0.0.0.0 0.0.0.0 192.168.20.1

VPC Configuration

Go to PC0 and Enter the following command

VPC> **IP 192.168.30.2/24 192.168.30.1**

```
PC0                                                    —    □    ×

Welcome to Virtual PC Simulator, version 1.0 (0.8c)
Dedicated to Daling.
Build time: Dec 31 2016 01:22:17
Copyright (c) 2007-2015, Paul Meng (mirnshi@gmail.com)
All rights reserved.

VPCS is free software, distributed under the terms of the "BSD" licence.
Source code and license can be found at vpcs.sf.net.
For more information, please visit wiki.freecode.com.cn.
Modified version supporting unetlab by unetlab team

Press '?' to get help.

VPCS> ip 192.168.30.2/24 192.168.30.1
Checking for duplicate address...
PC1 : 192.168.30.2 255.255.255.0 gateway 192.168.30.1

VPCS> 
```

Go to PC1 and Enter the following command

VPC> **IP 192.168.10.10/24 192.168.10.1**

Generate some traffic to verify the connectivity

VPC> **Ping 192.168.30.2**

```
PC1                                                        —   □   ×
Build time: Dec 31 2016 01:22:17
Copyright (c) 2007-2015, Paul Meng (mirnshi@gmail.com)
All rights reserved.

VPCS is free software, distributed under the terms of the "BSD" licence.
Source code and license can be found at vpcs.sf.net.
For more information, please visit wiki.freecode.com.cn.
Modified version supporting unetlab by unetlab team

Press '?' to get help.

VPCS> ip 192.168.10.10/24 192.168.10.1
Checking for duplicate address...
PC1 : 192.168.10.10 255.255.255.0 gateway 192.168.10.1

VPCS> ping 192.168.30.2

84 bytes from 192.168.30.2 icmp_seq=1 ttl=62 time=0.730 ms
84 bytes from 192.168.30.2 icmp_seq=2 ttl=62 time=1.339 ms
84 bytes from 192.168.30.2 icmp_seq=3 ttl=62 time=1.394 ms
84 bytes from 192.168.30.2 icmp_seq=4 ttl=62 time=1.507 ms
84 bytes from 192.168.30.2 icmp_seq=5 ttl=62 time=1.673 ms

VPCS>
```

Ping Successful.

Go to PC2 and Enter the following command

VPC> **IP 192.168.10.20/24 192.168.10.1**

```
PC2                                                        —   □   ×
Welcome to Virtual PC Simulator, version 1.0 (0.8c)
Dedicated to Daling.
Build time: Dec 31 2016 01:22:17
Copyright (c) 2007-2015, Paul Meng (mirnshi@gmail.com)
All rights reserved.

VPCS is free software, distributed under the terms of the "BSD" licence.
Source code and license can be found at vpcs.sf.net.
For more information, please visit wiki.freecode.com.cn.
Modified version supporting unetlab by unetlab team

Press '?' to get help.

VPCS> ip 192.168.10.20/24 192.168.10.1
Checking for duplicate address...
PC1 : 192.168.10.20 255.255.255.0 gateway 192.168.10.1

VPCS>
```

Verification:
Ping PC0 from PC1

```
PC1                                            —    □    ✕
84 bytes from 192.168.30.2 icmp_seq=5 ttl=62 time=1.452 ms

VPCS>
VPCS> ping 192.168.30.2

84 bytes from 192.168.30.2 icmp_seq=1 ttl=62 time=2.330 ms
84 bytes from 192.168.30.2 icmp_seq=2 ttl=62 time=1.384 ms
84 bytes from 192.168.30.2 icmp_seq=3 ttl=62 time=1.529 ms
84 bytes from 192.168.30.2 icmp_seq=4 ttl=62 time=1.476 ms
84 bytes from 192.168.30.2 icmp_seq=5 ttl=62 time=1.357 ms

VPCS>
```

Generating traffic from PC1

Ping Router 2 from PC2

```
PC2                                            —    □    ✕
VPCS> ping 192.168.20.2

84 bytes from 192.168.20.2 icmp_seq=1 ttl=254 time=1.188 ms
84 bytes from 192.168.20.2 icmp_seq=2 ttl=254 time=1.436 ms
84 bytes from 192.168.20.2 icmp_seq=3 ttl=254 time=1.330 ms
84 bytes from 192.168.20.2 icmp_seq=4 ttl=254 time=1.310 ms
84 bytes from 192.168.20.2 icmp_seq=5 ttl=254 time=1.492 ms

VPCS>
```

Generating traffic from PC2

Router# **show ip nat translation**

Router(config)# **do show ip nat translation**

```
Router1                                                    —  □  ×
Router(config)#do show ip nat translations
Pro Inside global        Inside local        Outside local        Outside global
icmp 200.200.200.1:29470 192.168.10.10:29470 192.168.30.2:29470 192.168.30.2:29470
icmp 200.200.200.1:29726 192.168.10.10:29726 192.168.30.2:29726 192.168.30.2:29726
icmp 200.200.200.1:29982 192.168.10.10:29982 192.168.30.2:29982 192.168.30.2:29982
icmp 200.200.200.1:30238 192.168.10.10:30238 192.168.30.2:30238 192.168.30.2:30238
icmp 200.200.200.1:30494 192.168.10.10:30494 192.168.30.2:30494 192.168.30.2:30494
--- 200.200.200.1         192.168.10.10       ---                  ---
icmp 200.200.200.2:33566 192.168.10.20:33566 192.168.20.2:33566 192.168.20.2:33566
icmp 200.200.200.2:33822 192.168.10.20:33822 192.168.20.2:33822 192.168.20.2:33822
icmp 200.200.200.2:34078 192.168.10.20:34078 192.168.20.2:34078 192.168.20.2:34078
icmp 200.200.200.2:34334 192.168.10.20:34334 192.168.20.2:34334 192.168.20.2:34334
icmp 200.200.200.2:34590 192.168.10.20:34590 192.168.20.2:34590 192.168.20.2:34590
Pro Inside global        Inside local        Outside local        Outside global
--- 200.200.200.2         192.168.10.20       ---                  ---
Router(config)#
```

The result shows dynamic network address translations

Router(config)# **do show ip nat statistics**

```
Router1                                                    —  □  ×
Router(config)#do show ip nat statistics
Total active translations: 7 (0 static, 7 dynamic; 5 extended)
Peak translations: 17, occurred 00:04:18 ago
Outside interfaces:
  Ethernet0/1
Inside interfaces:
  Ethernet0/0
Hits: 50  Misses: 0
CEF Translated packets: 50, CEF Punted packets: 0
Expired translations: 20
Dynamic mappings:
-- Inside Source
[Id: 1] access-list 10 pool CompTIA refcount 7
 pool CompTIA: netmask 255.255.255.0
        start 200.200.200.1 end 200.200.200.200
        type generic, total addresses 200, allocated 2 (1%), misses 0

Total doors: 0
Appl doors: 0
Normal doors: 0
Queued Packets: 0
Router(config)#
```

Debugging.

```
Router1                                                    —    □    ✕

Router(config)#
*May 14 23:36:58.467: NAT*:  s=192.168.10.10->200.200.200.1, d=192.168.30.2 [7578]
*May 14 23:36:58.467: NAT*:  s=192.168.30.2, d=200.200.200.1->192.168.10.10 [7578]
*May 14 23:36:59.469: NAT*:  s=192.168.10.10->200.200.200.1, d=192.168.30.2 [7579]
*May 14 23:36:59.469: NAT*:  s=192.168.30.2, d=200.200.200.1->192.168.10.10 [7579]
Router(config)#
*May 14 23:37:00.470: NAT*:  s=192.168.10.10->200.200.200.1, d=192.168.30.2 [7580]
*May 14 23:37:00.471: NAT*:  s=192.168.30.2, d=200.200.200.1->192.168.10.10 [7580]
*May 14 23:37:01.473: NAT*:  s=192.168.10.10->200.200.200.1, d=192.168.30.2 [7581]
*May 14 23:37:01.473: NAT*:  s=192.168.30.2, d=200.200.200.1->192.168.10.10 [7581]
Router(config)#
*May 14 23:37:02.475: NAT*:  s=192.168.10.10->200.200.200.1, d=192.168.30.2 [7582]
*May 14 23:37:02.476: NAT*:  s=192.168.30.2, d=200.200.200.1->192.168.10.10 [7582]
Router(config)#
*May 14 23:37:27.928: NAT*:  s=192.168.10.20->200.200.200.2, d=192.168.20.2 [7607]
*May 14 23:37:27.928: NAT*:  s=192.168.20.2, d=200.200.200.2->192.168.10.20 [7607]
*May 14 23:37:28.930: NAT*:  s=192.168.10.20->200.200.200.2, d=192.168.20.2 [7608]
*May 14 23:37:28.931: NAT*:  s=192.168.20.2, d=200.200.200.2->192.168.10.20 [7608]
Router(config)#
*May 14 23:37:29.933: NAT*:  s=192.168.10.20->200.200.200.2, d=192.168.20.2 [7609]
*May 14 23:37:29.933: NAT*:  s=192.168.20.2, d=200.200.200.2->192.168.10.20 [7609]
*May 14 23:37:30.935: NAT*:  s=192.168.10.20->200.200.200.2, d=192.168.20.2 [7610]
*May 14 23:37:30.935: NAT*:  s=192.168.20.2, d=200.200.200.2->192.168.10.20 [7610]
Router(config)#
```

Port forwarding

Port forwarding is a technique that can serve a remote computer to a computer that is connected to a private IP network. This service enables the dedication of port numbers. Port forwarding usually operates on routers that allow the user to enter a port number and IP address. Therefore, all the incoming traffic automatically forward to the matched port number and continue its services. The services allow the user to access data, tunneling, bypass a filter and any other.

Features and Benefits of WAN Technologies

Nowadays, organizations use many WAN technologies according to their needs. It is important to know the attributes and benefits of these technologies for better deployment of the network.

Fiber

The optical fiber is an advanced technology in the network cable; it transmits light waves between the two ends of fiber along the long distance with high data rates.

Optical fiber is consists of surrounding part cladding and central part core through which the light is propagated by following the phenomenon of total internal reflection. Optical fiber provides flexibility and speed of 150 Mbps with less attenuation as compared to electrical cables. Optical fiber mostly used for long distance communication where

ordinary cable wires do not install. However, its installation and maintenance are quite difficult.

Common implementations of fiber include SONET, DWDM, and CWDM.

Synchronous Optical Networking (SONET)

Synchronous Optical Networking (SONET) is a standardized protocol in optical communication that is used to push data at 150 Gbps over fiber optic medium. SONET adds synchronization of time in multiple digital data flows transmitted over fiber optic using lasers and LEDs. It usually provides an STS-1 link of 50 Mbps bandwidth and multiples of it, so STS-3 provides approx. 150 Mbps bandwidth.

Dense Wavelength Division Multiplexing (DWDM)

Dense Wavelength Division Multiplexing (DWDM) is an optical technology used to increase the bandwidth of the existing fiber-optic backbones. It multiplexes the multiple transmitted signal at different wavelengths on the same fiber. After the implementation of DWDM, a single fiber can transmit data at 400 Gbps speed.

Coarse Wavelength Division Multiplexing (CWDM)

Coarse Wavelength Division Multiplexing (CWDM) follows DWDM, but it is used in the small coverage area and used fewer channels as compared to DWDM.

CWDM is appropriate for small business and regional areas. It can provide wider spacing of 20 nm and can bear higher temperature fluctuations as compared to DWDM.

Frame Relay

Frame relay is a powerful WAN technology that operates at physical and data link layer of the OSI model. It is the simplified way of packet switching as it follows the principle of X.25 in which data frames are routed to various destinations as described in the header information.

Frame relay was designed to use over Integrated Service Digital Network (ISDN) interfaces. Frame relay does not guarantee the integrity of data, but its switching speed is much faster.

Satellite

Satellites are the peak of modern communications technology. They provide worldwide access to information by transmitting radio waves from orbit about the earth. The communication satellite is located in geostationary orbit. Satellite communications provider gets satellite signals from the antenna, this signal used to provide for downloading while for uploading purpose they provide traditional telephone dial-up

connections. Satellite communications provider offers high data rates as compared to their competitors.

Broadband Cable

Broadband cable is a special type of cable that is connected to deliver high bandwidth services such as Internet access, TV channels, telephony cable and other electronic interactive services.

Broadband cables are a coaxial cable that is connected to the cable modem. Connecting to the Internet, the Internet service provider configures the cable modem and then connected to their central offices.

Broadband cable provides great bandwidth speed, 30 Mbps for downstream and greater than 1 Mbps for upstream.

Digital Subscriber Line (DSL)

Digital Subscriber Line (DSL) is an advancement in copper wire technology, usually used to achieve high-speed digital transmission over standard copper public telephone network access lines, specifically used for high-speed Internet connection.

Asymmetric Subscriber Line (ADSL)

Asymmetric Subscriber Line (ADSL) the most common types of DSL, in ADSL the total capacity of the high-speed digital subscriber line is divided asymmetrically between the downstream and upstream way of transmission. The speed of downloading is 20 times greater than the uploading speed.

Integrated Service Digital Network (ISDN)

Integrated Service Digital Network (ISDN) is a combination of digital telephony and data transport services delivered by telephone carriers. It handles the digitization of telephone network, which offers voice, data, text, video, etc. over existing telephone lines.

Two most important aspects of ISDN include ISDN BRI, ISDN PRI. ISDN BRI service offered two B channels and one D channel (2B+D) B channel operated at 64 Kbps and used to carry user data, and D channel operates at 16 kbps used for control and signaling information. While ISDN PRI offers 23 B channels and 1 D channels, both of them operates at 64 kbps.

Asynchronous Transfer Mode (ATM)

Asynchronous Transfer Mode (ATM) is the transfer mode in which information is organized into 53 bytes of fixed cells for multiple services like voice, video, or data. ATM network is connection oriented; it handles multiple applications by integrating

multiplexing and switching functions at different data rates. ATM technology is much faster and able to transfer voice, data, and video signals up to 500 Mbps.

Point-to-point protocol (PPP)/multilink PPP

Point-to-point protocol (PPP) is the standard remote access protocol that provides methods for authentication, error checking and multiple protocol support. PPP is dealing with different network layer protocols such as IP, IPV6. PPP offers several authentication methods including PAP (Password Authentication Protocol), CHAP (Challenge Authentication Protocol), and EAP (Extensible Authentication Protocol).

PPP follows three steps to establish a session:

1. Framing rules are set between the client and server that covers the size of frames and data rates are acceptable.
2. Authentication of the client by the server using authentication protocol.
3. Network control protocols (NCPs) enable the remote client for different network layer protocol.

After following these steps, PPP is able to interchange data. If it requires multiple physical links, multilink PPP could be used to send frames, and it improves the throughput of the connection.

Multiprotocol Label Switching (MPLS)

Multiprotocol Label Switching (MPLS) offers an efficient encapsulation technique. It uses 'Label' attach to packets before transportation of data. MPLS packet can run on layer 2 technologies such as ATM, PPP, Ethernet. MPLS is responsible for the delivery of IP services. It provides greater flexibility in network planning and preference of traffic.

Global System for Mobile (GSM)

The Global System for Mobile (GSM) is the first group of wireless technology that has been widely utilized in mobile devices. It uses time division multiple access techniques to share the same channels among the users at different time spaces. GSM operates by SIM cards that enables access to the cellular networks and hold some information. GSM operates at 900 MHz in Asia and Europe and 1900 MHz in the USA. GSM provides features like phone call encryption, data networking, caller ID, call forwarding, call waiting, SMS, and conferencing.

Code Division Multiple Access (CDMA)

Code Division Multiple Access is the technology developed just after the GSM, it uses spread spectrum codes to communicate with the users in which different codes have been

assigned to users to time and frequency allocations. CDMA provides better voice quality, efficient use of spectrum and facilitates more users at the same time.

Long Term Evolution LTE/4G

Long Term Evolution is the latest wireless technology standard for high speed used by various wireless devices such as mobile phones, Tablets, Android devices, etc. It provides 300 Mbps and 75 Mbps for downlink and uplink rates respectively. It provides flexibility to use internet applications.

High-Speed Packet Access (HSPA+)

High-Speed Packet Access (HSPA+) introduced LTE for wireless networks and follows the third-generation product (3G) products. It can provide downlink and uplink speed up to 168 Mbps and 22 Mbps respectively. HSPA+

Third Generation (3G)

3G is the Third Generation of wireless technology. It comes with improvements over past wireless technologies. It provides high-speed communication, advanced multimedia access and supports global roaming. 3G is commonly used with mobile phones and handsets having an internet connection. It offers voice and video calls, uploading and downloading data, and web surfing services.

Enhanced Data Rates for GSM Evolution (Edge)

Enhanced Data Rates for GSM Evolution (Edge) is a high-speed 3G technology that was formed to the GSM standard. EDGE networks designed to provide multimedia applications such as streaming television, audio, and video to mobile phones at speeds up to 384 Kbps.

Dial-up

Dial-up technology is wired communication technology also known as Public Switch Telephone Network (PSTN) or Plain Old Telephone Service (POTS). A dial-up connection is a regular phone line used in homes that are connected by the RJ11 jacks from the central office to the local exchange.

Dial-up connection offers painfully slow 56 kbps lines. Although it is highly available and cost-effective. That's why it is used in business as a backup for a management connection for a router, switch, or computer.

WiMAX

Worldwide Interoperability for Microwave Access (WiMAX) is identified by 802.16 standards. WiMAX brought a new enhancement in wireless services as it replaced DSL and cable to provide high-speed Internet to the masses. WiMAX provided the concept of Wireless Metropolitan Area Networks (WMANs). Initially, WiMAX was running at the

speed of 40Mbps, but now it can provide speed up to 1 Gbps. WiMAX has some applications including a broadband network; it covers a large distance area like a small city.

Metro-Ethernet

Metro-Ethernet is an extension of Ethernet to Metropolitan Area Network. It is defined as a network that connects geographically isolated enterprise LANs and WANs networks that are usually held by service providers. Metro-Ethernet can increase network capacity and coverage area in a flexible, economical and scalable manner.

Leased lines

Leased lines are a private two-way circuit between two or more geographical distant area provided in exchange for a monthly lease. The services of leased lines include Telephone and Internet. The network of leased lines deployed in WAN environment.

T1/E1

T1/E1 is the digital transmission lines are used to connect public and customer equipment such as PABx, routers, and switches, etc. T1/E1 connections presented by service providers as point-to-point leased lines and switched for the usage of private WAN and public switch data and voice communication, internet access and video conferencing. T1 lines used in the United States and offer 1.54 Mbps dedicated bandwidth divide into 24 channels, whereas E1 lines used in Europe and offers 2.048 Mbps connection which divides into 32 channels.

T3/E3

T3/E3 is as similar as T1/E1 but used in large organizations that required high bandwidth. T-3 provides 44.736 Mbps for 672 DSos or the equivalent of 28 T-1s. Although E-3 provides 34.368 Mbps for the equivalent of 512 DSos or approximately 17 E-1s.

OC3/OC12

Optical Carrier (OC) is the standardized unit to measure transmission bandwidth of the data carried by SONET and fiber optics. The original speed of an OC trunk is approx. 50 Mbps was known as OC1, so OC3 is multiple of OC1 that has 150 Mbps speed. Therefore, OC12 delivers 600 Mbps. The fastest considered standard is OC-7144F which will offer exciting speed of 300Gbps.

Circuit switching Vs. Packet Switching

Circuit Switching	Packet Switching
The physical path between source and destination	No physical path followed
Reserve the complete bandwidth in	Does not reserve

advance	
Wastage of Bandwidth	No wastage of bandwidth
Does not store and forward transmission	Store and forward transmission
Capacity is wasted if Data is burst	Efficient use of capacity
Constant delay, no reordering, no packet drops	Packets delayed, reordered, or dropped
The route is established for the entire conversation	The route is established for each packet

Table 1-01: Circuit switching Vs. Packet Switching

Installation and Termination of Cables and Connectors

Copper Connectors

Copper connectors are used to connect copper cable; copper connectors are not certainly made up of copper. There are many types of copper connectors but discuss the most common types here.

RJ-11

Registered Jack (RJ)-11 connector used to connect UTP cables and mainly used to connect telephone lines and DSL connection. RJ-11 can accommodate two pairs of wires. RJ connectors attach UTP cable with the help of crimper.

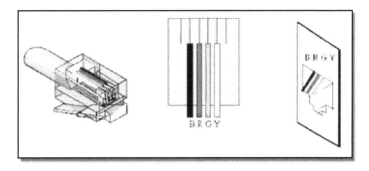

Figure 1-05: RJ 11 connector with cables

RJ-45

Registered Jack (RJ)-45 connector is the most common connector for all networks. It is used to connect all physical layer devices like Network Interface Cards (NICs). RJ-45 provides communication and control factor in network devices. The RJ-45 connector can accommodate four pairs of UTP cable and mainly used in LANs for a shorter distance (100 meters).

Figure 1-06: RJ 45connector with cables

RJ-48C

Another type of copper connector is RJ-48C that is similar to the RJ-45 connector. RJ -48c has four pairs shielded wire. It is used for long distance Wide Area Network (WAN) with the T1 connection.

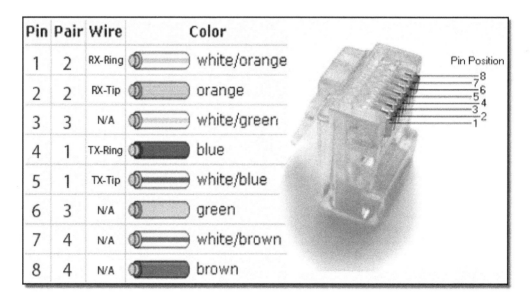

Figure1-07: RJ 48c connector with cables

DB-9/RS-232

DB-9 cable standard mostly used for serial data signals to provide a connection between data terminal and data communications equipment. DB-9 often used to connect computer's serial port to an external modem. DB-9 female connector might be used in RS-232 connections that widely used in modern networks such as USB.

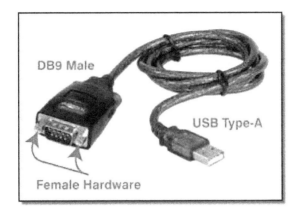

Figure 1-08: DB 9 connector

DB-25

DB-25 connectors have been used mostly in everything from modems to printers. In DB-25, 25 indicate the number of pins that can be used. It is configured in such a way to provide serial communication as well as parallel communication.

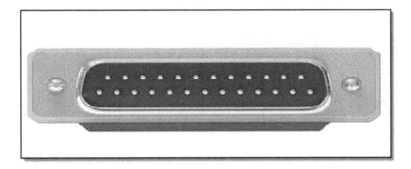

Figure 1-09: DB25 connector

UTP coupler

Universal Twisted Pair (UTP) coupler is a small plastic box that has two female RJ-45 or RJ-11 ports on any side of it. UTP coupler usually used to extend the length of a cable by installing another cable to it.

Figure 1-10: UTP coupler with cables

BNC coupler

A Bayonet Neill–Concelman (BNC) coupler is similar to UTP coupler. BNC coupler used to extend the length of a coaxial cable. BNC coupler contains two female connectors on any one end. It is used for general purpose networking and also sees their application in security cameras.

Figure 1-11: BNC connector

BNC

Bayonet Neill–Concelman (BNC) connector used to connect coaxial cables. BNC is not very useful in today's networking. The BNC connector is pushed in and then locked onto the connection to hold it securely in place while connecting the core wire.

Figure 1-12: BNC

F-connector

The F-connector is a coaxial type connector used to connect cable TV and cable modems. It mostly attached to RG-6 or RG-59 cable. It is responsible for providing a solid connection to promote the carrying of data or television signal

Figure 1-13: F connector

110 Block

110 block is a type of wiring distribution point. 110 block has replaced 66 block telephone wire installation and is used for computer networking. On either side of it, wires are punched down while the other side of it connected with RJ-11 or RJ-45. 110 block supports variable sizes from 25 to 500 wire pairs. It delivers 1 Gbps connections when connected with CAT6 cables.

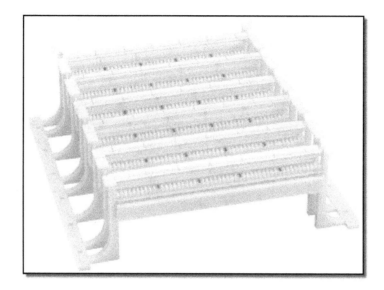

Figure 1-14: 110 Block

66 Block

The 66 Block wiring distribution was the standard for telephone companies. It is used for terminating sets of telephone wires with the help of punch down tool. It was mainly designed in multiple sizes to facilitate the sizes of the business telephone lines system. It was bounded for analog voice communications. Therefore, it has been replaced by new hardware like 110 blocks.

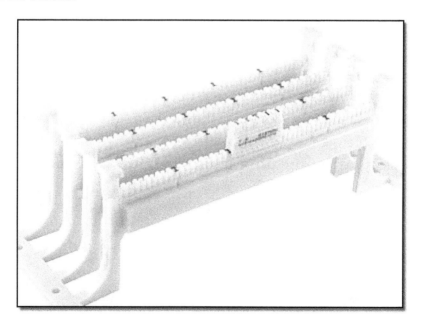

Figure 1-15: 60 Block

Copper Cables

In networking, multiple types of cables from copper to fiber have been utilized according to their requirements. This section described the various copper cables technology.

Shielded Vs. Unshielded

Shielded Twisted Pair Cable	Unshielded Twisted Pair Cable
STP is more expensive than UTP	UTP cable is cheapest
Harder to install as thick and heavy	Easy to install
STP reduces EM interference by a braided shield	Affected by external EM interference
Used in computer networking	Used in ordinary telephone wires

Table 1-02: Shielded Vs. Unshielded

CAT 3, 5, 5e, 6, and 6a

CAT 3, 5, 5e, 6, and 6a is the category of a twisted-pair cable. The following category defines the tightness of the twist applied to the wire pairs in the cable. Twisting in wires prevents them from electrical interference or crosstalk. This cable can transmit the information as faster as the twists are tighter without the interference of crosstalk. CAT5e (enhanced) is the most recommended type.

CAT3	CAT5	CAT5e	CAT6	CAT6a
10 Mbps	100 Mbps	**1000 Mbps**	1000 Mbps	1000 Mbps

Table 1-03: Cable categories and Maximum Speeds

Plenum Vs. PVC

The main difference between PVC and Plenum cable is in the construction and its applications. Plenum spaces are those that consist of a drop and standard ceiling. In these spaces where air circulates in a building, plenum-rated cable is used. Plenum spaces permit fire and smoke to travel swiftly. Plenum cable is coated with a jack that is usually made of a flame-resistant material such as Teflon.

Polyvinyl Chloride (PVC) cable is a non-plenum. It is used everywhere except plenum. PVC cables are low-cost then plenum cables. Therefore, many organizations use plenum cable only in the plenum for a prominent reason.

RG-59/RG-6

RG stands for Radio Guide. Coaxial cable uses RG ratings to distinguish among different cable types. RG 59 cable is thinner and has minimum shielded. It is used for low bandwidth and lower frequency usage such as CCTV installation. Whereas, RG 6 cables

are thicker and maximum shielded. It is good for high bandwidth and high-frequency requirements such as Cable TV, Internet, and Satellite signals.

Straight-through Vs. Crossover Vs. Rollover Cable

Cable Types	Standard	Application
Straight-Through	Both ends T568A or both ends T568B	-Used to connect dissimilar network devices -Connecting a network host a network device e.g., Switch or Hub
Crossover	One end T568A and another end 568B	-Used to connect similar network devices -Connecting two network hosts, network intermediary devices e.g., switch to switch, router to router
Rollover	Cisco Proprietary	Connecting a workstation serial port to a router console port.

Table 1-04: Straight-Through Vs. Crossover Vs. Rollover

Fiber Connectors

There are many types of connector used to connect fiber optics cables to the network device. This section will describe the various fiber connectors and their general purpose.

ST

Straight Tip (ST) connectors are similar to small BNC connector but made up of small hard plastic. ST uses a half-twist bayonet type of lock to hold in place securely. ST connectors are most commonly used with single-mode fiber-optic that travels long distances.

SC

Standard connector is another type of fiber-optic cable connector. It is based on push-pull connector mechanism identical to common audio and video plugs. SC connectors usually used with a multimode fiber-optic cable that is providing a backbone section for Local Area Network.

LC

Local connector (LC) is a fiber-optic cable connector that is made into the body of an RJ-style jack. The LC connector is perfect for organization's telecom room connected with Local Area Network.

MTRJ

Mechanical Transfer Registered Jack (MTRJ) is becoming popular because of its flexible sizes and stability. It consists of two fibers adjacent to each other and similar to an RJ-45

connector. It was designed to replace the SC, it is half in size of SC and provides two fibers connection.

FC

Ferrule Connector (FC) is a thread like structure that is designed for use in the vibrational environment. It is usually used with single-mode fiber-optic cable. It is less used than SC and LC connectors.

Fiber Coupler

The fiber coupler performs the function as a UTP coupler and BNC coupler. It is used to extend the cable length. Fiber coupler fuses two fibers together to the extended thread while working with high-powered light.

Fiber Cables

Fiber-optic cables are often used in network backbones to provide high bandwidth for fast and stable communications. Two main types of fiber-optic cable:

Single Mode Fiber

Single-mode fiber-optic cable (SMF) is a high-speed, long coverage media. Typically consist of a single strand or rarely two strands of glass fiber that carries the signal. SMF usually used Laser as a light source or sometimes uses Light Emitting Diodes (LEDs). A single light source is transmitting from end to end and provide communication by creating pulses. SMF is used for long distance because it can transmit data at a much faster rate as 50 times greater than multimode fiber.

Multimode Fiber

Multimode fiber-optic cable (MMF) provides communication by using light signal and spread it into multi-paths as it travels from the core and is reflected back through the cladding. MMF provides high bandwidth transmission at high speed as it travels along the medium distance about 3000 feet, but it cannot be suitable for long-distance communication. MMF is available in glass fiber as well as plastic fiber. Plastic fiber installation is easier and flexible, and MMF provides immunity to electrical interference.

APC Vs. UPC

By the time, the quality of fiber cable and connectors is increasing day by day and improving the ability to connect to devices without signal loss due to back reflection of light. The first quality of a connector is a physical contact which provides the physical connection with devices. Which improvement in this quality makes the Ultra Physical Contact (UPC) which has an additional feature of polish that gives a smoother physical contact and fewer signal losses. Whereas, Angled Physical Contact (APC) which has

tightened feature makes the physical connection more strong. The industry standard of APC is 8 degrees.

Media Converters

Media converters convert one media technology into another according to their requirement. If the requirement is to change the media from fiber to Ethernet or Ethernet to copper, a media converter is used to convert. Some common media converters are described below:

Single Mode Fiber to Ethernet

A single Mode Fiber uses among the building campuses. In this situation, Single-Mode Fiber to Ethernet converter used in each building because the light based fiber signal comes into the building to be carried farther through the building in the form of electricity.

Multimode Fiber to Ethernet

Multimode fiber is used as the backbone of the network across the building that allows the backbone to carry more data at a much faster speed that is fulfilled by copper cables. Multimode Fiber to Ethernet converter would be used between the backbone section and patch panels that connect with wall jacks and finally to the computers themselves.

Fiber to Coaxial

At early times, coaxial cables are used as a backbone in some buildings but today, they ate not used anymore. Coaxial cables are used to connect cable modems to provide internet connections. Fiber to coaxial converters used to provide high-bandwidth communications from a cable provider and divides it through the entire network backbone.

Single Mode Fiber to Multimode Fiber

As you know, single mode fiber is used between buildings for long distance area, whereas multimode fibers provide some channels for communication. Single Mode Fiber to Multimode Fiber converter, the signal pulses of light from the single-mode fiber in one stream convert the signal into multiple channels in multimode fiber.

Tools

Some common tools used in networking to attach the cables to cable connectors. Some common tools are discussed below:

Cable crimpers

The cable crimper and stripper attach an RJ-45 connector to the end of a cable. The eight wires inside the cable strip about an inch of the outer cable insulation then press down hard on the right place of the RJ-45 to close the connector around the cable and hold all

of the wires trapped into place so that the end of the cable sheath is safely tucked inside the connector as well. All this process is accomplished by cable crimpers and stripper.

Punch down tool

Punch down tool is a hand tool used to connect network wires to a patch panel. The process of properly punching down a wire requires some force if do it without any special tool it probably breaks the wire or not connected properly. So, by using a punch down tool help in connecting the wire in the right place.

Wire strippers

A wire stripper is a small hand-held device use to strip electrical insulation from wires. Usually, wire strippers are used in networking to remove only the outer sheath of the cable and bare the individual wires at the proper length of a connector or to punch down to a 110-block.

Snips

Wire snips are also called wire cutters used to cut the wire to the correct length for installation. It makes it easy to customize a cable according to requirement.

TDR

A Time Domain Reflectometer (TDR) is a sophisticated tool of network-troubleshoot equipment. It sends a low- level electromagnetic pulse and listens for any reflection of that pulse finding breaks or weak connections in copper cables. If troubleshooting a problem with the copper cable, a TDR tells the exact position even if wires are buried or in the wall. When the problem is accessible then able to fix it.

OTDR

An optical time domain reflectometer (OTDR) is a more sophisticated device as TDR. OTDR performs the same function as TDR, but it deals with light in fiber-optic cable. An OTDR test the cables within several kilometers but TDR test the copper cables shorter than 100 meters. For this reason, OTDR becomes a vital tool in today's networking as dealing with long distances fiber-optic cable flows.

Cable Certifier

Cable certifier certifies the cable after installation and properly connected with their respective connectors. It certifies that the installed cables perform properly and ready to provide the result as per their characteristics. Many cable certifiers available for all cable types and even for wireless networks.

Differentiate Between Common Networks Topology

Mesh Topology

Any network that has multiple paths or redundant connection in network topology is referred to as Mesh topology. Two types of Mesh topology, i.e., Full Mesh and Partial Mesh

Full Mesh	Partial Mesh
Every device connected to all devices in a network	Devices are grouped into nodes that connected to other nodes
Direct communication between devices	Allows communication between devices but not every device is directly connected to each other
Difficult to scale	Typically used for larger networks

Table 1-05: Full Mesh Vs. Partial Mesh

Bus Topology

The bus topology used in old networks are not in use today. In a bus topology, all computers are connected to each other by a single coaxial cable with BNC connector, and T connectors were used. T connectors were used to provide an independent connection for each computer on the bus.

Ring

A ring topology is a network topology that connects network devices in a circular path. Each network device is connected to two other devices. In the most ring network, data packets travel only in one direction to avoid a collision, but some networks allow data packets to travel in both directions.

Star

A star topology is the most common topology in use today. A star topology is consists of a group of computers connected to a central point such as hub or switches. The flow of information must pass through the central device. Each device present in star topology has an individual connection with the central device. So, if one connection fails do not affect the network, but a central device fails all the connections will be affected

Hybrid

The hybrid network topology is a combination of two networks topologies. It can be Star-Ring, Star-Bus topologies, etc. Hybrid network topology has many advantages like flexibility, reliability, and maximum fault tolerance.

Point-to-Point Vs. multipoint

Point-to-point and point-to-multipoint are the two types of the line pattern. The main difference between point-to-point and the multipoint connection is that in a point-to-

point connection the link connects only two devices, i.e., a sender and a receiver. On the other hand, in a multipoint connection, the link is between many devices, i.e., a sender and multiple receivers.

BASIS FOR COMPARISION	POINT-TO-POINT	MULTIPOINT
Link	The dedicated link between two devices	The link is shared between two or more devices
Channel Capacity	Entire channel capacity is shared between two devices	Channel capacity is shared among the connected devices
Sender and Receiver	The single transmitter and a single receiver	The single transmitter and multiple receivers
Example	Frame relay, T-carrier, X.25, etc.	Frame relay, token ring, Ethernet, ATM, etc.

Table 1-06: Point-to-Point Vs. multipoint

Client-server Vs. Peer-to-peer

There are two common network models for use in networking. Client-server and Peer-to-peer network, The Client-Server network model concentrates on information sharing whereas, the Peer-to-Peer network model concentrates on connectivity to the remote computers.

BASIS FOR COMPARISON	CLIENT-SERVER	PEER-TO-PEER
Basic	Specific server and specific clients connected to the server.	No specific server, no specific client, each node act as client and server.
Service	client request for service and server respond with the service	Each node can request for services and can also provide the services.
concentration	Sharing the information	Connectivity
Expense	Expensive to implement	Less expensive
Stability	More stable and scalable	Stability affected if the number of peers increases

Table 1-07: Client-server Vs. Peer-to-peer

Differentiate between Network Infrastructure Implementations

A computer network allows networking devices to connect and communicate with different computers. LAN, MAN, and WAN are the three types of the network designed to operate over the coverage area.

BASIS OF COMPARISON	LAN	MAN	WAN
Acronym	Local Area Network	Metropolitan Area Network	Wide Area Network
purpose	Connects a group of computers in a small geographical area	Covers relatively large region such as cities, towns.	Connect larger area such as countries.
Deployment and maintenance	Easy	Difficult	Difficult
Speed	High	Moderate	Low
Fault Tolerance	More	Less	Less
Congestion	Less	More	More
Application	College, school, Hospital	Small towns, City	Country, Continent

Table 1-08: LAN Vs. MAN Vs. WAN

WLAN

WLAN is an extended form of LAN with wireless technology. It is not difficult to connect to the wired networks wirelessly. Wireless LANs are designed to operate in license-free bands making their operation and maintenance costs effective than cellular and PCS networks. The use of the license-free band increases the risk of network security and spectral interference. The key advantages of wireless networks are mobility, flexibility, ease of installation and maintenance, and reduced cost.

Hotspot

A hotspot is any location where internet access available usually using Wi-Fi through a Wireless Local Area Network (WLAN). WLAN using a router connected to an internet service provider.

PAN

Personal Area Network (PAN) is a wireless LAN that is designed by an individual to invite others to join for a specific purpose. PAN is implemented for personal need and no one able to access it without permission.

Bluetooth

Bluetooth is designed for short-range connectivity for mobile personal devices. Operational frequency of Bluetooth is 2.45 GHz and coverage area are less than 10 meters.

Infrared (IR)

Infrared is the PAN technology use over short distances. The infrared (IR) initially offered a 115.2-kbit/s data rate over a range of up to 1 m. A 4-Mbit/s version was soon developed and has been widely integrated into laptops and PDAs for printer connections and short-range PANs. A 16-Mbit/s version is also available. The problem with IR isn't its very short range, but also its need for a line-of-sight (LOS) connection.

Near Field Communication (NFC)

Near field communications (NFC) is a special standard designed for smartphones that qualifies them to dynamically form a mini PAN by touching them together only a few centimeters away from each other. This network can then be used to exchange data for such things as a door key, a ticket for a train, a payment for services rendered, a photo, a telephone number and contact information, etc.

Supervisory Control And Data Acquisition (SCADA)

Supervisory control and data acquisition (SCADA) is a system consisting of software and hardware elements that allow remote control of industrial equipment by telemetry, usually wireless or satellite data. These procedures might include power generation, fabrication, water treatment, oil and gas pipelines, electrical power transmission, civil defense systems, air-conditioning and ventilation systems, lighting, and so on. The main part of this type of system might include an ICS server, DCS/closed network, remote terminal unit, and programmable logic controller.

Industrial Control Server (ICS) Server

The Industrial Control Systems (ICS) server is the data acquisition software part that uses industrial protocols to connect software to the other components of the system.

DCS/Closed Network

Additional sophisticated applications use a smart system called a DCS or closed network system. It can autonomously execute simple logic processes without including the master computer or the human operator.

Remote Terminal Unit (RTU)

Remote terminal units (RTUs) connect to sensors and convert telemetry signals into digital data. They can send and receive data from the ICS server and prepare it for use with the next component in the system, which will essentially modify something.

Programmable Logic Controller (PLC)

Programmable logic controllers (PLCs) can also process data into digital signals, but they use sensors installed by the creator and not telemetry data.

Medianets

A medianet is a modern network that was built with media delivery in mind. It can spontaneously adjust to different types of media needs such as video surveillance, desktop collaboration, streaming video, and even telepresence. It guarantees that new services can be quickly established and set the resources that they require (bandwidth, RAM, CPU, and so on) and also keep in mind the current services that are running on it so as not to reduce their performance.

Video Teleconferencing (VTC)

Video Teleconferencing (VTC) is a communication technology that allows users at two or more different locations to interact by making a face-to-face conference using audio and video technology. VTC uses either Integrated Services Digital Network (ISDN) or IP networks to establish a connection. Video teleconferencing (VTC) mainly established in **Integrated Service Digital Network (ISDN).** By the time, most calls are made over **Internet Protocol (IP)** networks due to increased bandwidth and lower cost brought about by the accessibility of these networks. Later, expanded bandwidth-enhanced IP technologies, and specialized protocols like the **Session Initiation Protocol (SIP)** have made video conferencing clear and easy to use.

IP Addressing schema

IP addressing is used to close together the network of computers and routers and connect it to other networks and the Internet. This section has details of IPv6, IPv4, private addresses, public addresses, NAT, PAT, and so on. Additionally, it discusses the services to resolve MAC addresses to IP addresses and to use IP addresses in more creative ways such as multicast addressing. There is also a need to understand the different types of communication that the network will use such as unicast and broadcast and the almost automatic domains of communication that will result from network schema.

IPv6

Internet Protocol v6 (IPv6) are in hexadecimal format. This address format has been shortened using the address compression rules for IPv6. Each hexadecimal character in the address is read as a 4 bits binary number by the network device. The below table illustrates the relationship of each decimal, binary, and hexadecimal character.

IPv6 address in this case as the following hexadecimal number

fe80::218:deff:fe08:6e14

The device will use a 128-bit number that looks like the following:

1111 1110 1000 0000 : 0000 0000 0000 0000 : 0000 0000 0000 0000 : 0000 0000 0000
0000 : 0000 0010 0001 1000 : 1101 1110 1111 1111 : 1111 1110 0000 1000 : 0110 1110 0001 0100

This huge addressing can be represented as

$2^{128} = 3.4028367 \times 10^{38}$

The addressing method of IPv6 use on interfaces of routers and network interface cards is same as IPv4 addressing while some new method has been introduced which are discussed below.

Auto-configuration

In auto-configuration method, the client can obtain a unique IPv6 address by using its own media access control (MAC) address and adding FF: FE into the middle of the address. It usually assures that the client has a unique address, as its MAC address is unique within that network segment.

EUI-64

Extended Unique Identifier 64 (EUI-64) addresses that are in use in many organizations today provide an address space that far exceeds that of our current MAC-48 addresses. In the coming years, EUI-64 addresses used more often, essentially replacing MAC-48 addresses, when companies begin the transition to IPv6.

Types of IPv6 address

IPv6 also has different types of addresses. The following are the three main types:

- **Anycast:** Very different from an IPv4 broadcast—one-to-the-nearest interface, where many interfaces can share the same address. These addresses are taken from the unicast address space but can represent multiple devices, like multiple default gateways. For example, using an anycast address as a default gateway address on your routers, user devices only have to know of one address, and you do not need to configure a protocol like HSRP or VRRP.

- **Multicast:** Address of a set of interfaces. One-to-many delivery to all interfaces in the set.

- **Unicast:** Address of a single interface. One-to-one delivery to a single interface.

The five types of unicast addresses are listed in below table. Interestingly enough, multiple addresses of any type can be assigned to a device's interface: unicast, multicast, and Anycast.

Address	Value	Description
Global	2000::/3	These are assigned by the IANA and used on the public networks. They are equivalent to IPv4 global (sometimes called as public) address. ISPs summarize these to provide scalability in the internet
Reserved	(range)	Reserved addresses are used for specific types of Anycast as well as for future use. Currently, about 1/256 of the IPv6 address space is reserved.
Private	FE80::/10	Like IPv4, IPv6 originally supported private addressing, which is used by devices that do not need to access a public network. The first two digits are FE, and the third digit can range from 8 to F
Loopback	::1	Like the 127.0.0.1 address in IPv4, 0:0:0:0:0:0:0:1, or ::1, is used for local testing function; unlike IPV4, which dedicates a complete class A block of addresses for local testing. Only one is used in IPv6
Unspecified	::	0.0.0.0 In IPv4 means "unknown" address. In IPv6, this is represented by 0:0:0:0:0:0:0:0, 0 ::, and is typically used in the source address field of the packet when an interface doesn't have an address and is trying to acquire one dynamically.

Table 1-09: IPv6 Unicast Address Types

IPv6 Header

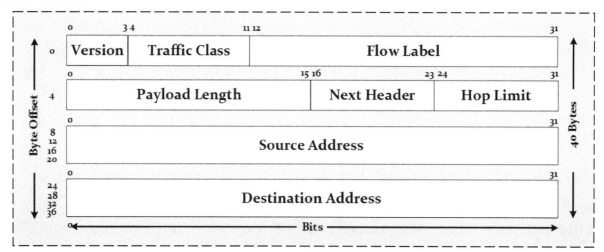

Figure 1-16: IPv6 Header Details

Version: Version of IP Protocol. 4 and 6 are valid. This diagram represents version 6 structure only.

Traffic Class: 8-bits traffic field.

Flow Label: 20-bits flow label.

Payload length: 16-bits unsigned integer length of the IPv6 payload, i.e, the rest of the packet following this IPv6 header in octets. Any extension header is considered part of the payload.

Source Address: 128-bits address of the originator of the packet.

Next Header: 8-bits selector, Identifies the type of header immediately following the IPv6 header. Uses the same values as the IPv4 protocol field.

Destination Address: 128-bits address of the intended recipient of the packet (possibly not the ultimate recipient. If a routing header is present).

Hop Limit: 8-bits unsigned integer decremented by 1 by each node that forwards the packet. The packet is discarded if hop limit is decremented to zero.

Points to Remember

- IPv6 addresses are 128-bits in length.

- IPsec is built into the IPv6 protocol and allows for device roaming without losing connectivity.

- IPv6 addresses use eight sets of four hexadecimal addresses (16 bits in each set), separated by a colon (:), like this: xxxx:xxxx:xxxx:xxxx:xxxx:xxxx:xxxx:xxxx .

- If you have successive fields of zeroes in an IPv6 address, you can represent them using two colons (::), but this can be used only once in an address.

- An Anycast address represents the nearest interface to a device, where many devices can share an Anycast address. Multicast addresses begin with FF.

- Global unicast addresses begin with 2000::/3. Private addresses range from FE8 through FFF. A loopback address is ::1.

- The subnet ID is the first 64 bits, and the interface ID is the last 64 bits. EUI-64 allows dynamic creation of the interface ID portion by using the MAC address on the interface.

DHCP6

As discussed earlier, Dynamic Host Configuration Protocol (DHCP) server is used to configure IP addresses, DNS servers automatically, and so on for clients joining a network.

DHCP6 works similar to DHCP4, with the exception that DHCP uses anycast communication instead of broadcast communication. Anycast communication is a more efficient type of signaling that is unique to IPv6. In anycast, a packet is sent to the addresses of the anycast members. By using anycast, a router can become a DHCP server for a client or direct it to a DHCP server.

Link Local

Same as IPv4, IPv6 comes with global address and link local address. Simply put, any address that starts with FE:80 has been set aside for unicast link local addressing on a private network. These addresses may be manually assigned or may be assigned using a DHCP server.

Tunneling 6to4, 4to6, Teredo, and Miredo

One of the nicest features about IPv6 is the conversion options that don't need to convert the entire network at one time but convert some part of the network and then coming back to the previous. If you connect two dissimilar networks to each other using a router in the middle that has both IPv6 and IPv4 addresses on it. It is referred to as 6to4 tunneling or 4to6 tunneling depending on which direction you are traveling. If you are using network address translation (NAT), then you might also use Teredo tunneling with a Miredo client. This type of tunneling is designed to allow full IPv6 connectivity to computer systems that have no direct connection but instead are coming through NAT or even port address translation (PAT).

IPv4

An IPv4 address is a 32-bits binary address represented in dotted decimal format. The following is an example of an IPv4 address:

192.168.1.1

IPv4 comes with a subnet mask that distinguishes which portion belongs to host portion and which belongs to network portion. IPv4 is in the dotted decimal format, but the network devices show the IPv4 addresses as binary numbers.

In fact, 192.168.1.1 ends up looking like the following:

11000000	10101000	00000001	00000001

It happens as the dotted decimal form uses the first 8 bits of binary over and over four times. The bits of the address are then valued based on the following template of values:

| 128 64 32 16 8 4 2 1 | 128 64 32 16 8 4 2 1 | 128 64 32 16 8 4 2 1 | 128 64 32 16 8 4 2 1 |

The address would then line up with the template as follows:

Everywhere there is not a 1 is a 0.

Subnetting

Subnetting allows a large network block to be logically subdivided into multiple smaller networks, or subnets. The use of multiple smaller networks allows the use of varying physical networks, such as Ethernet or Token Ring, which could not otherwise be combined. Additionally, the smaller subnets can improve the speed of traffic and permit easier management.

Subnet masks provide the logical segmentation required by routers to be able to address logical subnets. A default gateway IP address on a router interface allows clients to access networks outside their local subnets. The number of bits used in a subnet mask determines the number of subnets available.

APIPA

All client computers are configured by default to obtain their IP address from a DHCP server but when a DHCP server is not available. In this case, clients can configure by default to use an address in the range of 169.254.0.1 to 169.254.255.254. These addresses are called Automatic Private Internet Protocol Addressing (APIPA) addresses. The advantage of using APIPA is that the clients in the same network segment that could not obtain a true IP address from a DHCP server can still communicate with each other. The disadvantage is that the clients can communicate with each other but not with the true network.

Classful A, B, C, D

IPv4 develop a class-based system of IP addresses that have five classes of addresses. First three bits in the addresses identify the type of class. Remember that all class A addresses begin with 000, all Class B addresses begin with 100, all Class C addresses begin with 110, and all Class D addresses begin with 111. Since Class D addresses are used for multicasting. Also, there is a class E that begins at 240 in the first octet and is used only for experimental purposes.

Class	First octet range	Subnet mask	No. of networks	No. of Hosts/network
A	00000001-01111111 1-126	255.0.0.0	126	16,777,214
B	10000000-10111111 128-191	255.255.0.0	16,384	65,534

| C | 11000000-11011111 192-223 | 255.255.255.0 | 2,097,152 | 254 |
| D | 11100000-11101111 224-239 | NA | NA | NA |

Table 1-10: IP addressing

Private vs. public

A public IP address is an IP address that can be accessed over the Internet. A public IP address is the globally unique IP address assigned to a computing device. Your public IP address can be found at What is my IP Address page. Private IP address, on the other hand, is used to assign computers to your private network without letting them directly lead to the Internet. In a scenario, if you have multiple computers within your home you may want to use private IP addresses to address each computer within your home, your router gets the public IP address, and each of the devices connected to your router gets a private IP address from your router by DHCP protocol.

Internet Assigned Numbers Authority (IANA) is the organization responsible for assigning IP address ranges to organizations and Internet Service Providers (ISPs). To allow organizations to assign private IP addresses freely, the Network Information Center (InterNIC) has reserved certain address blocks for private use.

The following IP blocks are reserved for private IP addresses.

Class	Starting IP Address	Ending IP Address	No. of Hosts
A	10.0.0.0	10.255.255.255	16,777,216
B	172.16.0.0	172.31.255.255	1,048,576
C	192.168.0.0	192.168.255.255	65,536

Table 1-11: Private IP address

MAC addressing

The MAC address is a 48-bit binary address that is represented as a hexadecimal format. The below figure illustrates the structure of a MAC address in which the first 2 bits on the left represent whether the address is broadcast and whether it is local or remote. The next 22 bits are assigned to vendors that manufacture network devices, such as routers and NICs. This is the Organizational Unique Identifier (OUI). The next 24 bits should be uniquely assigned to the OUI.

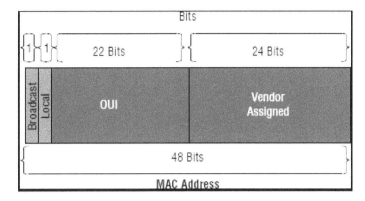

Figure 1-17: The structure of a MAC address

Multicast vs. Unicast vs. Broadcast

Three major types of addressing schemes are used on IPv4 networks. These are unicast, multicast, and broadcast. Unicast addressing is said if it has one source address and one destination address. Multicast addressing can be much more complex than unicast. With multicast addressing there is still only one source address, but there can be multiple destination addresses. The last one is broadcast addressing there has one source address that sends the data to all the devices that are connected with them.

Every IPv4 network or subnet has a broadcast address, which is the last numerical address before the next network. In the binary form of a broadcast address, you will notice that all the host bits are 1s. For example, the broadcast address of the network 192.168.1.0/27 is 192.168.1.31.

Broadcast Domains vs. Collision Domains

Collision domains occur when network devices share the same transmission medium, and their packets can collide. Collisions increase as the number of devices in a collision domain increase.

Broadcast domain occurs in the network where computers can receive frame-level broadcasts from their neighbors. Increasing devices on a network segment increases broadcast traffic on a segment

Device	Collision Domain	Broadcast Domain
Hub	All devices connected to the hub are in the same collision domain.	All devices are in the same broadcast domain.
Bridge or Switch	All devices connected to a single port are in the same collision domain; each port is its collision domain	All devices connected to the bridge or the switch are in the same broadcast domain.

Router	All devices connected to a single interface are in the same collision domain.	All devices accessible through an interface (network) are in the same broadcast domain. Each interface represents its broadcast domain if the router is configured to not forward broadcast packets.

Table 1-12: Broadcast Vs. Collision Domain

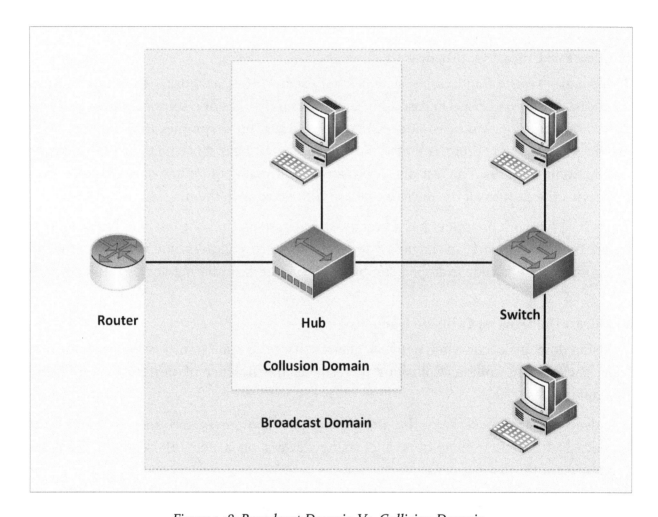

Figure 1-18: Broadcast Domain Vs. Collision Domain

Basic Routing concepts and Protocols

This section describes the various routing concepts and protocols.

Loopback interface

A logical interface is a virtual interface. It is not a physical interface like fast Ethernet interface or Gigabit Ethernet interface. A loopback interface is a software interface which

can be used to imitate a physical interface. The router doesn't have any loopback interfaces default, but they can easily be created. Loopback interfaces created by assign IP addresses to the router. Loopback interface has many advantages; it is used for redirecting traffic and loopback interface's IP Address determines an OSPF Router ID.

Routing Loops

Routing loops are issues that must be avoided in networks. Routing Loops makes the routing path more difficult, so the properly configured static routes and dynamic routes avoid routing loops by assuring that only most efficient paths are used.

Routing Tables

Routing Table is a set of rules used to determine the path of the data packet traveling over an Internet Protocol network. The routing table is consists of specific routing destinations, next hop, interface, metric, and routes. Routing tables can be maintained manually or automatically. Routing tables for static network devices do not change until the network administrator changes them manually. In dynamic routing, devices update its routing table automatically by using routing protocols to exchange information about the neighborhood network topology.

Static Vs. Dynamic Routing

Specification	Dynamic Routing	Static Routing
Configuration complexity	Independent of the network size	Increases in network size
Required administrator knowledge	Advanced knowledge required	No extra knowledge required
Topology	Automatically adapts to topology changes	Administrative intervention required
Scaling	Suitable for simple and complex topologies	Suitable for simple topologies
Security	Less secure	More secure
Predictability	Route depends on the current topology	The route to the destination is always the same

Table 1-13: Dynamic Routing Vs. Static Routing

Lab 1-5: Static Routing

Case Study: A Company requires the installation of two new routers to deploy a small static network. Being a network administrator, you have to configure static routing on these routers. Requirements are as follows:

Router 1 Ethernet interface 0/0: 10.10.1.1/24

Router 1 Ethernet interface 0/1: 10.10.2.1/24

Router 2 Ethernet interface 0/1: 10.10.2.2/24

Router 1 Ethernet interface 0/0: 10.10.3.1/24

PC1 IP Address: 10.10.1.2/24

PC2 IP Address: 10.10.3.2/24

Topology Diagram:

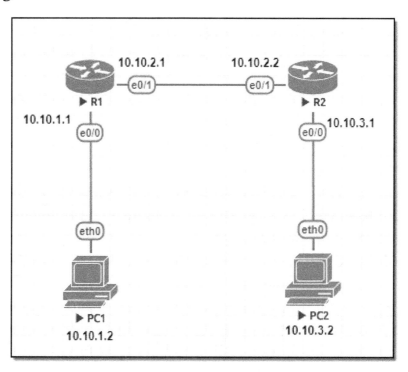

Router 1 Configuration:
Router>en
Router#config t
Enter configuration commands, one per line. End with CNTL/Z.
Router(config)#int e0/0
Router(config-if)#ip address 10.10.1.1 255.255.255.0
Router(config-if)#no shutdown
Router(config-if)#exit

```
*May 10 00:47:21.146: %LINK-3-UPDOWN: Interface Ethernet0/0, changed state to up
*May 10 00:47:22.150: %LINEPROTO-5-UPDOWN: Line protocol on Interface Ethernet0/0,
changed state to up
```

Router(config)#int e0/1

Router(config-if)#ip address 10.10.2.1 255.255.255.0

Router(config-if)#no shutdown

Router(config-if)#exit

```
*May 10 01:05:34.662: %LINK-3-UPDOWN: Interface Ethernet0/1, changed state to up
*May 10 01:05:35.662: %LINEPROTO-5-UPDOWN: Line protocol on Interface Ethernet0/1,
changed state to up
```

Router(config)# ip route 10.10.3.0 255.255.255.0 10.10.2.2

Router 2 Configuration

Router>

Router>en

Router#config t

```
Enter configuration commands, one per line.  End with CNTL/Z.
```

Router(config)#int e0/0

Router(config-if)#ip address 10.10.3.1 255.255.255.0

Router(config-if)#no shutdown

Router(config-if)#exit

```
*May 10 00:56:00.888: %LINK-3-UPDOWN: Interface Ethernet0/0, changed state to up
*May 10 00:56:01.892: %LINEPROTO-5-UPDOWN: Line protocol on Interface Ethernet0/0,
changed state to up
```

Router(config)#int e0/1

Router(config-if)#ip address 10.10.2.2 255.255.255.0

Router(config-if)#no shutdown

Router(config-if)#exit

```
*May 10 01:07:49.996: %LINK-3-UPDOWN: Interface Ethernet0/1, changed state to up

*May 10 01:07:50.996: %LINEPROTO-5-UPDOWN: Line protocol on Interface Ethernet0/1,
changed state to up
```

Router(config)# ip route 10.10.1.0 255.255.255.0 10.10.2.1

Virtual PC Configuration

Go to PC1 and enter the following command

VPC> **IP 10.10.1.2/24 10.10.1.1**

Similarly, Go to PC2 and enter the following command

VPC> **IP 10.10.3.2/24 10.10.3.1**

In case you are using Windows PC. Go to Control Panel > Network and Internet > Internet and Sharing > Change Adapter Settings > Select Adapter and go to Properties > Select IPv4 and Click properties > Select Manual IP addressing > Enter your IP address, Subnet and Default gateway. This process is defined in Lab 1.1 DHCP Configuration, instead of using Automatically obtain IP address option, you have to select manual configuration.

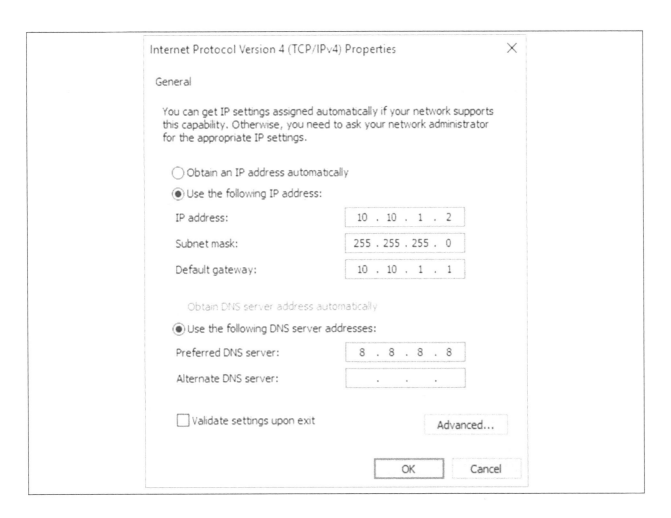

Verification
Go to PC1 and ping PC2 (10.10.3.2)

VPC> **ping 10.10.3.2**

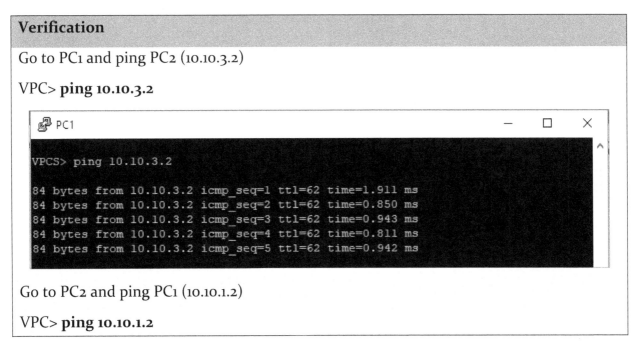

Go to PC2 and ping PC1 (10.10.1.2)

VPC> **ping 10.10.1.2**

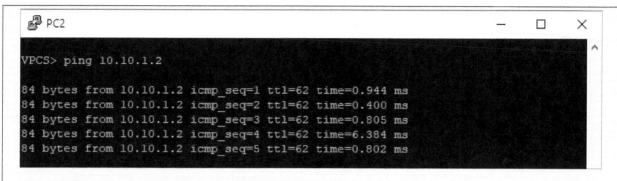

Go to Router and Enter the following command

Router# **show ip interface brief**

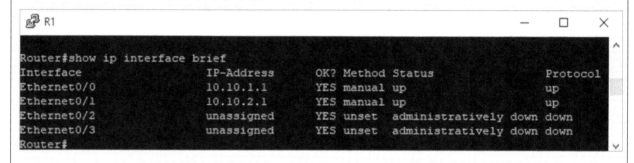

Interface	IP-Address	OK?	Method	Status	Protocol
Ethernet0/0	10.10.1.1	YES	manual	up	up
Ethernet0/1	10.10.2.1	YES	manual	up	up
Ethernet0/2	unassigned	YES	unset	administratively down	down
Ethernet0/3	unassigned	YES	unset	administratively down	down

//As shown in the output, we configured Ethernet 0/0 and 0/1 interfaces. Both interfaces are holding the configured IP address, a method is manual, status is up, and protocol is up.

Router# **show ip route**

```
R1                                                        —    □    ✕
Router#show ip route
Codes: L - local, C - connected, S - static, R - RIP, M - mobile, B - BGP
       D - EIGRP, EX - EIGRP external, O - OSPF, IA - OSPF inter area
       N1 - OSPF NSSA external type 1, N2 - OSPF NSSA external type 2
       E1 - OSPF external type 1, E2 - OSPF external type 2
       i - IS-IS, su - IS-IS summary, L1 - IS-IS level-1, L2 - IS-IS level-2
       ia - IS-IS inter area, * - candidate default, U - per-user static route
       o - ODR, P - periodic downloaded static route, H - NHRP, l - LISP
       a - application route
       + - replicated route, % - next hop override

Gateway of last resort is not set

      10.0.0.0/8 is variably subnetted, 5 subnets, 2 masks
C        10.10.1.0/24 is directly connected, Ethernet0/0
L        10.10.1.1/32 is directly connected, Ethernet0/0
C        10.10.2.0/24 is directly connected, Ethernet0/1
L        10.10.2.1/32 is directly connected, Ethernet0/1
S        10.10.3.0/24 [1/0] via 10.10.2.2
Router#
```

From the above output, as shown "**S   10.10.3.0/24 [1/0] via 10.10.2.2** " shows that network 10.10.3.0/24 is connected via 10.10.2.2. Here "**S**" denotes Static route.

Default route

A default route is a route that adopts when there is no other routing path available for an IP destination address. The default route usually has a next-hop address of another routing device present in a network, which performs the same process. The process repeats until a packet is delivered to the destination.

Types of Routing Protocol

There are basically three types of routing protocols which are as follows:

1. Distance Vector Routing Protocol
2. Link State Routing Protocol
3. Path Vector Routing Protocol

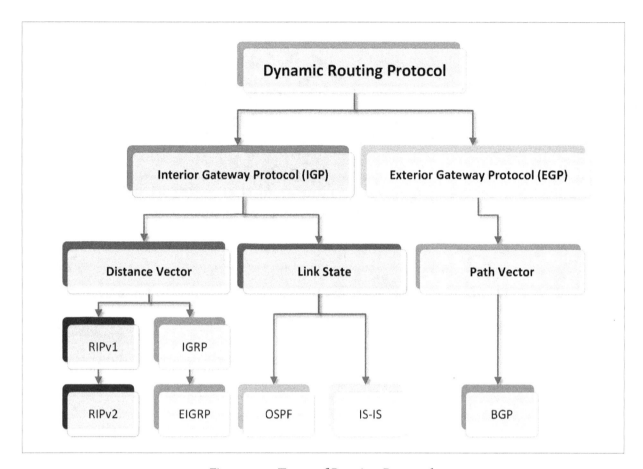

Figure 1-19: Types of Routing Protocol

Distance Vector Routing Protocol

Distance Vector is one of the two Interior Gateway Routing Protocols. It uses Bellman-Ford, Ford-Fulkerson, or DUAL FSM (Cisco only) algorithm for the calculation of its paths. In Distance Vector, router informs about topology changes periodically. There are two main parameters in distance vector routing protocol:

- Distance (Cost to the destination)
- Direction (Next Hop and the exit interface)

RIP and EIGRP are the two known Distance Vector Protocols. The others are DSDV and Babel. RIP uses hop count, EIGRP uses delay and Bandwidth as a cost to reach the destination. RIP UDP as a transport protocol with port number 520. It uses Poison reverse and Split Horizon to prevent routing loops. EIGRP, DSDV, and Babel are the loop-free routing protocols of Distance Vector. EIGRP runs over IP using Protocol no **88** (it does not use TCP or UDP).

Routing Information Protocol (RIP)

Routing Information Protocol (RIP) is a standardized Distance Vector protocol, designed for use on smaller networks. RIP was the first true Distance Vector routing protocols. RIP has two versions RIPv1 and RIPv2. RIPv1 is a class-full protocol and does not support Variable Length Subnet Masks (VLSMs). RIPv2 is a classless protocol and include the subnet mask with its routing table updates. RIPv2 supports VLSMs, and still based on hop count metric because of this limitation RIPv2 cannot be used effectively in today's network.

Hybrid routing protocols (EIGRP)

A hybrid routing protocol is the combination of two routing protocols Distance Vector Routing Protocol and Link State Protocol. Enhanced Interior Gateway Routing Protocol (EIGRP) belongs to hybrid routing protocols and Cisco proprietary protocol. EIGRP uses more sophisticated metric than RIPv1 RIPv2. This metric depends upon the bandwidth of a connection and delay. The only drawback of EIGRP is that it operates only on Cisco routers and Cisco layer 3 switches.

Link State Routing Protocol

Link state Routing protocol including OSPF (Open System Shortest Path First) and IS-IS (Intermediate System to Intermediate System) is the second main type of Interior Gateway Routing Protocols. In link state routing protocol, each node prepares a table or map of connectivity about which node is connected to another. Each node independently calculates the best logical path to every destination. This collection of best path forms the Routing table. Link state Routing uses Dijkstra Algorithm for calculating its shortest path. OSPF does not use TCP/UDP as a transport protocol. It is encapsulated on IP with Protocol no 89; whereas IS-IS is OSI Layer 2 Protocol.

Comparison of distance vector and Link State Routing protocols are given below:

Distance Vector	Link State
Distance vector means that routes are advertised by providing two characteristics:	In link-state protocols, also called shortest-path-first (SPF) protocols, the routers each create three separate tables. One of these tables keeps track of directly attached neighbors, one determines the topology of the entire internetwork, and one is used as the routing table.
Distance: ⟶ Identifies how far it is to the	a router configured with a link-state routing protocol can create a complete

	destination network and is based on a metric such as the hop count, cost, bandwidth, delay, and more.	view or topology of the network by gathering information from all of the other routers.
Vector: ⟶	Specifies the direction of the next-hop router or exit interface to reach the destination.	Link-state routing tables are not exchanged periodically. Instead, triggered updates containing only specific link-state information are sent.
A router using a distance vector routing protocol does not know the entire path to a destination network.		Periodic keepalives that are small and efficient, in the form of hello messages, are exchanged between directly connected neighbors to establish and maintain neighbor relationships.
Distance vector protocols use routers as signposts along the path to the final destination.		
The only information a router knows about a remote network is the distance or metric to reach that network and which path or interface to use to get there.		
Distance vector routing protocols do not have an actual map of the network topology.		
RIP is a distance-vector routing protocol and periodically sends out the entire routing table to directly connected neighbors.		

Table 1-14: Difference between Distance Vector & Link State

Basis for Comparison	Distance Vector				Link-State	
	RIPv1	**RIPv2**	**IGRP**	**EIGRP**	**OSPF**	**IS-IS**
Speed Of Convergence	Slow	Slow	Slow	Fast	Fast	Fast
Scalability	Small	Small	Small	Large	Large	Large
VLSM	No	Yes	No	Yes	Yes	Yes
Resource Usage	Low	Low	Low	Medium	High	High
Implementation and Maintenance	Simple	Simple	Simple	Complex	Complex	Complex

Table 1-15: Link-State and Distance-Vector Routing Protocol Comparison

Note:

While EIGRP is an advanced routing protocol that combines many of the features of both link-state and distance-vector routing protocols, EIGRP's DUAL algorithm contains many features which make it more of a distance vector routing protocol than a link-state routing protocol.

Open Shortest Path First (OSPF)

Open Shortest Path First (OSPF) is the most common link state protocol use in today. OSPF operates on algorithm Shortest Path First (SPF) developed by Dijkstra. The main advantage of EIGRP is that it updates the routing table immediately if any changes occur in the network. OSPF can easily use on small, medium and large networks.

Intermediate System to Intermediate System (IS-IS)

Another important routing protocol is Intermediate System to Intermediate System (IS-IS). IS-IS is designed for large networks like Internet Service Providers. It selects the routing path by packet switched network and also follows Dijkstra's algorithm.

The below-mentioned table describes the difference between Distance Vector, Link state, and Hybrid routing protocol.

IGP vs. EGP

Basis for Comparison	Interior Gateway Protocols	Exterior Gateway Protocols
Routing	Routing inside an autonomous system	Routing across an autonomous system
Configuration	Fast convergence and easy configuration	Slow convergence and complex configuration
Routing Decisions	Administrator influence is low on routing decisions	Administrator influence is high on routing decisions
Examples	RIP, IGRP, OSPF, and IS-IS	BGP

Table 1-16: IGP Vs. EGP

Path Vector Routing Protocol

Border Gateway Protocol (BGP)

Path Vector Routing Protocols are those dynamic routing protocols which operate over path information. This path information is dynamically updated throughout the autonomous system. It is different from the distance vector routing and link state routing. Each entry in the routing table contains the destination network, the next router, and the path to reach the destination.

Autonomous system numbers

An Autonomous System (AS) is a group of networks under a single administrative. When Border Gateway Protocol (BGP) was in progress and standardization stage, a 16-bit binary number was used as the Autonomous System Number (ASN) to identify the Autonomous Systems. 16-bit Autonomous System Number (ASN) is also known as 2-Octet Autonomous System Number (ASN). By using a 16-bit binary number, represented as (2^{16}) numbers, which is equal to 65536 in decimals. The Autonomous System Number (ASN) value 0 is reserved, and the largest ASN value 65,535, is also reserved. The values, from 1 to 64,511, are available for use in Internet routing, and the values 64,512 to 65,534 is selected for private use.

BGP also was known as Border Gateway Routing Protocol is a dynamic routing protocol, which is mostly used in the global internet. Typically, the connection between the ISP's is BGP. Because of its complex path selection method, it allows more flexibility to configure best path selection. IBGP and EBGP are interior and exterior BGP's, which are used within

an autonomous system and with different autonomous systems respectively. BGP uses TCP port number 179 to send its routing information. The main difference of BGP is it does not need neighbors to be connected to the same subnet. ASN stands for Autonomous System Number or a unique number that defines the autonomous System number different from others. IANA or ICANN also provide ASN.

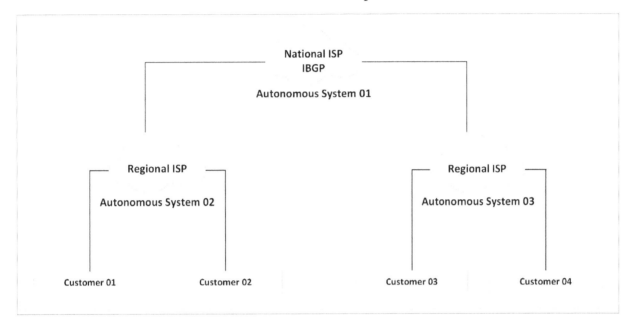

Figure 1-20: Autonomous System

BGP is a very robust and scalable routing protocol, as evidenced by the fact that BGP is the routing protocol employed on the Internet. Internet BGP routing tables gas more than 600,000 routes. To achieve scalability at this level, BGP uses many route parameters, called attributes, to define routing policies and maintain a stable routing environment.

Route Redistribution

Route redistribution is when you take a route from one routing protocol and distribute it into another protocol. By default, routers only promote and share routes with other routers running the same protocol. So, if you have 2 routers running on different protocol can't share the information, but by using routing redistribution, they can share information with each other.

High availability

High Availability is the method to prevent the failure of the router from causing a long-term connectivity issue. The three most common high-availability solutions for routers are:

Virtual Router Redundancy Protocol (VRRP)

Virtual Router Redundancy Protocol (VRRP) placed and connected a virtual router at any physical router in a network. VRRP provides for the automatic assignment of IP addresses to the virtual router. If a physical router fails, the virtual router performs its function. The physical router forwards its packet at any instant is called Master router.

Virtual IP

Virtual IP is a similar concept to VRRP; it is consists of a virtual IP address assigned to any physical router present in the network. Therefore, the traffic coming to the virtual IP addresses may be sent to any router behind it. It provides load-balanced to increase traffic throughput and also increase stability.

Hot Standby Router Protocol (HSRP)

Hot Standby Router Protocol (HSRP) is a Cisco proprietary routing redundancy protocol. HSRP establishes a fault-tolerant default gateway between network routers. This gateway automatically created when the current gateway becomes inaccessible because interfaces on the router failed.

Route Aggregation

Route Aggregation is also known as supernetting, is a method of using multiple addresses or block of addresses. It based on the principle of subnetting but subnetting moves from left to right whereas route aggregation moves from right to left.

Routing Metrics

The routing metric is the data that every routing protocol used to make decisions. Different routing metrics use different routing protocols. There are six routing metrics described below:

Hop counts

Hop counts is the process of a packet passing through some router interfaces to reach its final destination. Hop counts are used by only two protocols RIP and RIPv2 because it is less intelligent. Hop count does not depend upon the bandwidth link and current traffic.

MTU, Bandwidth, Delay

Maximum Transmission Unit (MTU) is considered as a legacy metric that is used to signify the largest packet could be sent across the entire route. EIGRP uses MTU but not used in the calculation of the best route. EIGRP uses bandwidth and delays to make decisions.

Bandwidth is the idea belongs to the weakest link in a chain determines its strength. Practically, defines that the lowest configured bandwidth of an interface in a proposed route.

Delay is the time taken by the packet to travel across the link.

These types of metrics are more intelligent than hop counts:

Costs metrics used by the OSPF routing protocol. OSPF cost metric is calculated by taking 10 to the power of 8 and dividing it by the bandwidth in bits per second. If the connection has a bandwidth of 100 Mbps has a cost of 1.

Latency metric is similar to delay metric that defines the amount of time taken by the data packets to travel from a source to destination. The difference is that delay is only a routing metric whereas latency also deals with outside of routing such as in hard drive or memory.

Administrative Distance

Administrative Distance (AD) of any specific route is an indication of the honesty of the route, the lowest AD value indicating the most trustworthy route. It is a useful metric when network connected to more than on one routing protocol is promoting a path to a destination, and the paths are different.

SPB

SPB Shortest path bridging (SPB) is standardized by the 802.1aq standard and is designed to simplify the creation of robust networks by enabling multipathing routing.

Basics Elements of Unified Communication Technologies

VoIP

Voice over Internet Protocol (VoIP) is the transmission of voice and multimedia content over IP networks. The content may be in many forms, including files, voice communication, pictures, fax or multimedia messages. VoIP is most often used for telephone calls, which are almost free of cost.

Video

Video calling is a technology that facilitates the communication and interaction of one or more users through a combination of high-quality audio and video over Internet Protocol (IP) networks.

Real-Time Services

Real-time network services are designed to deliver real-time information with a high quality of real-time service. Real-time information is live voice and video. Real-time services are designed to deliver real-time information concerning time. There are a lot of real-time services going around. For examples; Online learning, Online games, Online banking and so on.

QoS

Quality of service assures that Unified Communication (UC) services are treated with a higher priority than other traffic. This quality of service edge can be modeled at Layer 2 or Layer 3 of the OSI model. Two types of QoS deployed on a network.

DSCP

Differentiated Services Code Point (DSCP) is a method for differentiating and managing network traffic. It operates at the network layer (layer 3) using 6-bit code point within an 8-bit field. Each frame from an application is dedicated to a class of traffic, and each router on the network is configured to recognize that class.

COS

Class of Service (COS) is an old method of classifying network traffic. It operates at Data-Link layer (layer2) using a 3-bit designator, so there are only eight designations for traffic (0–7). Routers and switches can be configured to recognize the classification of packets and react thus applications that need more from the network will get a higher priority.

Devices

To implement these services, devices are required to handle these services. Some Unified Communication (UC) devices are described here:

By using authorized **UC servers** and applications connected to specially configured **UC devices** like routers and switches with QoS to connect to the network. It is also possible to use the **UC gateway** and configure DSCP in it for specific types of traffic, thereby giving it a different and perhaps more advantageous route into and out of your network. All of this can combine to provide the performance that needs for the UC application that is using.

Technologies Using in Cloud and Virtualization.

Virtualization

In computing, virtualization defines to create a something that is not an actual or virtual version of a device or resources like servers, storage devices or operating systems.

Virtual Switch

A virtual switch (vSwitch) is a software application that allows communication between virtual machines. A vSwitch provides more than just forward data packets; it intelligently directs the data packets by checking it before moving them to a destination.

Virtual switches are usually embedded into installed software, but they may also be included in a server's hardware as part of its firmware. The vSwitch combines physical switches into a single logical switch. It helps to increase bandwidth and create an active mesh between server and switches.

Virtual Router

A virtual Router is a software-based routing structure that allows the host machine to perform as a typical hardware router over a local area network.

A virtual router can enable a computer/server to have the abilities of a complete router by performing the network and packet routing functionality of the router through a software application.

Virtual Firewall

A virtual firewall is a firewall device or service that provides network traffic filtering and monitoring for virtual machines. A virtual firewall is installed, executed and operated from a virtual machine.

Virtual NIC

A virtual NIC that is linked to a physical NIC is a true Ethernet link in the firmest sense. Its packets are sent on the wire with its own unique MAC address. A virtual NIC that is connected to a virtual network does not require an Ethernet interface on the host.

Software-defined Networking

The idea of programmable networks has newly regained substantial momentum due to the emergence of the Software-Defined Networking (SDN) paradigm. Outdated network architectures are ill-suited to meet the requirements of today's enterprises, carriers, and end users. SDN often referred to as a key enabler that promises dramatically simplify network management and enable innovation through network programmability.

Software Defined Networking (SDN) is an emerging network framework where network control is decoupled from forwarding and is directly programmable. Previously, the network control is firmly bound in individual network devices. This way is dramatically changed into accessible computing devices enables the underlying infrastructure to be abstracted for applications and network services, which can treat the network as a logical or virtual entity.

SDN architecture

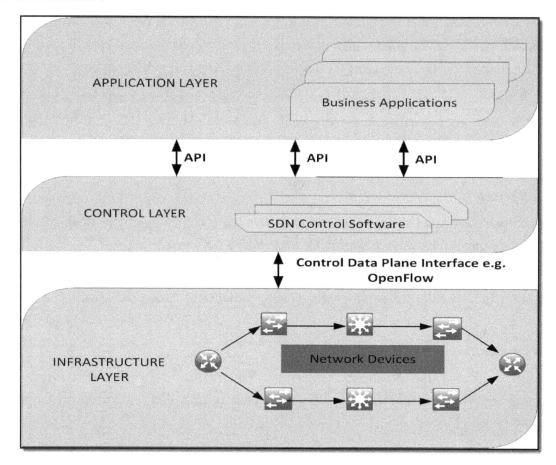

Figure 1-21: Software-Defined Network Architecture

Figure 1-21 represents a logical view of the SDN framework. Network brainpower is logically integrated into software-based SDN controllers, which maintain a global view of the network. SDN also significantly simplifies the network devices themselves, as they no longer need to understand and process thousands of protocol standards but only accept instructions from the SDN controllers.

OpenFlow is the first standard communications interface defined between the control and forwarding layers of an SDN framework that allows directing access and manipulation of the forwarding plane of physical as well as virtual network devices.

SDN architecture will provide a set of Application Programming Interfaces (APIs) that simplifies the implementation of common network services like routing, multicast, security, access control, bandwidth management, traffic engineering, QoS, energy efficiency, and various forms of policy management. Therefore, enterprises, network operators, and carriers gain exceptional programmability, automation, and network

control, enabling them to build highly scalable, flexible networks that cheerfully familiarize with changing business needs.

Storage Area Network

To realize the SDDC, the network must have shared storage among the physical servers that host the virtual servers and virtual network devices. Three methods can create this storage:

iSCSI

Internet Small Computer Systems Interface (iSCSI) is a storage transport methodology that is fast and reliable and can help organization leverage the network cables, switches, and connections that they already have in place. It is used on 10 Gbps networks to leverage bandwidth. If any network has 10 Gbps bandwidth, the network can be served for storage purpose by installing iSCSI cards on the servers.

Jumbo frame

The MTU of network components used for 9000 frames instead of 1500 frames. It is to allow for larger frames, called jumbo frames, used with iSCSI to reduce overhead.

Fibre Channel

Fibre Channel is another technology that can use to transfer data from your SAN. It uses either fiber-optic cables and switches or a 10 Gbps network with particular cards. Fibre Channel uses a special type of address called a worldwide name (WWN). Each node in the Fibre Channel network has its own specific WWN.

Network Attached Storage

Network Attached Storage (NAS) belongs to storage area network in theory. NAS is a form of dignified mapped drive in which a shared data is connected to by a client to obtain and use data. The NAS server usually a Unix or Linux server, which provides the client has its access to the data but never access to the disk.

Cloud Concepts

Cloud computing is a service that delivers computing resources that can be provided when needed. Major cloud concepts include public, private, hybrid, and community relating to Infrastructure as a Service (IaaS), Software as a Service (SaaS), and Platform as a Service (PaaS) individually.

Types of Cloud Computing Services

Cloud Computing Services are categorized into the following three types: -

- Infrastructure-as-a-Service (IaaS)
- Platform-as-a-Service (PaaS)

- Software-as-a-Service (SaaS)

Infrastructure-as-a-Service (IaaS)

Infrastructure services, (IaaS) also known as Cloud infrastructure service is basically a self-service model. IaaS is used for accessing, monitoring and managing purpose. For example, instead of purchasing additional hardware such as firewall, networking devices, server and spending money on deployment, management, and maintenance, IaaS model offers cloud-based infrastructure to deploy remote datacenter. Most popular examples of IaaS are Amazon EC2, Cisco Metapod, Microsoft Azure, Google Compute Engine (GCE).

Platform-as-a-Service (PaaS)

Platform as a service is another cloud computing service. It allows the users to develop, run and manage applications. PaaS offers Development tools, Configuration management, Deployment Platforms, and migrate the app to hybrid models. It helps to develop and customize applications, manage OSes, visualization, storage and networking, etc. Examples of PaaS are Google App Engine, Microsoft Azure, Intel Mash Maker, etc.

Software-as-a-Service (SaaS)

Software as a Service (SaaS) is one of the most popular types of Cloud Computing service that is most widely used. On-demand Software is centrally hosted to be accessible by users using client via browsers. An example of SaaS is office software such as office 365, Cisco WebEx, Citrix GoToMeeting, Google Apps, messaging software, DBMS, CAD, ERP, HRM, etc.

Cloud Deployment Models

The following are the deployment models for Cloud Services.

Deployment Model	Description
Public Cloud	Public clouds are hosted by a third party offering different types of Cloud computing services.
Private Cloud	Private Clouds are hosted personally, individually. Corporate companies usually deploy their private clouds because of their security policies.
Hybrid Cloud	Hybrid Clouds are comprised of both Private and public cloud. Private cloud is for their sensitive and public cloud to scale up capabilities and services.
Community Cloud	Community Clouds are accessed by multiple parties having common goals and shared resources.

Public: The philosophy behind the public cloud is to get the computing resources immediately. In public cloud, the client has a choice to decide from a variety of offerings from a public cloud vendor such as Amazon Web Service or Microsoft's Azure.

Private: Individual can make the platform for the private cloud using virtualization software from VMware and other companies. The cloud gives complete authority and decision making. However, it takes some time to develop but complete authority in IaaS, PaaS, and SaaS components of the system.

Hybrid: To get the services of both public and private cloud hybrid cloud can be used. In hybrid cloud infrastructures like public cloud and control like private cloud.

Community: A community cloud is used by a group of organizations from the business community that share the same common content such as compliance, security, and so on. Therefore, the costs to create the cloud are divided over a few organizations to save money for each organization but still maintain more control over IaaS, PaaS, and SaaS decisions than with a public cloud.

Set of Requirements to Implement a Basic Network

This section discusses the list of requirements to implement a basic network design.

List of Requirements

The network that we will discuss must be able to perform the following functions:

- Successfully and securely connect six separate departments with 1–30 hosts in each department in the main building.
- Dynamically assign IP addresses to all clients.
- Use a private addressing scheme that can also connect to the Internet.
- Provide for WAN connectivity to two remote locations.
- Provide monitored web access to employees in all locations.
- Detect threats to the network and automatically close ports when appropriate.
- Provide for high availability and high performance for a customized database server system used by the sales department.
- Leverage an existing 10 Gbps infrastructure for storage and networking.
- Provide for secure wireless connectivity for users in the main building.
- Use an easy-to-configure-and-manage open-source protocol in the main building network.

Device Types/Requirements

To create a network design, you firstly need a router and some switches, which can handle 10 Gbps bandwidth, a DHCP server, which could be a separate server or could be

configured on the router. Additionally, need a proxy server and an IPS server to meet the security goals. Also, we will need a load balancer to meet the performance and high-availability goals of our custom database application for sales and need an iSCSI array for storage. Finally, you need a WAP or two to handle the wireless connections in the main building.

Environment and Equipment Limitations

Most of the network installation, configuration, and so on will be in the main building. For example, use plenum cable whenever in the plenum to meet that legal standard and make the fire marshal happy. Build the cables appropriately for straight-through to connect dissimilar devices and crossover to connect similar devices. Use the appropriate number of switches and other devices to meet the requirements and allow for a little growth.

Compatibility, Wireless, and Security Considerations

The network design must be capable of separating six different departments into their broadcast domains, so it can manage them separately from each other. By using a private addressing structure of 192.168.1.0/27. The networks will be the 0, 32, 64, 96, 128, and 160 subnets. The WAN links to the remote offices will be subnets of the 192 subnets and will, therefore, be 192.168.1.192/30 and 192.168.1.196/30, since need only two hosts on each of those links.

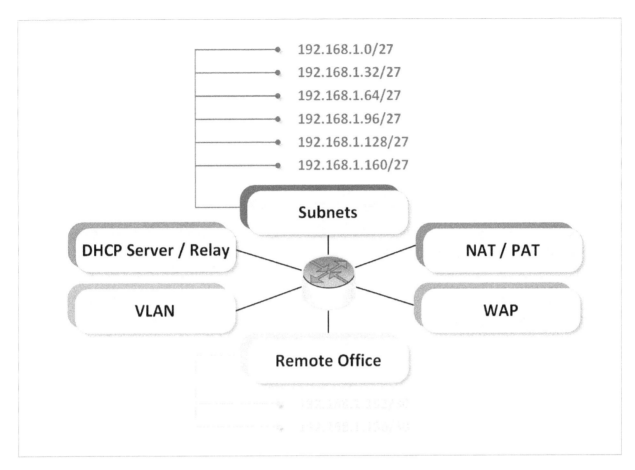

Figure 1-22: IP Schema of a Little Network

The client addresses will be obtained through a DHCP server that will have the scopes listed for each of the clients. Using a DHCP relay agent server in each subnet that does not contain the DHCP server, so the client can obtain an appropriate address dynamically. Also, use the DHCP server to configure the clients with the address of the proxy server to be used for monitored Internet access. Also, configure an IPS to close connections when inappropriate anomalies are detected in the network traffic.

Finally, use a router or a switch with VLANs configured to divide the network into the logical segments that created with the subnetting. Also, the switches will be connected to a router configured with PAT for Internet access and to a WAP for wireless access.

Mind Map

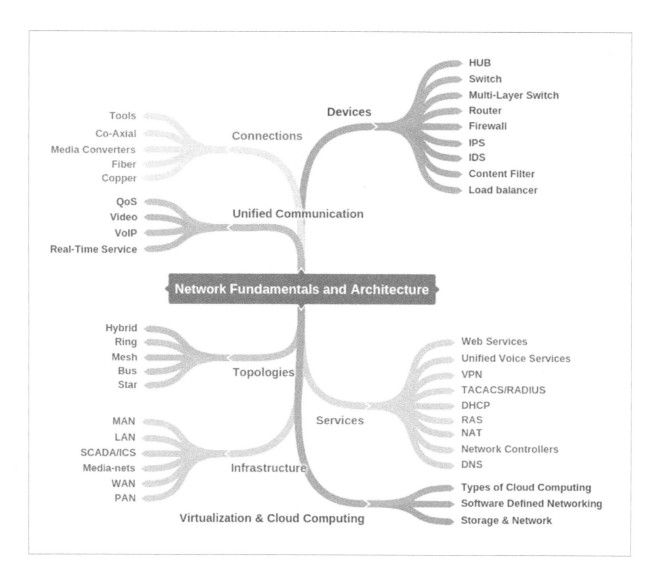

Chapter 2: Network Operations

Application of Monitoring Tools

A network administrator needs to know the behavior of the network, analyze the network performance to manage and troubleshoot the network in a better way. For this, they require the appropriate tools that monitor the overall network's activity.

This section will describe such tools that will help analyze the network's performance. It may include packet/network analyzers, interface monitoring tools, port scanners, SNMP management software, alerts, packet flow monitoring, SYSLOG, and SIEM. It also includes environmental monitoring tools for temperature and humidity, power monitoring tools, and even some wireless survey and analysis tools.

Network/Packet Analyzer

A packet analyzer is like an electron microscope for IT administrators as it inspects the network traffic. Network analyzers are also valuable tools for testing protocols, diagnosing network problems, identifying configuration issues, and resolving network bottlenecks. Finally, information security teams rely on these tools to discover network misuse, vulnerabilities, malware, and attack attempts.

There are many types of packet analyzer but the most commonly used is Wireshark. Wireshark is the world famous and widely used network protocol analyzer. The figure next page shows the operation of DHCP on Wireshark by searching DHCP offer and DHCP ACK packet.

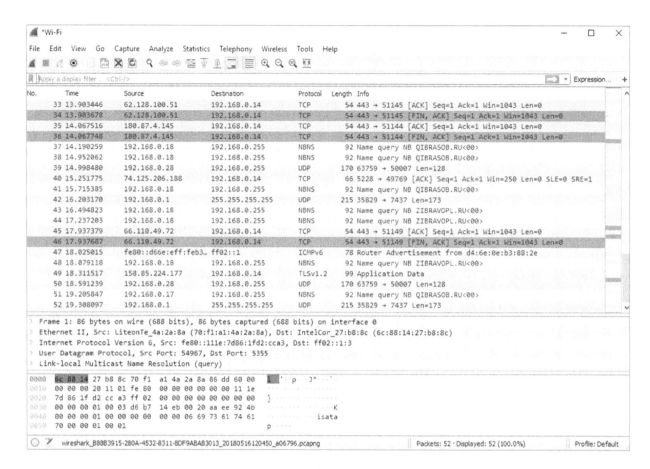

Figure 2-01: Wireshark Packet Analyzer

Interface Monitoring Tools

Interface monitoring tools used to monitor the traffic flow across the specific network interfaces. Using a common tool like PuTTY on a specific router interface examine the traffic flow. For example, if you PuTTY into a router, and you can enter the following command

"debug packet display interface Nic_o port-8o."

This would show you any HTTP (port 80) traffic that was on that interface.

Port Scanner

A port scanner is a software application designed to examine a server or clients for open ports. It is used as a weapon or as a useful tool depends upon the way it handles. Port scanner use to verify the security policies on a network. Without prior permission, nobody can use a port scanner on another organization's network. Common port scanners are Nmap, Pentest, and others.

Figure 2-02: Nmap in Action

Top Talkers/Listeners

Top talkers are the computers sending the most data, whereas top listeners are the ones receiving the most data. Some network software like ObjectPlanet analyze the top talkers and top listeners of network traffic. This type of software can usually break down this information by using IP address, hostname, protocol, port, and so on. By using this information, finding bandwidth hogs that are unauthorized to be on the network is easier.

SNMP Management Software

Simple Network Management Protocol (SNMP) is a tool that can help in identifying devices called agents in the network such as routers, switches and also determining the status and configuration of these devices.

SNMP consists of complex jumble of object IDs (OIDs) and management information base (MIBs) to contain data with Network Management Stations (NMSs).

SNMP performs following main functions:

The NMS occasionally queries or polls the SNMP agent on a device to collect and analyze statistics via GET messages. These messages can be sent to a console or alert you via email or SMS. The command snmpwalk uses the SNMP GETNEXT request to query a network for a tree of information. End devices running SNMP agents will send an SNMP TRAP to the NMS if a problem occurs.

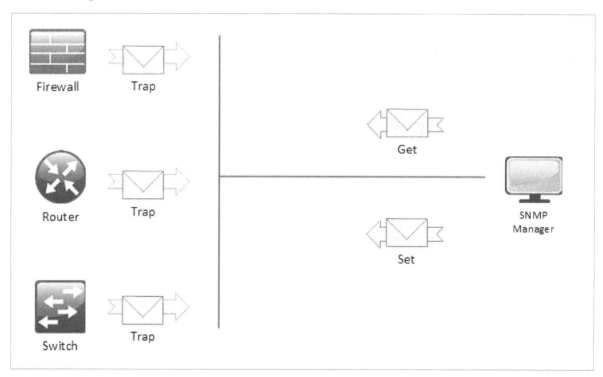

Figure 2-03: SNMP GET and TRAP messages

Administration can also use SNMP to provide some configuration to agents as well, called SET messages. In addition to polling to obtain statistics, SNMP can be used in analyzing information and compiling the results in a report or even a graph. Thresholds can be used to trigger a notification process when exceeded. Graphing tools are used to monitor the CPU statistics of devices like a core router. The CPU should be monitored continuously,

and the NMS can graph the statistics. Notifications will be sent when any threshold set has been exceeded.

SNMP has three versions:

SNMPv1: Supports plaintext authentication with community strings and uses only UDP.

SNMPv2c: Supports plaintext authentication with MD5 or SHA with no encryption but provides GET BULK, which is a method to collect many types of information at once and minimize the number of GET requests. It offers a more detailed error message reporting method, but it's not more secure than v1. It uses UDP even though it can be configured to use TCP.

SNMPv3: Supports strong authentication with MD5 or SHA, providing confidentiality (encryption) and data integrity of messages via DES or DES-256 encryption between agents and managers. GET BULK is a supported feature of SNMPv3, and this version also uses TCP.

Alerts

A network alert provides information to a network administrator that a key health or performance indicator has exceeded a threshold to facilitate the detection, diagnosis, and resolution of network performance issues.

These alerts can be generated in the form of Email and SMS to the network administrator.

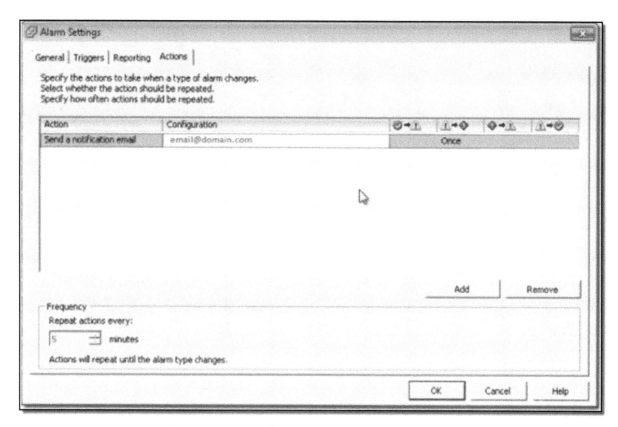

Figure 2-04: An alert on VMware's vCenter server

Packet Flow Monitoring

Packet flow monitoring analyzes the flow of data packet throughout the network carefully. Packet flow monitoring is accomplished with a set of tools related to general packet sniffers and analyzers, tracks traffic flowing between the specific source and destination devices. Cisco developed the concept of packet flow monitoring and consequently incorporated in routers and switches. The most prevalent packet flow monitoring tool is NetFlow. It consists of flow caching, a flow collector, and a data analyzer. It depends on requirement what to examine incoming flows, just outgoing, or both. Also, the user can specify the interface, IP address, protocol, and ports about which they are interested in collecting data.

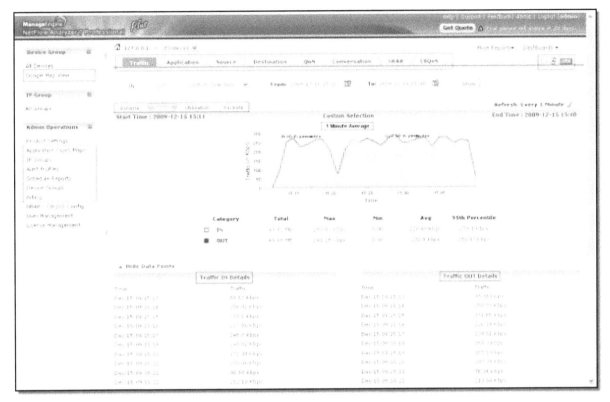

Figure 2.05: Packet Monitoring in NetFlow

Syslogs

Syslog is a standard for all message logging for Unix and Unix-based computers as well as Unix-like systems such as printers, routers, switches, and so on. It provides a central place for messages to be collected after they are generated by the software on each of these devices. Messages in the SYSLOG are labeled with a facility code that directs the type of software that generated the message and the severity or importance of the message. By monitoring the SYSLOG, it can easily detect the weak points and improve overall performance.

Security Information and Event Management (SIEM)

Security Information and Event Management (SIEM) is an industry standard term used to monitor and manage networks. SEIM is a combination of two related technologies Security Event Management (SEM) and Security Information Management (SIM).

SEM deals with the real-time monitoring and notifying the security events such as authentication failures and intrusion events generated by the security systems while SIM is responsible for collecting and managing security-related log data from firewalls, antivirus software, network routers, DNS servers, databases and another origin.

Therefore, SIEM is referred to as the System Information and Event Management strengthen the effect on the whole system, particularly on security.

Some popular SIEM options include

- ArcSight Express
- McAfee ESM (Enterprise Security Manager)
- IBM Security QRadar
- Splunk Enterprise software or virtual machines
- LogRhythm's appliance, software, and virtual machines

Environment Monitoring Tools

In IT industries cooling environment is more important as servers, routers, switches, and other networking devices are running and generating heat. So, the recommended temperature range for a datacentre is between 68 and 75 degrees Fahrenheit and recommended relative humidity is 50 to 60 percent.

Power monitoring tools

Since all the networking devices run on electricity, so the failure of electricity will cause a big problem. Power monitoring tools are made to help in controlling and providing uninterrupted power supply across the devices. In large organization and large datacentres, companies like Schneider Electric also popular as APC offers a wide range of power monitoring tools that are responsible for saving money by providing operational and clean power to all the networking devices.

Wireless survey tools

Before creating a wireless network, need to do a wireless survey of the place where the wireless network will deploy. So, for this purpose wireless survey tools helps in collecting real-world data by performing unique true end-user experience measurements such as wireless LAN throughput, data rates, retries, and losses. It can also assist in minimizing the costly impact of RF interference sources on wireless 802.11n/a/b/g/ac LAN performance by performing real-time wireless spectrum analysis in a single walk-through.

Wireless analyzers

The wireless analyzer has similar functions as network analyzers. The wireless analyzer can find the reserved channels, number of clients and bandwidth used, top talkers/listeners and more. Wi-Fi analyzers recognize networks by inactively collecting packets and detecting standard named networks, detecting hidden networks, and inferring the presence of nonbeaconing networks by data traffic.

Analyze Metrics and Reports from Monitoring and Tracking Performance Tools.

Network administrations perform their work much better if they have a complete understanding of network performance. To evaluate network performance, they must have a baseline of network performance that is reflected in their logs and maybe even in graphs. By this, they can easily spot issues that affect network utilization and bottlenecks.

Baseline

In networking, the baseline can refer to the standard level of performance of a certain device or the normal operating capacity for your whole network. Specifically, server's baseline defines standards for factors like how busy its processors are, how much of the memory it uses, and how much data usually goes through the NIC at a given time. A network baseline bounds the amount of bandwidth available and when.

For networks and networked devices, baselines include information about four key components:

- Processor
- Memory
- Hard-disk (or other storage) subsystem
- Wired/wireless utilization

Bottleneck

A network bottleneck refers to a discrete condition in which data flow is limited by network resources. There are four vital resources on any network or any devices on the network: processor, memory, disk subsystem, and a network subsystem. A serious weakness in any of the network resources can easily spread and affect the other resources. It will cause a network bottleneck.

Log management

All system that generates automatic log files facing two issues. One is security and other is maintenance. Log files are important for the information they provide and its stores on mass storage and continuously increases until they fill. The job of providing proper security and maintenance for log files is called log management. Log management can manage system logs, history logs and event logs.

Graphing

The graph is an important tool to express the performance of any network visually. The graph included in mostly all performance monitoring software.

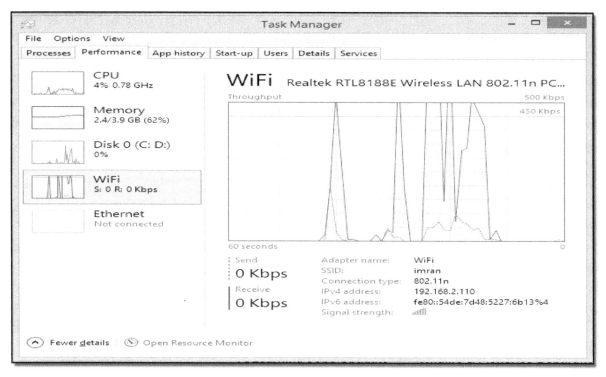

Figure 2-06: Network Utilization Graph

Utilization

Utilization represents the efficient use of available resources of the network. In case of bandwidth utilization, wired and wireless analyzers represent the bandwidth used on network segments or wireless area. There are various tools to find the stats on storage, network device CPU, and device memory for servers and hosts.

For example, if you have a MAC, you can use the built-in activity monitor, which provides the CPU usage, memory statistics, energy used by the applications, disk usage, and network bytes sent and received, as shown in below figure:

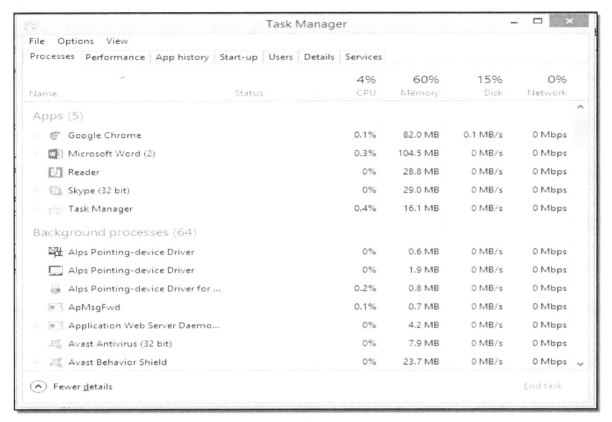

Figure 2-07: MAC's Activity Monitor

Link status

Link status detects the physical layer carrier which primarily means copper feels light and fiber see the light. All network devices use lights or software to show the link status. If it shows the positive link status on one side then it also assures the other side of the device is on, it means the connectivity is established, and the network is ready to send and receive data. This can be moved to the next layer (layer 2, 3) of the OSI model.

Interface monitoring

A network interface monitor collects and analyzes performance, traffic, and bandwidth data for network interfaces. It is used to detect, diagnose, and resolve network performance issues.

Interface monitor carefully monitors the errors, utilization, discards, packet drops, reset, speed and duplex in the interface.

To monitor these interface issues, there is a range of interface monitoring tool available in the market. The most popular and useful interface monitoring tool is LogicMonitor.

Supporting Resources for Configuration Management.

For the network administrator, configuration management is the part of their job. To accomplish it, they need to understand the entire network configuration. Some tools will help them to look up and secure the entire network include Archives and Backups, Baselines, management of mobile devices, Network Access Control (NAC) and various types of documentation.

Archives/Backups

The network administrator should keep track of all the documentation in the form of archives and backups. Although it is not an easy task to update the archives and backups as upgrade and replacement is a part of network infrastructure. If any changes in configuration on routers, switches or add new VLAN will require a change in the logical diagram and the backup. To track these updates and documentation, many organization uses software, and some hire a team member to perform this responsibility. It archived and backed up information can be used to troubleshoot or restore the part of a network.

On-boarding and off-boarding of mobile devices

By the explosion of mobile devices such as smartphones and tablets, nowadays, many organizations have encouraged to BYOD (Bring Your Own Device) policy that allows employees to use their devices on the organization networks. IT administrator must configure the network in such a way that the mobile devices easily connect and work on the organization's network. This is called On-boarding mobile devices. When the employees completed their job period and left the company, it is necessary to make their devices as like they won't be able to use organization's network this is called off-boarding mobile devices.

Network Access Control (NAC)

Network Access Control (NAC) is an evolution in security protocols and methods. In recent days NACs are available in high processing CPU with high bandwidth connection. When a new computer wants to connect to the network it first examines the network access control if it approves then it allows to connect to the network. NAC prevents the computer from viruses and unwanted threats.

Documentation

Documentation about the network is very important for the network administrator that it bears a lot of useful information, so it should be up to date with the following record.

Network Diagrams: A network diagram is a visual representation of network architecture. It maps out the structure of a network with a variety of different symbols and line connections. It is the ideal way to share the layout of a network because the visual presentation makes it easier for users to understand how devices are connected.

Network diagrams can be made with Microsoft Visio or cisco works that provide remarkable visibility.

Asset Management: Asset management is a technical word as well as a system that monitors and manages all networking device of any worth. IT asset management includes standards and processes for the deployment, maintenance, lifecycle management, updating, and ultimate clearance of equipment such as routers, switches, servers, appliances, and others.

IP Address Utilization: Documentation about the IP address utilization is beneficial, especially for the flexible network. Knowledge about the which IP address is allocated to the router must be properly documented, and it will help not only for new IT technician but also helpful in identifying IP addressing issues that might occur. Appropriate IP address design can also simplify the routing tables and make routing process fast. The smart network cannot be designed without proper IP address documentation.

Vendor Documentation: Vendor documents often have beneficial clauses that were negotiated during the purchase process. It may include vendor specifications, safety issues, environmental conditions, warranties, and deadlines. So, these documents should be well maintained as it has the information about the performance, monitoring, and troubleshooting.

Internal operating procedures/policies/standards: Documenting network policies on each feature of network behavior from the acceptable use of a vendor to the standard level of performance. Each policy should be carefully documented.

Importance of Implementing Network Segmentation

This section will discuss the importance of network segmentation concerning SCADA systems, legacy systems, private and public networks, honeypots and honeynets, and testing labs. It will also discuss the concepts of load balancing, performance optimization, security, and compliance and their significance to network segmentation.

SCADA systems/industrial control systems

An industrial control system (ICS) is a general term that incorporates several types of control systems used in industrial production. The most common is Supervisory Control and Data Acquisition (SCADA). SCADA is a system working with coded signals over communication channels to provide control of remote equipment.

It includes the following components:

- Sensors: usually contains digital or analog I/O, and these types of signals cannot be easily communicated over long distances
- Remote terminal units (RTUs): connect to the sensors and convert sensor data to digital data includes telemetry hardware.
- Programmable logic controllers (PLCs): connect to the sensors and convert sensor data to digital data exclude telemetry hardware
- Telemetry systems: connect RTUs and PLCs to control centers and the Enterprise
- Human interface: presents data to the operator

Data acquisition server (ICS Server) uses coded signals over communication channels to acquire information about the status of the remote equipment for display or recording functions.

Legacy Systems

Legacy systems are older and incompatible with more modern systems and equipment. They may be less secure and also be no longer supported by the vendor. In most cases, these legacy systems, especially concerning industrial control systems use propriety protocols that prevent them from communicating on the IP-based network. It's a good way to segment these systems to protect them from security issues they aren't capable of handling or even just to permit them to function correctly.

Separate Private/Public Networks

This type of network segmentation separate public networks and private networks. This can be done by NAT, PAT, and Firewalls. Network Address Translation (NAT) services assist in converting traffic of a private IP address to the public IP address when the traffic enters the internet, it also served as the network segmentation between a private network and public network. Firewalls make the private network secure by using three-pronged devices which allows for some devices to be accessed from inside, outside and inside or outside depends upon the functionality and security requirement.

Honeypot/Honeynet

Honeypots are security devices used as a decoy to act as a valuable server target to an attacker. When they are monitored and are inaccessible from any truly sensitive computer data, it also appears to be vulnerable to attack and quite undefended. The idea is to get the attacker to take the lure, and then while they are wasting their time in the honeypot, network's real data is safe, and then gather information about the attacker and give it to the authorities.

Two or more honeypots on the same network make a honeynet. It is used in a large organization where a single honeypot server won't do the job. The honeynet simulates a

production network but is deeply monitored and isolated from the true production network.

Testing Lab

Testing labs is a place where you test the performance of new hardware and software before implementing in the production environment. It gives a lot of benefits as you have the freedom to learn from your mistakes in a forgiving environment so that you hopefully won't make that mistake in the production environment.

Load Balancing

Nowadays, networks often have multiple connections from a source to destination. This type of configuration has been managed by load balancing. When more than one path exists from a source to destination, it can use all the multiple paths by spreading the traffic flows and the available bandwidth to each connection. Load balancing can accomplish this during segmentation network. Some common traffic that is load balanced in today's network include websites, FTP, DNS, and Internet Relay Chat.

Performance Optimization

The main function of a network is to make its resources available to the end user. End users don't want to know the network is functioning. All they want to do is to get the services so that they can do their job. On the other hand, network administrators must be aware of the latest networking technologies so that they can continue to make the resources transparently available to end users. To enable this, they can employ many methods to make the network more efficient, such as quality of service (QoS), traffic shaping, caching engines, and many more.

Security

The most important thing that network never compromise is network security. In reality, a network computer is responsible for sharing resources that have to face security issues and threats. These security issues can be resolved by hardware and software. To make the resources secure, first segmenting it then decide the allotment of resources.

Compliance

To comply means to meet an established standard. That standard might be enforced by the organization such as password complexity rules. In this case, it's unlikely that the same standard will apply in the same way to all parts of network or users. It provides more flexibility to apply a higher standard to areas that permit it and a lower standard to areas that don't. Network segmentation may be required to comply with industry regulation.

Installation and Application of Patches and Updates

To enhance the level of network performance and security, the system must be up to date. These updates may include OS, firmware, drivers, and others.

OS Updates

Operating system updates perform on a daily basis on the systems. It is because most of the software are not fully tested and debugged at the time of release as it takes a long time. Usually, this bug will discover when the customer uses this software. So, the software company will respond with a fix in the form of patches or updates.

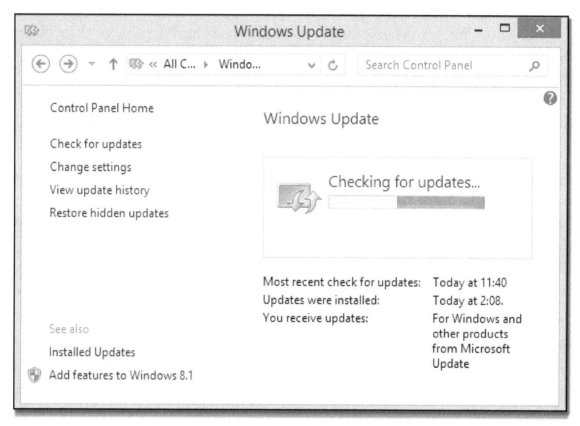

Figure 2-08: Windows Updates

Firmware Updates

Firmware is the midway between the software and hardware. BIOS on a PC and the bootstrap that handles routers and switches are the examples of firmware. Firmware updates are designed to increase the performance of a device. Firmware is a form of program code, and their related data is stored in some insistent memory like Non-Volatile RAM (NVRAM). The firmware update is not necessary with a software update. Usually, the firmware will be updated on a router, switch or even PC by simply replacing the hardware and attaining the new firmware with new hardware.

Driver Updates

Drivers are software that allows the hardware to communicate with the operating system. Drivers are usually specified with hardware and their related operating system. Drivers can be updated by installing the new driver, and some new operating system provides a rollback option if the installed driver fails to update.

Feature Changes/Updates

Feature changes/updates define the purpose itself. To add new functionality to the system not only because it is available but also keep in mind that it supports the system.

Major vs. Minor Updates

Major update belongs to the overall change in the installed hardware and software. It could be the effect on security or efficiency should be planned to be performed whenever the software or hardware vendors require. Major updates should not leave over chance or worry about whether they will break something. Minor updates that only twist a setting or service should be performed simply when that service or twist is needed or beneficial.

Vulnerability Patches

When a major vulnerability to an OS or other system is discovered, vendors incline to respond quickly by generating a fix in the form of a vulnerability patch. If the vulnerability is major, that patch is usually made available as soon as it is complete. Sometimes, these high-priority security patches are even pushed to the end user right away. Minor vulnerabilities get patched as part of a regular patch cycle.

Upgrading vs. Downgrading

Operating system updates are not always beneficial for the system as it doesn't give something new that is of value to the system. Whenever the new version of operating system releases, it may have some security and compatibility issues. So, before upgrading the system waiting until all the bugs are removed in the released version.

In most cases, the system was upgrading and then facing substantial issues in the production environment. So, it is necessary for the system to downgrading the system to the previous version. In many cases, the administration should have back up of all the task before performing any updates.

Configuring Switch Features

As discussed earlier, switches are the devices that segment a network at data link layer of the OSI model. Switches first make a MAC table of all the connected devices then forwarding frames by following their MAC table. In a scenario, the responsibility of that in charge of any organization's switches including Virtual Local Area Network (VLAN),

Spanning tree Protocol (STP), VLAN trunking, default gateway, and PoE. This section will provide the information of this.

Virtual Local Area Network (VLAN)

Switches and Routers have physical interfaces commonly known as a physical port; these ports can be configured in a variety of ways depending upon the topology, design, type of encapsulation, duplex, and speed of the link. On switches, still, additional configuration is VLAN port assignment.

- **Native VLAN:**
  When enabling IEEE 802.1Q tunneling on an edge switch, you must use IEEE 802.1Q trunk ports for sending packets into the service-provider network. However, packets pass through the core of the service-provider network can be carried through IEEE 802.1Q trunks, ISL trunks, or non-trunking links. When IEEE 802.1Q trunks are used in these core switches, the native VLANs of the IEEE 802.1Q trunks must not match any native VLAN of the non-trunking (tunneling) port on the same switch because traffic on the native VLAN would not be tagged on the IEEE 802.1Q sending trunk port.

- **VTP:**
  VTP is a Layer 2 messaging protocol that maintains VLAN configuration consistency by managing the databases of VLANs within a VTP domain. A VTP domain is made up of one or more network devices that share the same VTP domain name and that are interconnected with trunks. VTP can make configuration changes centrally on one or more network devices and have those changes automatically communicated to all the other network devices in the network.

Spanning tree (802.1d)/rapid spanning tree (802.1w)

Spanning tree is used to ensure that only one active path exists between two nodes at one time on the network. If a network has more than one active paths, you can block all the redundant paths by enabling spanning tree. STP prevents network switching loops. STP has two main types the original spanning tree 802.1d and the improved Rapid spanning tree 802.1w. The leading advantage of 802.1w is much faster convergence on link failure. It is accomplished by the protocol automatically determining the designated ports that will be used as well as the backups and alternates that might be used in case of a link failure.

Flooding

When a switch does not know what to do with traffic or the switches or it does not have specific destination address, then it forwards the data to all the connected ports except the host address. This process is called flooding.

Forwarding/blocking

When switches learns the destination of the data, then it forwards it. Alternatively, if you do not allow the traffic from unknown ports, then it is blocking.

Filtering

If switches want to allow traffic from only the specific port, then configure the switches according to it this process is called filtering traffic.

Interface configuration

A VLAN is a subnet created using a switch instead of a router. For this reason, VLANs have many advantages over subnets created by routers. One of the main advantages of VLANs is that the logical network design does not have to follow the physical network topology. It gives administrators much more flexibility in network design and in the subsequent changes of that design. All the administrator has to do is configure the interface with the right VLAN and connect the appropriate cables.

Trunking/802.1q

VLAN Trunking (802.1Q) allows physical network interfaces in a computing environment to be shared. As data centers become more complex and the number of interconnected services become increases. So, it is expensive to provide dedicated cabling and network switch ports to allow for all the required connections. VLAN trunking allows for multiple virtual network connections to be maintained on a small number of physical adapters.

Tag vs. Untag VLANs

Tagged VLAN means frame can be tagged from which VLANs the frame belongs that can happen in trunk port of the switch. Trunk Tagging protocol 802.1Q, ISL and DTP are the types of Tag VLAN.

Untagged VLAN. Frame can't be tagged while traveling from one switch to another switch. e.g., VLAN1, Native VLAN or Management VLAN. Frame can't mention which VLAN the frame belongs. Untag VLAN is a port-based VLAN.

Port bonding (LACP)

Link Aggregation Control Protocol (LACP) is a protocol used to create one logical link from multiple physical links. It is used to increase the bandwidth and the reliability of a

connection. It has been replacing STP in many organizations. LACP in CompTIA term is referred to as Port Bonding.

Port mirroring (local vs. remote)

Port mirroring, also known as Switch Port Analyzer (SPAN) and Remote Switch Port Analyzer (RSPAN), allows you to sniff traffic on a network when using a switch.

Local SPAN supports a SPAN session entirely within one switch; all source ports or source VLANs and destination ports are on the same switch. Local SPAN copies traffic from one or more source ports in any VLAN or from one or more VLANs to a destination port for analysis.

Remote SPAN supports source ports, source VLANs, and destination ports on different switches. The traffic for each RSPAN session is carried over a user-specified RSPAN VLAN that is dedicated for that RSPAN session in all participating switches.

Speed and duplexing

Switches support various level of speed such as 10 Mbps, 100 Mbps, and 100 Mbps. Most switches can also automatically sense the speed of the NIC which is connected and use different speeds on various ports.

Duplexing has two types: half duplexing and full duplexing. In full duplexing, transmission and reception occur at the same time as a telephone. While in half duplexing transmission and reception occur at a different time like Walkie-talkie.

IP address assignment

Switches work on a MAC address, but it is typically configured with IP address when using a Remote network like VLAN.

VLAN Assignment

As we know, switches belong to native VLAN by default but if we add new VLANs we have to assign VLAN other than VLAN1 and then assign the specific ports to the VLAN then connect to the appropriate cables to the port to segment the devices.

Default gateway

Default Gateway is the gateway used by the network device to send packets unless the specific gateway is defined. It allows the network devices to communicate with other networks.

PoE and PoE+ (802.3af, 802.3at)

Power over Ethernet PoE (802.3af) and PoE+ (802.3at), technologies describe a system for transmitting electrical power along with data to remote devices over twisted-pair cable in an Ethernet network. Many switches, IP telephones, embedded computers, wireless

access points, cameras, and so on can use this technology for convenient installation. The main difference between PoE and PoE+ is an increase in the wattage, PoE (802.af) provides 15.4W; whereas PoE+ (802.at) provides 25.5W from the same source.

Switch Management

A common switch does not need for configuration as it is built into Application-Specific Integrated Circuits (ASICs). You should configure the switch with a secure password so that only the authorized person can access the switch. It also includes console connections, virtual terminal ports, auxiliary ports, and so on. You can also make the switch more securable configure with Authentication, Authorization, and Auditing mechanism.

Managed vs. Unmanaged

The managed switch gives you complete control over your LAN traffic and offers advanced features to control, configure and manage the traffic. Whereas, unmanaged switches cannot configure and support any advanced features. They are like plug-and-play devices, and you need to connect your computer or other network devices directly to the unmanaged switch.

Lab 2.1: Virtual Local Area Network (VLAN)

Case Study: Configure a Switch Using Virtual Local Area Network (VLAN)

Topology Diagram:

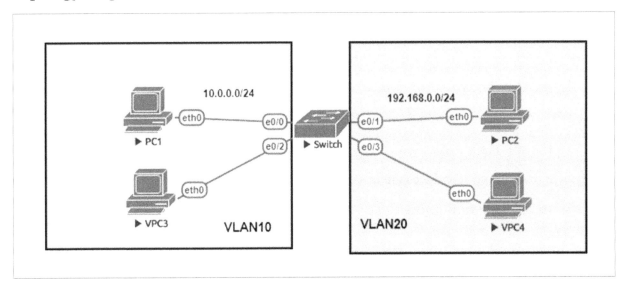

Configuration:
Switch>
Switch>en
Switch#config t

```
Enter configuration commands, one per line.  End with CNTL/Z.
Switch(config)#vlan 10
Switch(config-vlan)#exit
Switch(config)#vlan 20
Switch(config-vlan)#exit

Switch(config)#int range ethernet 0/0, ethernet 0/2
Switch(config-if-range)#switchport mode access
Switch(config-if-range)#switchport access vlan 10
Switch(config-if-range)#ex

Switch(config)#int range ethernet 0/1 , ethernet 0/3
Switch(config-if-range)#switchport mode access
Switch(config-if-range)#switchport access vlan 20
Switch(config-if-range)#ex
Switch(config)#
```

Configuring VPC

Go to PC1 and assign IP address 10.0.0.1/24

VPC> **ip 10.0.0.1/24 10.0.0.100**

Go to PC2 and assign IP address 192.168.0.1/24

VPC> **ip 192.168.0.1/24 192.168.0.100**

Go to PC3 and assign IP address 192.168.0.2/24

VPC> **ip 192.168.0.2/24 192.168.0.100**

Go to PC4 and assign IP address 10.0.0.2/24

VPC> **ip 10.0.0.2/24 10.0.0.100**

Verification:

Switch#**show VLAN brief**

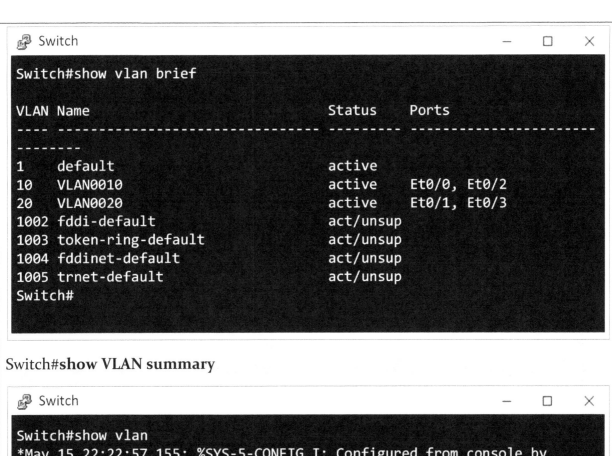

Switch#**show VLAN summary**

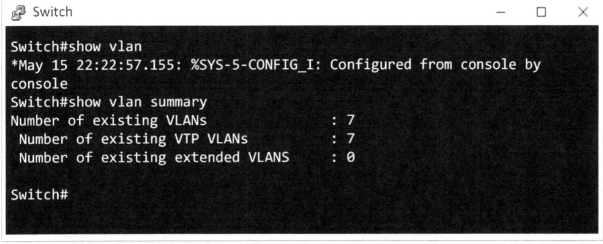

Ping PC3 from PC1 (Same VLAN)

VPC> **ping 10.0.0.2**

```
PC1                                                    —    □    ×

VPCS>
VPCS> ping 10.0.0.2

84 bytes from 10.0.0.2 icmp_seq=1 ttl=64 time=0.561 ms
84 bytes from 10.0.0.2 icmp_seq=2 ttl=64 time=0.395 ms
84 bytes from 10.0.0.2 icmp_seq=3 ttl=64 time=0.955 ms
84 bytes from 10.0.0.2 icmp_seq=4 ttl=64 time=0.677 ms
84 bytes from 10.0.0.2 icmp_seq=5 ttl=64 time=0.819 ms

VPCS>
```

Ping PC2 & PC4 from PC1 (Different VLAN)

VPC> **ping 192.168.0.1**

VPC> **ping 192.168.0.2**

```
PC1                                                    —    □    ×

VPCS> ping 192.168.0.1

192.168.0.1 icmp_seq=1 timeout
192.168.0.1 icmp_seq=2 timeout
192.168.0.1 icmp_seq=3 timeout
192.168.0.1 icmp_seq=4 timeout
192.168.0.1 icmp_seq=5 timeout

VPCS> ping 192.168.0.2

192.168.0.2 icmp_seq=1 timeout
192.168.0.2 icmp_seq=2 timeout
192.168.0.2 icmp_seq=3 timeout
192.168.0.2 icmp_seq=4 timeout
192.168.0.2 icmp_seq=5 timeout

VPCS>
```

Ping PC4 from PC2 (Same VLAN)

VPC> **ping 192.168.0.2**

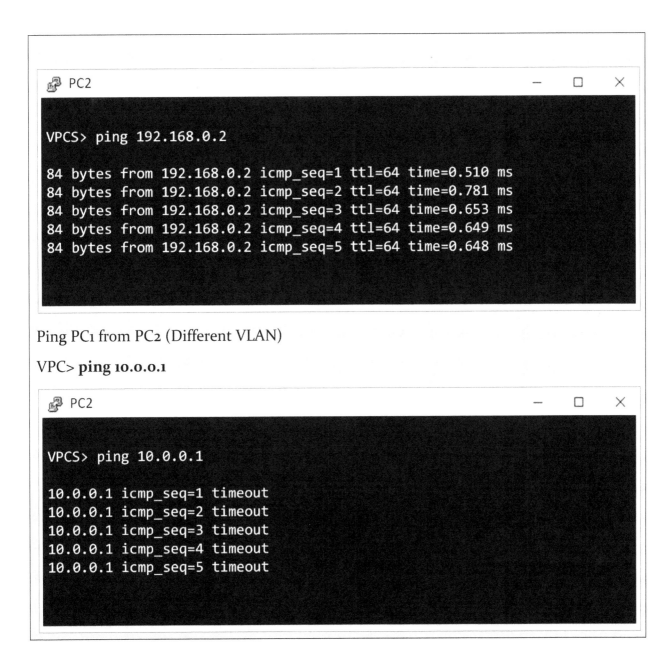

```
VPCS> ping 192.168.0.2

84 bytes from 192.168.0.2 icmp_seq=1 ttl=64 time=0.510 ms
84 bytes from 192.168.0.2 icmp_seq=2 ttl=64 time=0.781 ms
84 bytes from 192.168.0.2 icmp_seq=3 ttl=64 time=0.653 ms
84 bytes from 192.168.0.2 icmp_seq=4 ttl=64 time=0.649 ms
84 bytes from 192.168.0.2 icmp_seq=5 ttl=64 time=0.648 ms
```

Ping PC1 from PC2 (Different VLAN)

VPC> **ping 10.0.0.1**

```
VPCS> ping 10.0.0.1

10.0.0.1 icmp_seq=1 timeout
10.0.0.1 icmp_seq=2 timeout
10.0.0.1 icmp_seq=3 timeout
10.0.0.1 icmp_seq=4 timeout
10.0.0.1 icmp_seq=5 timeout
```

Lab2.2: Rapid Spanning –Tree Protocol

Case Study: Configure Rapid Spanning-Tree Protocol and observe the behavior

Topology Diagram:

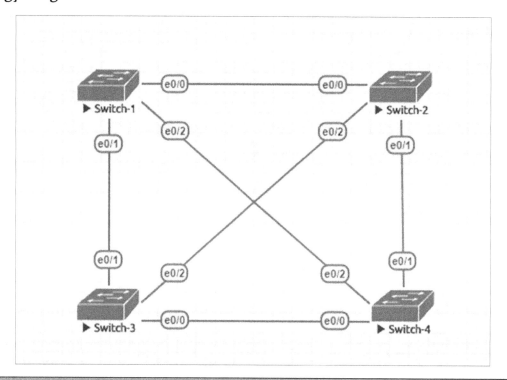

Switch 1 Configuration
Switch(config)#hostname Switch1
Switch1(config)#spanning-tree mode rapid-pvst
Switch1(config)#spanning-tree portfast default
Switch1(config)#spanning-tree portfast bpdufilter default
Switch1(config)#spanning-tree portfast bpduguard default
Switch1(config)#

Switch 2 Configuration
Switch(config)#hostname Switch2
Switch2(config)#spanning-tree mode rapid-pvst
Switch2(config)#spanning-tree portfast default

Switch 3 Configuration
Switch(config)#hostname Switch3
Switch3(config)#spanning-tree mode rapid-pvst
Switch3(config)#spanning-tree portfast default

Switch 4 Configuration
Switch(config)#hostname Switch4
Switch4(config)#spanning-tree mode rapid-pvst
Switch4(config)#spanning-tree portfast default

Verification:
Enter the command "**Show spanning-tree**" on switch 1

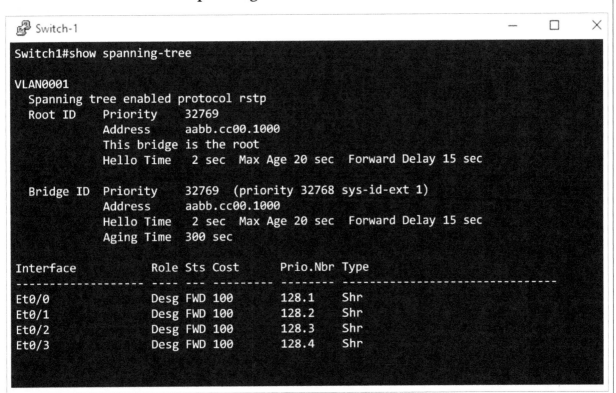

This switch is the root bridge; it's all ports are designated forwarding state.

Enter the command "**Show spanning-tree**" on switch 2

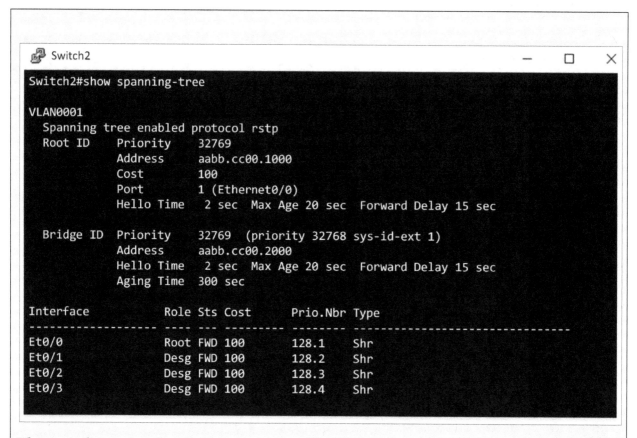

This switch is not a root bridge; however, all of its ports are designated forwarding state. Root ID is aabb.cc00.1000 which is the MAC address of Switch 1.

Enter the command "**Show spanning-tree**" on switch 3

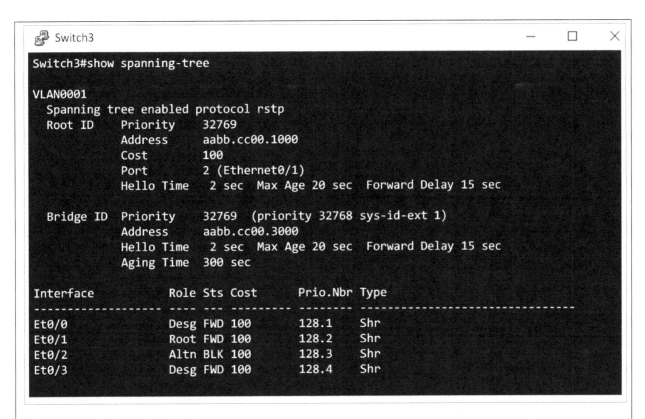

```
Switch3#show spanning-tree

VLAN0001
  Spanning tree enabled protocol rstp
  Root ID    Priority    32769
             Address     aabb.cc00.1000
             Cost        100
             Port        2 (Ethernet0/1)
             Hello Time   2 sec  Max Age 20 sec  Forward Delay 15 sec

  Bridge ID  Priority    32769  (priority 32768 sys-id-ext 1)
             Address     aabb.cc00.3000
             Hello Time   2 sec  Max Age 20 sec  Forward Delay 15 sec
             Aging Time  300 sec

Interface         Role Sts Cost      Prio.Nbr Type
----------------- ---- --- --------- -------- --------------------------------
Et0/0             Desg FWD 100       128.1    Shr
Et0/1             Root FWD 100       128.2    Shr
Et0/2             Altn BLK 100       128.3    Shr
Et0/3             Desg FWD 100       128.4    Shr
```

Ethernet 0/2 is in the block state

Enter the command "**Show spanning-tree**" on switch 4

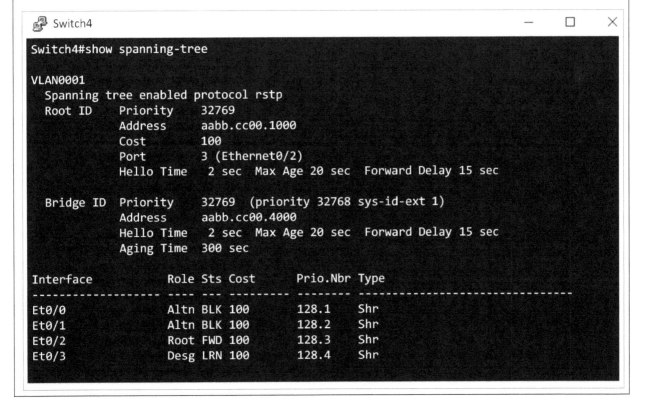

```
Switch4#show spanning-tree

VLAN0001
  Spanning tree enabled protocol rstp
  Root ID    Priority    32769
             Address     aabb.cc00.1000
             Cost        100
             Port        3 (Ethernet0/2)
             Hello Time   2 sec  Max Age 20 sec  Forward Delay 15 sec

  Bridge ID  Priority    32769  (priority 32768 sys-id-ext 1)
             Address     aabb.cc00.4000
             Hello Time   2 sec  Max Age 20 sec  Forward Delay 15 sec
             Aging Time  300 sec

Interface         Role Sts Cost      Prio.Nbr Type
----------------- ---- --- --------- -------- --------------------------------
Et0/0             Altn BLK 100       128.1    Shr
Et0/1             Altn BLK 100       128.2    Shr
Et0/2             Root FWD 100       128.3    Shr
Et0/3             Desg LRN 100       128.4    Shr
```

Ethernet 0/0 and Ethernet 0/1 is in a block state.

Lab2.3: VLAN Trunking Protocol

Case Study: Configure a VLAN Trunking Protocol on Switch

Topology:

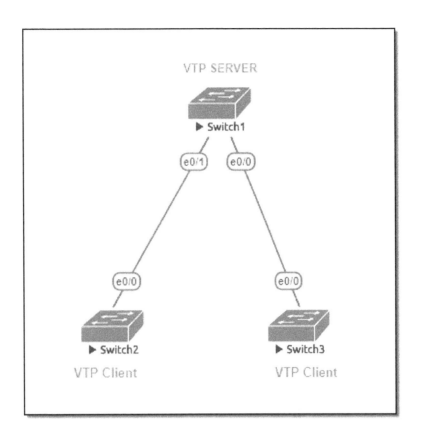

VTP Server Initial Configuration:

Switch>en

Switch#config t

Enter configuration commands, one per line. End with CNTL/Z.

Switch(config)#hostname VTP_Server

VTP_Server(config)#int range ethernet 0/1 , ethernet 0/0

VTP_Server(config-if-range)#switchport trunk encapsulation dot1q

VTP_Server(config-if-range)#switchport mode trunk

VTP_Server(config-if-range)#ex

VTP_Server(config)#vtp ?

  domain   Set the name of the VTP administrative domain.

   file   Configure IFS filesystem file where VTP configuration is stored.

   interface Configure interface as the preferred source for the VTP IP updater

```
            address.
 mode       Configure VTP device mode
 password   Set the password for the VTP administrative domain
 pruning    Set the administrative domain to permit pruning
 version    Set the administrative domain to VTP version
```

VTP_Server(config)#vtp domain ipspecialist.net

```
Changing VTP domain name from NULL to ipspecialist.net

*May 16 01:11:22.234: %SW_VLAN-6-VTP_DOMAIN_NAME_CHG: VTP domain name changed to
ipspecialist.net.
```

VTP_Server(config)#vtp mode server

```
Device mode already VTP Server for VLANS.
```

VTP_Server(config)#vtp password P@$$word:10

```
Setting device VTP password to P@$$word:10
```

VTP_Server(config)#vtp version 3

```
*May 16 01:12:06.424: %SW_VLAN-6-OLD_CONFIG_FILE_READ: Old version 2 VLAN
configuration file detected and read OK. Version 3 files will be written in the
future.
```

VTP-Client Configuration
<u>Switch 02</u>
Switch>en
Switch#config t
Enter configuration commands, one per line. End with CNTL/Z.
Switch(config)#hostname Switch2
Switch2(config)#int ethernet 0/0
Switch2(config-if)#switchport trunk encapsulation dot1q
Switch2(config-if)#switchport mode trunk
Switch2(config-if)#ex

Switch2(config)#vtp domain ipspecialist.net

```
Domain name already set to ipspecialist.net.
```

Switch2(config)#vtp version 3

Switch2(config)#

```
*May  16  01:14:37.855:  %SW_VLAN-6-OLD_CONFIG_FILE_READ:  Old  version  2  VLAN
configuration file detected and read OK.  Version 3 files will be written in the
future.
```

Switch2(config)#vtp password P@$$word:10

```
Setting device VTP password to P@$$word:10
```

Switch 03

Switch>en

Switch#config t

```
Enter configuration commands, one per line.  End with CNTL/Z.
```

Switch(config)#hostname Switch3

Switch3(config)#int ethernet 0/0

Switch3(config-if)#switchport trunk encapsulation dot1q

Switch3(config-if)#switchport mode trunk

Switch3(config-if)#ex

Switch3(config)#vtp domain ipspecialist.net

```
Domain name already set to ipspecialist.net.
```

Switch3(config)#vtp version 3

Switch3(config)#

```
*May  16  01:14:37.855:  %SW_VLAN-6-OLD_CONFIG_FILE_READ:  Old  version  2  VLAN
configuration file detected and read OK.  Version 3 files will be written in the
future.
```

Switch3(config)#vtp password P@$$word:10

```
Setting device VTP password to P@$$word:10
```

Creating VLANs on VTP Server

VTP_Server# vtp primary

```
This system is becoming primary server for feature VLAN

No conflicting VTP3 devices found.

Do you want to continue? [confirm]

*May 16 01:24:21.883: %SW_VLAN-4-VTP_PRIMARY_SERVER_CHG: aabb.cc00.1000 has become
the primary server for the VLAN VTP feature
```


VTP_Server(config-vlan)#name HR-Department

VTP_Server(config-vlan)#ex

VTP_Server(config)#vlan 20

VTP_Server(config-vlan)#name Finance-Department

VTP_Server(config-vlan)#ex

VTP_Server(config)#vlan 30

VTP_Server(config-vlan)#name IT-Department

VTP_Server(config-vlan)#ex

VTP_Server(config)#

Verification:

We have only created VLANs on VTP Server switch. Let's check if VLANs are configured correctly.

Enter the following command

VTP_Server# **Show VLAN brief**

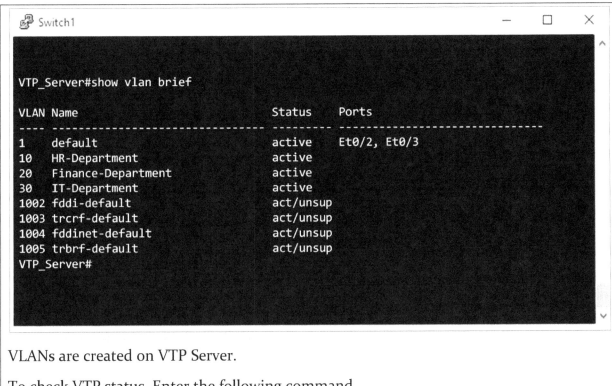

VLANs are created on VTP Server.

To check VTP status, Enter the following command

VTP_Server# **show vtp status**

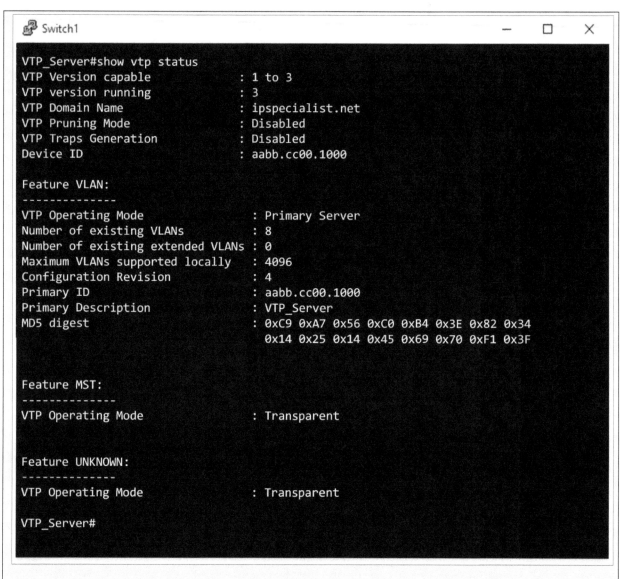

This Switch is the Primary VTP Server. VTP Domain is ipspecialist.net.

Now check Switch 2 and Switch 3 if VLAN Configuration is successfully transferred.

Enter the following command on switch 2

Switch2# **show VLAN brief**

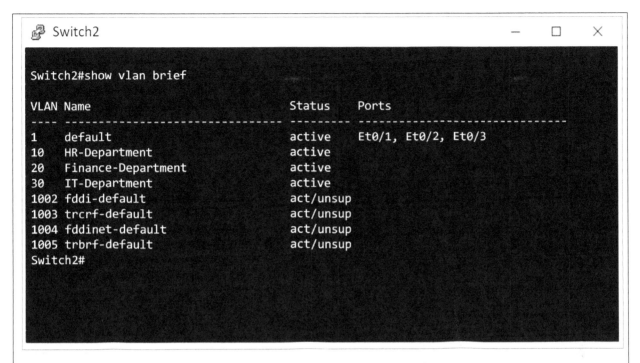

All VLANs are automatically created on VTP Client (Switch2)

Now, to check VTP Status of Switch 2, enter the following command

Switch2# **show vtp status**

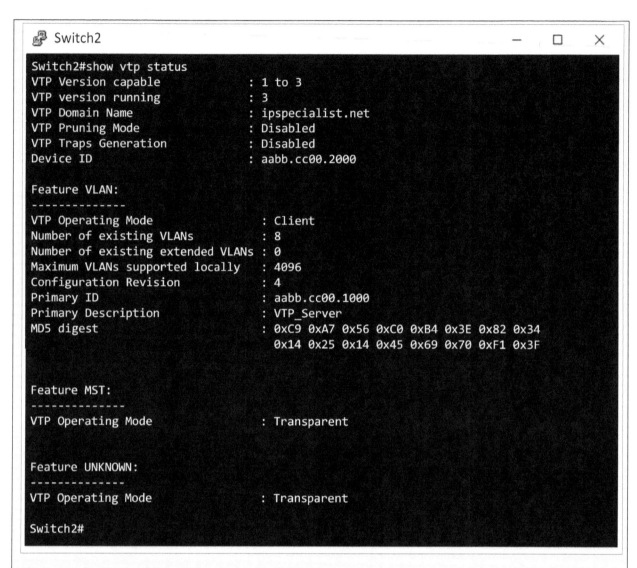

The switch is capable of Version 1-3 of VTP. Currently running version is version3. VTP domain is ipspecialist.net. VTP Operating mode is Client.

Now, to check VTP Status of Switch 3, enter the following command

Switch3# **show vtp status**

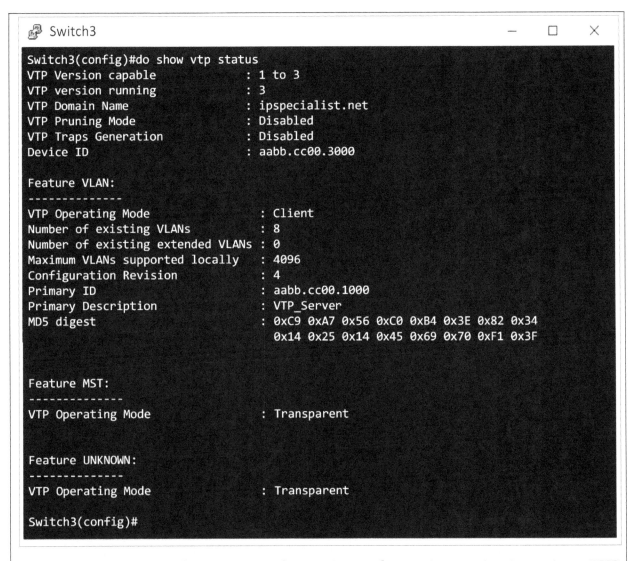

The switch is capable of Version 1-3 of VTP. Currently running version is version3. VTP domain is ipspecialist.net. VTP Operating mode is Client.

Enter the following command on switch 3

Switch3# **show VLAN brief**

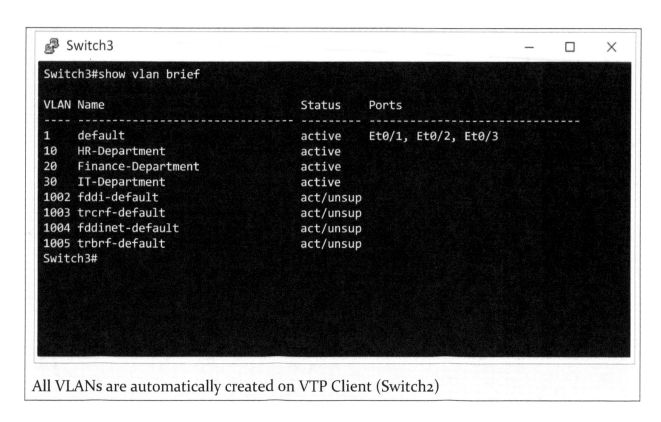

All VLANs are automatically created on VTP Client (Switch2)

Lab2.4: User/Password Configuration on Switch

Case Study: Configuring a Username and Password on Layer 2 Switch

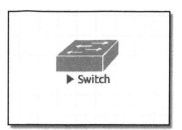

Configuration:
Switch>
Switch>en
Switch#config t
Enter configuration commands, one per line. End with CNTL/Z.
Switch(config)#username admin privilege 15 secret P@$$word:10
Switch(config)#username john privilege 5 password john@123

Switch(config)#line console o

Switch(config-line)#login local

Switch(config-line)#end

Switch# copy running-config startup-config

Switch#reload

Verification:

After reboot, Console will be prompt for Username to log in.

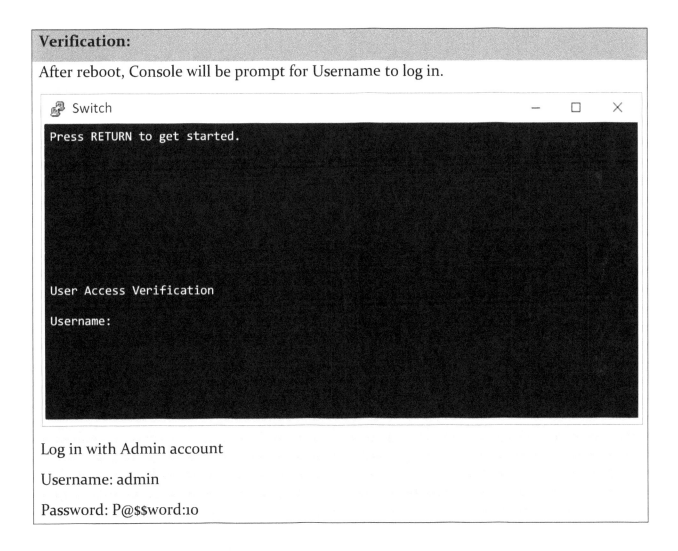

Log in with Admin account

Username: admin

Password: P@$$word:10

```
User Access Verification


Username: admin
Password:
Switch#en
Switch#config t
Enter configuration commands, one per line.  End with CNTL/Z.
Switch(config)#
```

To log out, Enter the command **Logout** as shown below

Switch# **logout**

Log in with John account

Username: John

Password: john@123

```
User Access Verification


Username: john
Password:
Switch#en
Switch#config t
Enter configuration commands, one per line.  End with CNTL/Z.
Switch(config)#
```

Wireless LAN Infrastructure and other Wireless Technologies

This section will describe the implementation of wireless LAN infrastructure and also discuss the challenges of the wireless network. Some of the challenges of installing a wireless network area are wireless access point (WAP) placement, antenna types, interference, frequencies, channels, wireless standards, SSID, and compatibility issues.

Small office, home office wireless router

Vendor companies like Cisco and Belkin introduce a router that is usually installed in small office and homes. The devices come with an intelligent wizard built into the router that questioning few to the installer and configure the appropriate settings for DHCP, DNS, Security, and so on. To make it easier the cables and connections are color-coded. The wireless network is affected by environmental factors such as the distance between the client and the wireless router, type of obstacles, and interference from other signals.

Wireless Access Points

Wireless Access Point (WAP) is a component that connects all wireless devices. WAP has at least one antenna sometimes usually have two antennas for better reception and an Ethernet port to connect them to a wired network.

Device density

To increase the density of wireless devices, use multiple access points to overlap with each other. The amount of overlapping depends upon the range of installation usually 10 to 20 percent overlapping is desired at a minimum.

Roaming

The overlapping in wireless access points provides roaming for the users, so they connect to them while moving around building or campuses.

Wireless controllers

The wireless controller collects all the data from the control plane and sends out streaming orders to the individual APs. Depending on the type of controller and how the network is configured, the controller may also process all data plane traffic as well, which has its benefits and limitations.

- **VLAN pooling**
  VLAN pooling is a feature that enables the user to group multiple wireless controller VLANs to form a VLAN pool. Configure a VLAN pool to load-balance sessions evenly across multiple VLANs. Individual VLANs are then assigned dynamically from the pool when a wireless client accesses the network it uses a round robin algorithm.

- **LWAPP**

  Lightweight Access Point Protocol (LWAPP) is a protocol proposed by a division of Cisco called Airespace. LWAPP is used by the wireless Access controller that organizes the hand-off signals among many WAPs.

Wireless bridge

A wireless bridge is a network device that connects Ethernet network to a wireless network and also connects one wireless network to another wireless network. The wireless bridge does not provide a wireless access point for end users; it only connects the different wireless and wired networks throughout an organization's premises.

Site surveys

Before the deployment of wireless LAN, infrastructure performs a site survey that will help in frequency planning, cost estimation, coverage area and other parameters.

Heatmaps

A diagram of signal strength in a Wi-Fi network is referred to as Heat Maps. It is like a wireless monitoring tool that provides a visual map of a workstation to the network administrator that will give invaluable knowledge about the adjustment of the access points (APs) for better coverage.

Frequencies

The wireless network operated on 2.4 GHz frequency band and 5 GHz band frequency. Sometimes these two frequency bands combined to form a band that provides greater bandwidth for the user.

Channels

Various frequency bands (2.4GHz, 3.6 GHz, 4.9 GHz, 5 GHz, and 5.9 GHz) have their range of channels. Usually, wireless routers will use the 2.4GHz band with a total of 14 channels, but in reality, it may be used 13 channels around the world. All Wireless versions through 802.11n (a, b, g, n) work between the channel frequencies of 2400 and 2500 MHz. This 100 MHz in between them are split into 14 channels 20 MHz each. Therefore, each 2.4GHz channel overlaps with two to four other channels as shown in below diagram. Overlapping makes wireless network throughput quite poor.

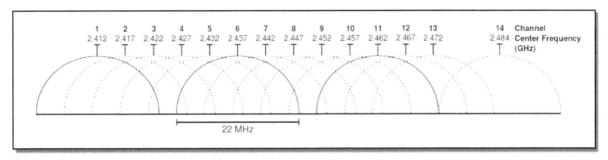

Figure 2-09: Channel Overlapping

Most popular channels for 2.4 GHz Wireless channels are 1, 6, and 11 because they don't overlap with each other.

Goodput

Goodput is an application level throughput that measures the number of useful bits per unit of time sent by the network from source to destination excluding protocol overhead such as retransmissions. The main goal of wireless communication is to configure all settings to maximize goodput. Some wireless software and firmware can manage and monitor goodput.

Connection types

Wireless networks have many standards that have developed over time, such as 802.11a, 802.11b, 802.11g, and 802.11n. Standards and connection types continue to develop that make wireless networks even faster and more powerful. Some standards are backward compatible with others while some are not. Some devices cannot be configured to be compatible with 802.11a standard because it uses 5 GHz frequency whereas 802.11 b and g use only 2.4 GHz frequency band.

Standard	802.11a	802.11b	802.11g	802.11n	802.11ac	802.11ad
Maximum Throughput	54 mbps	11 Mbps	54 Mbps	Up to 600 Mbps	3.2 Gbps	Up to 7 Gbps
Maximum Range	~ 150 feet	~ 300 feet	~ 300 feet	~ 300 feet	~ 100 feet	~ 15 feet
Frequency	5 GHz	2.4 GHz	2.4 GHz	2.4/5 GHz	5 GHz	60 GHz
Backward Compatibility			802.11b	802.11a/b/g	802.11a/b/g/n	802.11a/b/g/n

Table 2-01: Wireless Network Standards

Antenna placement

Optimal antenna placement varies according to the space to fill and security concerns. You can find the best place for antenna by site survey, also using wireless analyzer tools to find the dead spots and odd corners, and then use the right kind of antenna on each WAP to fill in space.

WAP antennas are available in many shapes and sizes. Previously, it was common to see WAPs with only one antenna. Some WAPs have two antennas, and some (802.11n and 802.11ac) have more than two antennas.

Antenna types

There are many types of the antenna, but the two common types of antennas are an omnidirectional antenna and unidirectional antenna. Antennas can even be placed away from the WAP but connected to it with a cable.

Omnidirectional

Omnidirectional antennas radiate its energy with equal strength in all direction. It has the advantage that any device within the signal radius can potentially access the network.

Unidirectional

Unidirectional antennas radiate its energy only in one direction. It is used to increase the strength of the signal.

MIMO/MU-MIMO

Multiple-input and multiple-output (MIMO) is an emerging technology that offers a substantial increase in speed and distance without additional need of transmission power. MIMO is a technique of using multiple antennas at both the transmitter and receiver to improve communication performance. MIMO is used with 802.11n and with 4G technologies.

When MIMO is used throughout a network with multiple users connecting to multiple antennas with multiple outputs, it is referred to as multiple-user multiple-input and multiple-output (MU-MIMO).

Signal strength

Signal strength is an important factor to consider while installing a wireless network. The signal strength varies according to many factors. Such as Distance between the client and WAPs, walls and other barriers, Protocol used and interference with another signal.

SSID broadcast

When a wireless device like mobile phones and laptops want to connect WAPs, it will scan for service set identifiers (SSIDs) in its instant area, which is a network name. In wireless LAN, if it wants the devices to find the SSID that are broadcasting, so it will make

sure that WAP's enabled for broadcast. For security purpose, SSID broadcasting can be disabled.

Topologies

The topology is an arrangement of a network including nodes and connections lines. The network topology may be physical or logical. Three basic types of wireless network topologies.

Ad hoc

A wireless device connecting to another wireless device with no need for a WAP is referred to as an ad hoc topology. It is also sometimes called an Independent Basic Service Set (IBSS) because it is independent of the WAP.

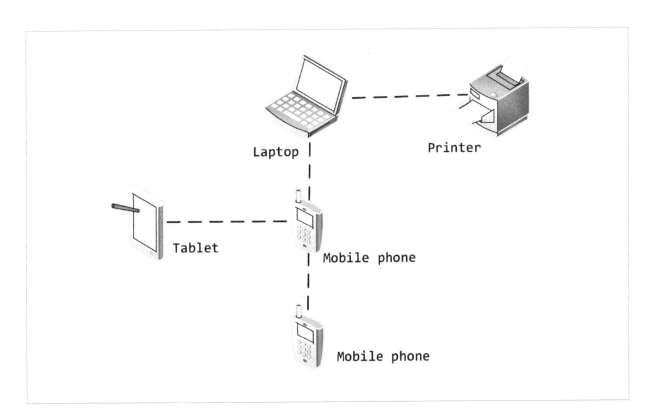

Figure 2-10: An ad hoc topology

Mesh

This is one of the complex wireless topologies as it involves one or more than one WAPs. The user can connect to the network through a specific WAP depending on the placement in premises. This type of topology is called Basic Service Set (BSS).

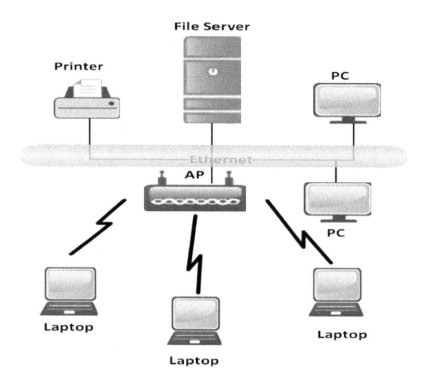

Figure 2-11: Mesh topology

Infrastructure

In infrastructure topology devices that are connected to one WAP can be automatically switched to another WAP. It is useful if the device will be used in many parts of your premises and needs to maintain connectivity throughout the entire area once connected. This type of topology is also called Extended Service Set (ESS).

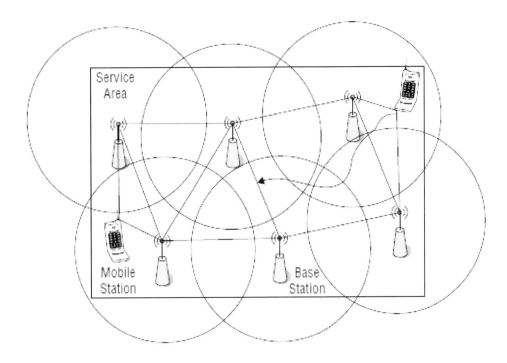

Figure 2-12: Infrastructure topology

Mobile devices

Mobile Devices such as Cell phones, Laptops, Tablets, Gaming devices and Media devices want to connect to wireless LAN infrastructure must be enabled Wireless features and capable of uploading and downloading data.

Mind Map:

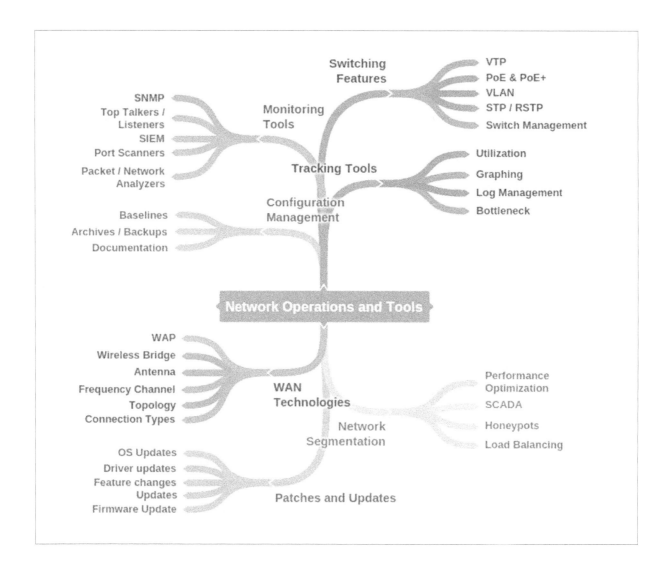

Chapter 3: Network Security

Risk Related Concepts

The main idea to understand regarding security is the assessment of risk. There is a risk in everything regarding networking, or anything else for that matter. The question is how much risk you are willing to take and how you will reduce that risk as much as possible. Concepts to understand regarding the reduction of risk include disaster recovery, business continuity, battery backups, first responders, data breach, end-user awareness and training, single point of failure, adherence to standards and policies, vulnerability scanning, and penetration testing. This section will discuss all of these concepts and more.

Disaster recovery

Disaster recovery (DR) is a set of rules and procedures that are designed to enable the recovery or replacement of vital IT and networking infrastructure. The disaster could be a natural disaster such as an earthquake, a human-caused disaster such as a fire or just a human mistake. DR is concerned with how fast normal operations can be restored.

Key metrics related to this concept include Recovery Point Objective (RPO). RPO depends upon the decision that how much data can tolerate risk losing. Recovery Time Objective (RTO) related to how much time will be allowed for restored to satisfactory operation. So, the need for metrics is lower than the DR strategy will be more complex and expensive.

Business continuity

Business continuity (BC) involves strategies to make sure that an unplanned event or outage does not cause a disaster in the first place. BC includes concepts such as resilience, recovery, and contingency. Business continuity has a direct relation with redundant servers, clustering, mirroring, and so on. BC attempts to make sure that the business itself remains workable whatever happens to the network and servers.

Battery backups/UPS

As all of the networking devices run on electricity. So, the servers, routers, and switches have power supplies that convert the electricity from the power company to power that they can use to operate. All these network devices should have an uninterruptible power supply (UPS) as a backup for each server or rack of servers. The batteries in UPSs fails, so it should be check periodically and replace as necessary.

First responders

First responders are the people or groups of people who are the first to look after the natural disaster or attack. They are typically employees of emergency service such as the

police department, fire department, or a governmental agency such as the Federal Emergency Management Authority (FEMA). First responders might know paramedics and emergency medical technicians. Their role is to protect the people and to restore order to the site. They are generally trained to coordinate with other agencies to guarantees that relevant evidence is preserved.

Data Breach

A data breach is the release of secure information to an unsecured environment. It can be intentional, or it can be unintentional. A data breach is a security incident in which sensitive, protected or confidential data is copied, transmitted, viewed, stolen or used without the knowledge of authorization. The storage of unencrypted data in any portion of the network is one of the main causes of a data breach.

Data breaches may involve financial information such as credit card or bank details, personal health information (PHI), Personally identifiable information (PII), trade secrets of corporations or intellectual property. Most data breaches involve overexposed and vulnerable unstructured data like files, documents, and sensitive information.

End User Awareness and Training

End users are possibly the main source of security problems for any organization. IT administration must increase end-user awareness and training, so they know how to look after their systems and how to act to avoid attacks. The following training policies helpful to develop end-user awareness.

Security Policies:

End Users need to read, understand, and sign all appropriate security policies when required.

Passwords:

Make sure users understand necessary password skills, such as sufficient length and complexity, refreshing passwords regularly, and password control.

System and workplace security:

Make sure users understand how to keep their workstations secure through screen locking and not storing written passwords in plain view.

Social Engineering:

Users need to identify typical social-engineering strategies and know how to counter them.

Malware:

Train users to recognize and deal with malware attacks.

Single Point of Failure

A single point of failure also known as SPOF is any component of a system that causes the whole system to stop working if it fails.

Critical assets - Redundancy

Every organization has assets that are critical to the operation of the organization. Critical assets can include patents/copyrights, corporate financial data, customer sales information, human resource information, proprietary software, scientific research, schematics, and internal manufacturing processes. Critical assets can be identified by using different methods, including risk assessments, asset tracking through a service or hardware inventory, and network traffic monitoring that discloses the most frequently used network and system components.

Critical nodes

Identifying critical nodes is generally much clearer than identifying critical assets because of the IT nature of critical nodes and the fact that the IT department is always going to be painfully responsive of what nodes are critical.

Critical nodes are very much unique to IT equipment. Some examples of critical nodes are:

- A file server that contains critical project files
- A single web server
- A single printer
- An edge router

Redundancy

Redundancy means that another component can handle the event when one component fails. This component might be SPOF. A well-designed system will attempt to reduce all single points of failure by redundancy. Redundancy is relatively easy to do, but the trick is to determine where the redundancy is needed to avoid single points of failure without too much complexity, cost, or administration. Redundancy can do this process by identifying two things: critical assets and critical nodes. It's beneficial to have redundancy on any critical nodes, or critical assets.

Adherence to Standards and Policies

Given the importance of company policies and standards; it's also vital for an organization to adhere to standards and policies strictly. For company policies, this can often be a challenge. Standards can be found on the websites maintained by the International Organization for Standardization (ISO) at www.iso.org as well as many

others. If you are the decision maker, you can review these standards and then decide what will be done for your specific organizational needs.

Vulnerability Scanning

Vulnerability scanning is a security technique used to identify security weaknesses in a computer system. Vulnerability scanning can be used by individuals or network administrators for security purposes, or hackers can use it.

No particular vulnerability scanner works for every aspect of the infrastructure. There is a variety of vulnerability scanners used for the specific purpose of the organization. Some of them described here:

Microsoft Baseline Security Analyzer (MBSA):

MBSA is designed to test individual systems. It's old technology, but still does a great job of testing Microsoft Windows system for vulnerabilities

Nmap Port Scanner:

Port scanners query individual nodes, looking for open or vulnerable ports and creating a report.

Figure 3.1 shows sample output from Zenmap, the GUI frontend for Nmap.

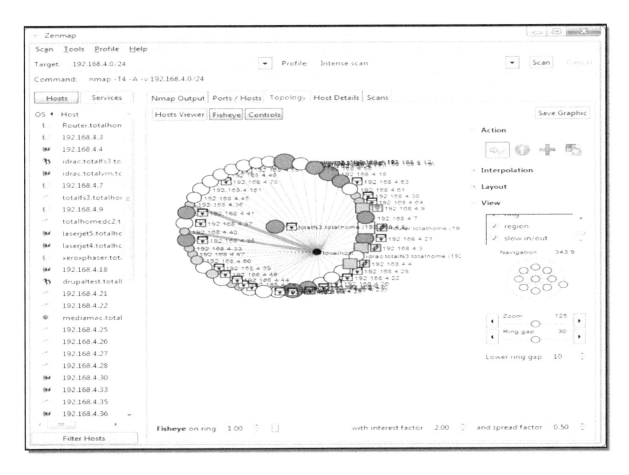

Figure 3-01: Output from Zenmap, the GUI frontend for Nmap

Penetration Testing

Penetration testing involves attacking your system or inviting someone else to attack it. The purpose of doing this is to determine the point of weaknesses. The best result of a penetration test would be that no weaknesses exist; although, any result can be turned into a positive because the penetration test is performed in a controlled environment to expose a vulnerability that can be mitigated before it is exploited by an attacker. Penetration testing can be done by a skillful operator who understands the target and knows potential vulnerabilities, it can also be done by the number of tools like Aircrack-ng and Metasploit. Aircrack-ng is an open source tool for pentesting pretty much every aspect of wireless networks. Metasploit, another unique open source tool, enables the pentester to use a massive library of attacks as well as tweak those attacks for unique penetrations.

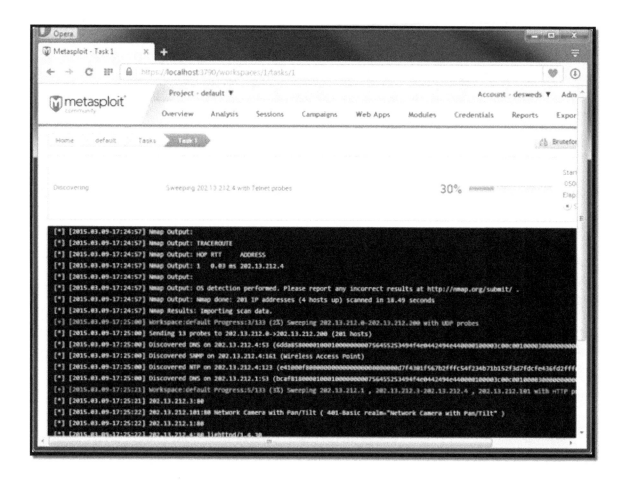

Figure 3-02: Metasploit Output

Common Network Vulnerabilities and Threats

This section will discuss the most common threats against the network and the computers that it contains. It will focus on the vulnerability that makes the threat a reality and especially on what can be done to mitigate the threat.

Attacks/threats

A network threat is any form of potential attack against the network. This threat in the form of a person sneaking into the offices and stealing passwords, or an ignorant employee deleting files that should not have access to in the first place.

This section will discuss the most common network threats and the attacks that can be launched against the network.

DoS

A denial of service (DoS) attack is a targeted attack on servers that make the server site unable to process any upcoming request by providing some form of service on the Internet such as a website.

Distributed DoS

A Distributed Denial of Service (DDoS) attack occurs when multiple systems under the control of the attacker are used in a coordinated attack to create a traffic spike on the system. The purpose of this type of attack is to flood the resources so that they are no longer available for legitimate use. A group of computers connected in a coordinated manner for malicious activities is termed as a botnet. Each computer in a botnet is called a bot. A botnet may also be known as a zombie army.

Reflective/amplified

One type of DoS attack involves manipulating a protocol so that a request is sent from one computer, but all replies are redirected to the target computer. One such type of attack that uses ICMP echo request is the SMURF attack. These types of attacks are often a diversion that leads to a larger attack. Other attacks might target DNS, NTP, or other essential protocols. In smurfing, the attacker flooded a network with ping packets sent to all target address. The return address of the pings was spoofed to that of the intended victim. When all the targeted address on the network respond to the initial ping, they sent their response to the intended victim. The attacker then amplified the effect of the attack by the number of responding machines on the network. Due to modern network management procedures and controls built into modern operating systems, the danger of the smurf attack has been largely mitigated.

Friendly/unintentional DoS

A different type of DoS event can be caused not by an attack but simply due to a sudden enormous spike in popularity that is not ready to handle the traffic. Sometimes an unexpected news event may cause a web server that normally has sufficient amount of resources to be completely overcome by a spike in traffic. This is normally a short-term event that tends to fix itself over time.

Physical attack

A permanent DoS (PDoS) is somehow referred to as Physical Attack. PDoS is an attack that damages the targeted device such as a router, server, and so on. The ultimate goal of PDoS to make the devices inoperable. All of the encryption protocols in the world won't stop if someone is pouring a cup of water into the server, switch, or router. It is possible

when the attacker has access to the physical network environment. Strong physical security will keep the system from happening such event.

ARP cache poisoning

The Address Resolution Protocol (ARP) resolves IP addresses to MAC addresses. After the IP addresses are resolved, they are stored in a cache for further use. If an attacker can poison the cache, then the IP address will be incorrectly resolved to a different MAC address. This type of attack may be just the beginning of a larger attack. ARP cache poisoning attacks target the ARP caches on hosts and switches. Every node on a TCP/IP network has an ARP cache that stores a list of known IP addresses with their MAC addresses.

On a Windows system; to show ARP cache, usie the arp –a command.

The result of typing arp –a on my system:

Interface: 192.168.0.25 --- 0x3

Internet Address	Physical Address	Type
192.168.0.1	d4-6e-0e-b3-88-2e	dynamic
192.168.0.39	80-56-f2-7c-3f-4f	dynamic
192.168.0.46	5c-ac-4c-07-6f-5c	dynamic
192.168.0.255	ff-ff-ff-ff-ff-ff	static
224.0.0.22	01-00-5e-00-00-16	static
224.0.0.251	01-00-5e-00-00-fb	static
224.0.0.252	01-00-5e-00-00-fc	static
239.255.255.250	01-00-5e-7f-ff-fa	static
255.255.255.255	ff-ff-ff-ff-ff-ff	static

If a device wants to send an IP packet to another device, it must encapsulate the IP packet into an Ethernet frame. An attacker can send an unsolicited ARP and associate his MAC address with the gateway's IP address. Now all packets will pass through the attacker before the destination address.

Packet/protocol abuse

Attackers can use protocols to attack the network that is old and unable to remember yet. Protocols that can be abused by an attacker include older versions of SNMP and UDP, as well as other classified protocol that uses Network Time Protocol (NTP). The Internet

keeps time by using NTP servers. Without NTP providing accurate time for everything that happens on the Internet and anything that is time sensitive would be in danger.

Spoofing

Spoofing is the concept of a program masquerading as another one by falsifying data in an attempt to gain an illegitimate benefit. Attackers use many types of spoofing attacks because many of the protocols in the TCP/IP suite do not provide a tool for authenticating the source and destination of a message. IP spoofing and ARP spoofing may be launched by man-in-the-middle attacks. Other types of spoofing include email and even GPS spoofing. The network can be prevented from spoofing attacks by enabling authentication as much as possible and by disabling old protocols or unusable protocol.

Wireless

Wireless threats come in all sort, from someone attaching to your WAP without authorization, to grabbing packets out of the air and decoding them by a packet sniffer.

This section will discuss wireless security protocols and configuration and their effect on the network.

1. Evil twin

An evil twin is a fake Wi-Fi connection that fools people into considering that it is an authentic connection for phishing attacks and exploitation of data transactions. Evil twins work best in unsecured networks such as those you see in airports and hotels that boasted "Free Wi-Fi here". They can affect you personally and professionally. You can protect against Evil Twin by educating yourself and also by using virtual private networks (VPNs) with SSL or TLS to certify that all email, passwords, and other sensitive information is encrypted during transmission.

2. Rogue AP

A rogue access point (rogue AP) is any wireless access point that has been installed on a network's wired infrastructure without the approval of the network's administrator thereby providing unauthorized wireless access to the network's wired infrastructure.

To prevent the installation of rogue access points, the users should know that these types of unsecured installations are not acceptable, and they also monitor their network for newly installed access points using wireless IDS/IPS systems that can detect changes in the radio spectrum that indicate a new access point is installed and operational.

3. War Driving

War Driving is a method of looking for wireless networks by using omnidirectional antennas connected to laptops or PDAs using wireless sniffing programs in a moving vehicle. War-driving can be best described as a new form of hacking into the network.

Once the car is installed, the crackers start driving and log data as they go. The specialized software logs the latitude and longitude of the car's position as well as the signal strength and network name.

4. War Chalking

War Chalking is creating a semantic for indicating free Internet access. It can be best described as marking a series of well-defined symbols on sidewalks, walls, pillars, and others structures to indicate nearby wireless access. Each symbol defines a specific wireless setting as sown below.

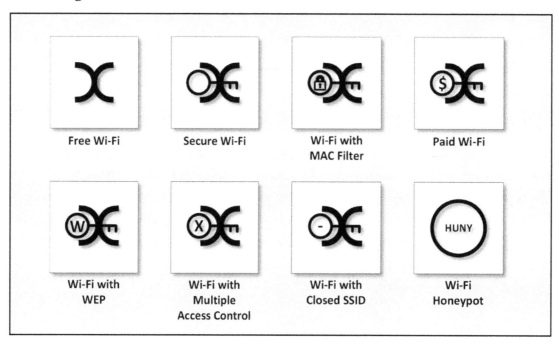

Figure 3.03: War Chalking Symbols

5. BlueJacking

BlueJacking is the process of sending unsolicited messages over Bluetooth-enabled devices. These messages would pop up on the screen. It has an insufficient range, usually only about 30 feet. It is generally harmless and has been used for advertising purposes. BlueJacking wasn't considered anything more than irritating,

6. Bluesnarfing

Bluesnarfing is a method of hacking a phone or other Bluetooth-enabled device through the Bluetooth connection. It used weaknesses in the Bluetooth standard to take

information from other Bluetooth devices. It might allow access to the calendar, contacts, private messages, and so on of a user. This information can then be used directly or to create an effective social engineering attack. The user can prevent this attack entirely by disabling Bluetooth on devices whenever they are in an unsafe area.

7. WPE /WPA/WPS attacks

Wired Equivalent Privacy has been gone through many WEP attacks because in WEP encryption has many flaws. The flaws in WEP make it susceptible to various statistical cracking techniques. WEP uses RC4 for encryption, and RC4 requires that the initialization vectors (IVs) be random. The implementation of RC4 in WEP repeats that IV about every 6,000 frames. If we can capture enough of the IVs, we can decipher the key.

WPA and WPA2 attacks occur especially with wireless networks using WPA-Personal or WPA2-Personal passphrases. When hackers attack, they use classy methods that make some assumptions about the passphrase, and the fact that certain passphrases are used quite often. To prevent these attacks from succeeding is to use long passphrases such as 16 or more characters, thus making the network hard to crack.

WPS is very easy to use but is susceptible to different forms of WPS attacks. By design, the WPS PIN numbers are short. When WPS attacks, hackers concentrate on hacking the PIN number. By hacking the PIN, they can easily take control of the WAP.

Brute force

Brute force is a method of hacking passwords where an attacker guesses every possible password until the correct combination is found and then attacker gained access. Brute force attacks were successful in the past, but the passage of time as the complexity of protocols increases, the difficulty of brute force attacks has increased exponentially. Brute force attacks can be eliminated by limiting the number of wrong attempts for a password to a fixed amount, i.e. five attempts and then locking the account.

Session hijacking

Session hijacking is abusing an established valid computer session to gain unauthorized access to information or services on a computer. Protocols that provide authentication during the process of establishing a session can prevent session hijacking. Some protocols that provide this type of authentication are SSL and TLS.

Social Engineering

Social Engineering in Information Security refers to the technique of psychological manipulation. This trick is used to gather information on different social networking and

other platforms from people for fraud, hacking and getting information for being close to the target.

You can understand the social engineering as an art of extracting sensitive information from peoples. Social Engineers keep themselves undetected, people are unaware and careless and share their valuable information. This information is related to the type of social engineering. In Information Security aspects, Footprinting through Social engineering gathers information such as: -

- Credit card information.
- Username and Passwords.
- Security devices and Technology information.
- Operating System information.
- Software information.
- Network information.
- IP address and name server's information.

Man-in-the-middle

A man-in-the-middle places between the two physical or logical communicating parties. The two communicating parties still assume that their communication is direct to each other, but in actually it is not like that man in the middle attacker sits between them and listen to the communication and learn new information, or it may begin to change the communication between the parties to confuse or interrupt the communication. In any case, man-in-the-middle attacks are harmful to an organization. So, most organizations adopt methods including strong authentication and the latest protocols such as L2TP/IPsec with tunnel endpoint authentication.

VLAN Hopping

VLAN hopping is a method of attacking computer resources that are connected to VLANs. There are mainly two ways to finish this. One way is by pretending to be a switch that has a trunk established and thereby gain all the information about all of the VLANs and all of the communication channels between switches. Another way is by using "double tags" to avoid security measures. VLAN hopping is almost no more because modern switches are all hardened against this attack.

Compromised system

Most of the time, compromised system is defined as the security of one system that is internal to a network can allow an attacker to avoid the security measures that are in place but focusing on attacks from the outside. The compromised system can be used from the inside to launch multiple attacks that appear to be originating from the system that is compromised. Therefore, security measures must include a means of protecting

the network from attack from devices and programs that are already internal to the network helpful to combat compromised systems.

Effect of malware on the network

Many types of malware can affect productivity not only by slowing the network but also by taking the time and resources of the IT department to destroy the virus. When personal computer winds up with a virus, that's an inconvenience. When a large organization winds up with the same virus on all of its computers and systems, that's more than just an inconvenience; it's a loss of productivity that could charge the company a large amount of money. For this reason, it's important to isolate the affected system until it can be cleaned so as not to spread the malware to the rest of the network.

Insider threat/malicious employee

The most exceptional hackers in the world are inside an organization, either physically or by access permissions. They do hacking much easily. Malicious employees are a huge threat because of their ability to destroy data, inject malware, and initiate attacks directly.

Zero-day attacks

A zero-day exploit is an attack that exploits a previously unknown security vulnerability. It is also sometimes defined as an attack that takes advantage of a security vulnerability on the same day that the vulnerability becomes usually known. In other words, there are "zero days" between the time the vulnerability is exposed and the first attack.

Vulnerabilities

The vulnerability is a cyber-security term that mentions a flaw in a system that can leave it open to attack. The vulnerability may also mention any weakness in a computer system itself, in a set of procedures, or in anything that leaves information security exposed to a threat. This section will discuss some of the measures that will take to eliminate the vulnerabilities in the system, so that threats don't have as much chance at becoming successful attacks.

Unnecessary running services

Any services that are running but not being currently used, usually forgotten by the user but still remember the attacker, are the perfect targets for an attacker. Legacy protocols such as NetBIOS might give an attacker a door into a system. The user should disable or at least stop any services that they are not using the network and servers.

Open Ports

Ports are doors into the network and the services that it offers. Any open ports that are not using should be disabled or closed. Firewalls should be configured to allow only the

ports that are specifically listed, rather than allowing all ports first and then blocking the useless ports.

Unpatched/legacy systems

Unpatched systems and legacy systems present an obvious security threat. It is needed to deal with such problems on live systems on your network. When it comes to unpatched Operating Systems, patch or isolate them.

Unencrypted channels

Unencrypted channels make the communication secure as it has not encrypted. So, use the encrypted channels for secure communication and as well as reliable delivery.

In general, look for the following unsecure protocols and unencrypted channels:

• Using Telnet instead of SSH for remote terminal connections.

• Using HTTP instead of HTTPS on websites.

• Using unsecure remote desktops such as VNC.

• Using any unsecure protocol in the clear. Run them through a VPN.

Clear text credentials

Legacy protocols like FTP, Telnet, and POP3 offers a username and password in clear text. Credentials can be captured, and because they're not encrypted. Clear text credentials can be gladly exposed. So, the use of the latest protocols will provide for the encryption of end-user credentials as well.

Unsecure protocols

Many protocols have become legacy due in great part to the fact that they do not offer any security. These protocols have been outdated by other protocols that do offer security. These protocols include Telnet, HTTP, SLIP, FTP, TFTP, SNMPv1, SNMPv2, and others.

- **TELNET:** A terminal emulation that enables a user to connect to a remote host or device using a telnet client. Telnet is measured insecure because it transfers all data in clear text. Users who want secure transmission of data consider SSH as opposed to telnet.

- **HTTP:** HTTP is a set of standards that allow users of the World Wide Web to exchange information found on web pages. HTTP has been dramatically changing by HTTPS that encrypted the information by transport-layer security.

- **SLIP:** Serial Line Internet Protocol (SLIP) to connect a modem to an Internet service provider (ISP). The SLIP was an unsecure protocol, and therefore it has been migrated to Point-to-Point Protocol (PPP)

- **FTP:** File Transfer Protocol (FTP) is the most common way of sending and receiving files between two computers. FTP is not very secure because data transfers are not encrypted by default, so add usernames and passwords to prevent all but the most severe hackers from accessing your FTP server.

- **SNMPv1 and SNMPv2:** Simple Network Management Protocol (SNMP) is a useful tool for network administrators, SNMPv1 sent all data including the passwords and unencrypted over the network. SNMPv2 had good encryption but was quite challenging to use. SNMPv3 is the standard version used today and combines robust, properly secure authentication and encryption.

TEMPEST/RF emanation

TEMPEST is a codename that refers to a method of spying on computer systems by exploiting RF emanations. Radio waves can penetrate walls to a specific range and accidental spill, called RF emanation, it can lead to a security vulnerability. Avoid this by placing some form of filtering between systems and the place where the attackers are going to be using their super-high-tech Bourne Identity spy tools to pick up on the emanations. To combat these emanations, the U.S. National Security Agency (NSA) developed a series of standards called TEMPEST. TEMPEST defines how to shield systems and exhibits in some different products, such as coverings for individual systems, wall coverings, and special window coatings.

Network Hardening Techniques.

Network-hardening techniques relate to using all new software, protocol, and practice to protect and secure the network. The network hardening techniques will consider in this section include anti-malware software, security policies, secure protocols and procedures, access lists, wireless security, user authentication, and hashing algorithms.

Anti-malware Software

There are different types of anti-malware software used to assist in network hardening. It works like a sword and shield, in active mode it finds, and in passive mode, it destroys the viruses. Whenever an Anti-malware software start, the program scans the computer's boot sector and files for viruses if it finds any threat, it appears the available options for removing or disabling them. Vendors that have created anti-malware software include Trend Micro, McAfee, Symantec, Malwarebytes, and many others.

Anti-malware software comes in many types some are Host-based, some are Network-based, and some are Cloud/ server-based.

Host-based

The standard host-based anti-malware is installed on individual systems. Host-based anti-malware works smartly, but it is hard to manage in multiple systems.

Cloud/server-based

Cloud/server-based anti-malware store the software on a remote location such as in the cloud or a local server, but it depends upon each host to access the software and operates. The advantage is it stores nothing on the host system and making update easier. But a disadvantage is it suffers from lack of administration because it all depends upon the user on each host to run the anti-malware program.

Network-based

Network-based anti-malware a single anti-malware server runs on some systems, i.e. each host has a small client. These network-based programs are much easier to update and manage.

Switch port security

The switch port security feature is a key implementation of the network switch security. It provides the ability to limit what addresses will be allowed to send traffic on individual switch ports within the switched network. Switch port security starts with understanding potential vulnerabilities and then addressing them through correct configuration. This address may include DHCP snooping, ARP inspection, MAC address filtering, and VLAN assignments.

DHCP snooping

DHCP snooping is a method of controlling IP address assignment to prevent the possibility of attacks related to ARP spoofing. It uses a series of Switches and ensures that only specific hosts with specific MAC addresses will receive specific IP addresses. It can consequently ensure that the recorded MAC address associated with an IP address will not approach the network. Furthermore, it can ensure than only authorized DHCP servers are added to the network.

ARP Inspection

ARP inspection is similar to DHCP snooping in that it confirms IP to MAC assignments of packets based on the trusted list. It can be used to fight against man-in-the-middle attacks and ARP poisoning attacks.

MAC Address Filtering

MAC address filtering is a method that creates a table of "accepted users" list called Whitelisting that limit access to the wireless network. A table stored in the WAP lists the MAC addresses that are allowed to participate in the wireless network. MAC address

filtering can also create a table of "blocking users" list called Blacklisting that denies specific MAC addresses from logging onto the network. A MAC address can easily be a spoof by a hacker, making the NIC report an address other than its own and then access the network, and disturbing blacklisting. For this reason, if MAC address filtering is used as part of network security, then it should be a single part of it, and additional physical security and Layer 3 security measures should also be used.

VLAN Assignments

VLANs on switches allow you to create network segmentation by creating multiple virtual subnets while maintaining a flexible network that is easy to modify when required. Alternatively, an improper VLAN assignment on a port will effectively place clients in a subnet that will not control by the administrator. It is not only a connectivity problem, but it could also create a security issue. While assigning a VLAN, it should be done with great care as to which client computer is connected to which VLAN interface.

Security Policies

A security policy is a written document that defines how an organization will protect its IT infrastructure. There are hundreds of different security policies. It should be clearly defined as acceptable behavior on the organization's computers and networks and the concerns for violating acceptable behavior standards.

Disable Unneeded Network Services

Disable the network services that are no longer in use for security concerns. There are two reasons to disable unnecessary services, one is many operating system use services to listen on open TCP or UDP ports then unintentionally leaving the systems open to attack, and the other reason is attacker often use services as a tool for the use and propagation of malware. Therefore, users should prevent their system by disabling TCP/UDP ports and legacy services such as NetBIOS, Telnet, and any other unsecure protocol or service.

Use Secure Protocols

When you have disabled the unsecure protocols, then you should use the secure protocols. For example, use SSH instead of Telnet, use SNMPv3 instead of earlier versions, use SFTP instead of FTP, use HTTPS, SSL/TLS, rather than HTTP, and use IPsec whenever possible.

SSH

Secure Shell (SSH) has replaced an unsecure protocol Telnet. SSH involves SSH servers that use public key infrastructure (PKI) in the form of an RSA key. When a client tries to log into an SSH server, the server sends its public key to the client first then the client

receives this key, it creates a session ID and encrypts it using the public key, and sends it back to the server. The server decrypts this session key ID and uses to forward all data. It is secure therefore only the client, and the server knows this session ID.

SNMPv3

SNMPv3 added additional security features with support for encryption and strong authentication. It also provided features for managing and controlling a large number of devices efficiently.

SSL

Secure Sockets Layer (SSL) requires a server with a certificate. When a client requests access to an SSL-secured server, the server sends to the client a copy of the certificate. The SSL client checks this certificate, and if the certificate checks out, the server is authenticated, and the client negotiates a symmetric-key cipher for use in the session.

TLS

TLS is an updated version of Secure Sockets Layer protocol; it is more robust and flexible than SSL. TLS works with all TCP application and provides secure communications on the Internet for such things as e-mail, Internet faxing, and other data transfers, securing Voice over IP (VoIP) and virtual private networks (VPNs). The TLS Handshake Protocol allows the server and client to authenticate each other and to negotiate an encryption algorithm and cryptographic keys before data is exchanged. Every web browser today uses TLS for HTTPS-secured.

SFTP

The SSH File Transfer Protocol (SFTP), also known as the Secure File Transfer Protocol, enables secure file transfer capabilities between networked hosts. Unlike the Secure Copy Protocol (SCP), SFTP provides additional functionalities such as remote file system management, allowing applications to continue interrupted file transfers, list the contents of remote directories, and delete remote files.

HTTPS

Hyper Text Transfer Protocol Secure (HTTPS) is the secure version of HTTP, the protocol over which data is sent between the browser and the connected website. The 'S' at the end of HTTPS stands for 'Secure.' It means all communications between the browser and the website are encrypted and secured. Web browsers such as Internet Explorer, Firefox, and Chrome, YouTube, Facebook also display a padlock icon in the address bar to indicate that an HTTPS connection is in influence visually.

IPSec

The IP Security (IPsec) design comprises a suite of protocols developed to ensure the reliability, confidentiality, flexibility, and authentication of data communications over an IP network. IPsec may be used in three different security domains: virtual private networks, application-level security and routing security. Now a day, IPsec is predominately used in VPNs. When it used in application-level security or routing security, IPsec must be tied to other security measures to provide a complete solution.

IPsec works in two different modes: Transport mode and Tunnel mode. In Transport mode, only the actual payload of the IP packet is encrypted, the destination and source IP addresses and another IP header information are still readable. In Tunnel mode, the entire IP packet is encrypted and then placed into an IPsec endpoint, where it is encapsulated inside another IP packet. By default, IPv6 will use the IPsec Transport mode.

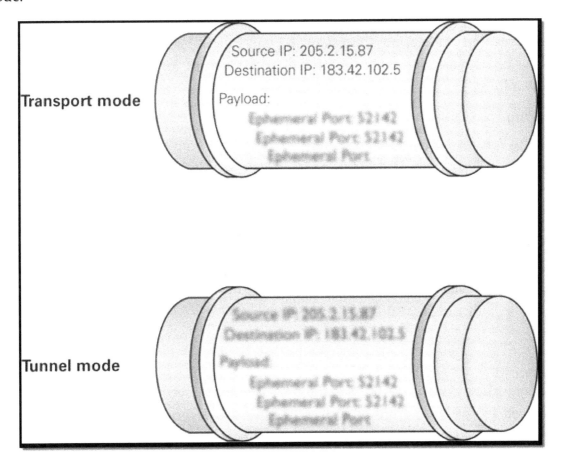

Figure 3-04: IPSec's Two Modes

Access lists

Access lists are used for identifying traffic to take a decision. They are not always for filtering traffic for security. Thereby, many types of the access list to filter traffic to and from a network. These may include web/content filtering, port filtering, IP filtering, and others. This section will discuss the main differences between web/content, port, and IP filtering access lists.

Web/content filtering

Web/content filters are proposed to offer or block access to specific types of content on web servers used within the network and to reach the Internet. The goal is to allow access to the content that is beneficial for the user, but at the same time, it blocks access to objectionable content. This type of filters may be used on browsers, email, client computers, search engines, network components, or a combination of any or all of these methods.

Port filtering

A port filtering access list does not read the whole content of the message but only read the header of the packets being sent. The header of the packets contains information such as the source and destination address of the packet and the ports that will be used for each. The list is generally made to deny all access except for the ports that have been explicitly allowed.

IP filtering

IP filtering creates access lists that allow or deny a source address or range of source addresses to a destination IP address or range of IP addresses. This type of filtering may be affected if a source address has been transformed by Network Address Translation (NAT) or Port Address Translation (PAT).

Wireless security

Wireless communication has become popular with each passing year. Therefore, it is essential to understand such protocols and procedures that can secure wireless networks. This section will discuss WEP, WPA, WPA2, TKIP/AES, 802.1x, TLS/TTLS, and MAC filtering.

WEP

Wired Equivalent Privacy (WEP) was the first attempt to secure wireless connections. It was secured by encrypting only the data transfer. However, WEP was found not to be equivalent to wired security because the security mechanisms that were used to establish the encryption were not encrypted. It used a key length that was originally 64-bit and then later upgraded to 128-bit. WEP also operates only at the lower layers of the OSI model and therefore cannot offer end-to-end security for applications.

WPA

Wi-Fi Protected Access (WPA) was designed to improve on WEP as a means of securing wireless communications. WPA is an upgradation on the system that currently uses WEP.

WPA offers two distinct advantages over WEP:

- Improved data encryption through the Temporal Key Integrity Protocol (TKIP), which scrambles the keys using a hashing algorithm.
- User authentication using the Extensible Authentication Protocol (EAP) and user certificates. It ensures that only authorized users can gain access to the network.

WPA2

Wi-Fi Protected Access version 2 (WPA2) further improves on WPA, offering additional advantages such as the following:

- Using Advanced Encryption Standard (AES) mode of encryption for much stronger security and longer security keys. It is usually installed in enterprise environments.
- Implementing Counter Mode Cipher Block Chaining Message Authentication Code Protocol (CCMP), which is based on the 802.11i standard and offers an enhanced data cryptographic encapsulation mechanism that replaces TKIP completely with a security method that is much stronger.

WPA Enterprise

WPA Enterprise is a wireless protocol that enhances security using IEEE 802.1x standard to enable you to set up a network with some seriously secure authentication using a RADIUS server and passwords encrypted with Extensible Authentication Protocol (EAP). WPA is used in medium to large size organization.

TLS

Transport Layer Security (TLS) provides secure communication among various network devices while avoiding eavesdropping, tampering, and message forgery. It is designed to allow end users to be sure about whom they are communicating with. To secure transmission of data, Clients can exchange the keys.

TTLS

Tunnel Transport Layer Security (TTLS) is a protocol that allows each client to authenticate to a server that has created a tunnel for communication. The clients have to authenticate only the server that created and authenticated the tunnel. It can save resources and provide for a more flexible setup of secure tunnels.

MAC filtering

MAC address has 48-bits hexadecimal address present on all network host. MAC filtering applied on switches working at Data-Link Layer of the OSI model. It focuses on source MAC address and destination MAC address in the packet and can be configured in such a way as to allow only specific MAC addresses through an interface on the switch. MAC filtering is usually applied at the access layer of a computer network, where the host computers are connected to the switches. Whether your network is wired or wireless, MAC address filtering is generally not used as the only means of security, because MAC addresses can easily be spoofed with the accurate software.

User authentication

User authentication is a process by which users prove their identity over the network. Generally, user authentication depends upon three factors.

The three factors by which users prove their identity are as follows:

<u>Something You know:</u> Something a user knows could be a password or the personal identification number (PIN) that corresponds to their smart card.

<u>Something You Have:</u> Something a user has could be a smart card or a cryptographic key.

<u>Something You Posses</u> Something a user is would relate to biometric authentication, such as a fingerprint, voiceprint, cornea or iris scan, or a hand geometry print.

Each of these factors of authentication uses different protocols.

Challenge Handshake Authentication Protocol (CHAP) and MSCHAP

Challenge Handshake Authentication Protocol (CHAP) is a remote access authentication protocol that uses a password that is a shared secret between the server and client. CHAP uses three-way handshaking in which the server sends the client a challenge to prove that it knows the secret by inserting it into a challenge string sent by the server using a hashing algorithm. The client uses the hashing algorithm on the secret to solving the challenge, called a message digest, which it sends back to the server. When the server receives the message digest from the client, it compares it with the message digest of the true secret and challenge using the same hashing algorithm. If the two message digests are the same, then the client knows the secret, and then communication can establish. If they are not the same, then the communication will be dismissed. CHAP is the strongest authentication method that can be used when deploying a mixture of Microsoft clients and other types of clients, such as Novell, UNIX, or Apple.

Microsoft Challenge Handshake Protocol (MS-CHAP) is Microsoft's variation on the CHAP protocol, which provides even greater security for authenticating Microsoft clients.

Password Authentication Protocol (PAP)

Password Authentication Protocol (PAP) is a legacy protocol that has been used in the past with Point-to-Point Protocol (PPP). It consists of two entities and a shared password. These two entities prove to each other by sending the password in clear text. Because of this, PAP is considered a very weak authentication mechanism and should not be used in today's networks.

Extensible Authentication Protocol (EAP)

Extensible Authentication Protocol (EAP) is an open set of standards that allows the addition of new methods of authentication. EAP use certificates from other trusted parties as a form of authentication. It is currently used for smart cards, and it is evolving in many forms of biometric verification using a person's fingerprint, retina scan, and so on.

Kerberos

Kerberos is a protocol for authenticating service requests between trusted hosts across an untrusted network, such as the internet. Kerberos was a three-headed dog who guarded the gates of Hades. The three heads of the Kerberos protocol represent a client, a server and a Key Distribution Center (KDC), which acts as Kerberos trusted third-party authentication service. Users, machines, and services using Kerberos want only to trust the KDC, which runs as a single process and provides two services: an authentication service and a ticket granting service. KDC "tickets" provide mutual authentication, allowing nodes to prove their identity to one another in a secure manner. Kerberos authentication uses conventional shared secret cryptography to prevent packets traveling across the network from being read or changed and to protect messages from eavesdropping and replay attacks. Kerberos is built into all major operating systems, including Microsoft Windows, Apple OS X, FreeBSD, and Linux.

Two-factor authentication

Two-factor authentication means to authenticate the user by something they have or something they know. For example, authentication by a smart card that also has pin numbers usually belongs to Two-factor authentication.

Multifactor Authentication

Multifactor Authentication means to authenticate the user by above two factors along with something they are. For example, authentication by a smart card that has pin numbers along with biometric verification such as thumb scanned, iris scanned, and others belong to Multifactor Authentication.

Single sign-on

The ability to log in only one time and use the same token to access any resource that is allowed on an entire network is called single sign-on.

Hashes

A hash function can be used to convert digital data of any size into a data string of a fixed and much smaller size. If the larger data is changed even in any small way, the resulting smaller data will change largely. It allows a system to quickly determine if the data sent through a network is the same as the data received, without having to examine the entire data stream or document. The two main hashing algorithms used in today's networks are MD5 and SHA.

Message Digest 5

Message Digest 5 (MD5) is a hashing algorithm that is still very commonly used, while some experts say that it has broken about the processing power that hackers can have today. It uses a 512-bit block and creates a 128-bit hash value that is typically expressed as a 32-digit hexadecimal number. It is often used to verify the integrity of data sent over network systems.

String	MD5
IPSpecialist...	a535590bec93526944bd4b94822a7625
IPspecialist...	997bd71ad0158de71f6e97a57261b9a7

Table 3-01: Comparing MD5 Values

Secure Hashing Algorithm (SHA)

Secure Hash Algorithm (SHA) belongs to cryptographic hash functions published by the National Institute of Standards and Technology. It currently has block sizes of 256 bits and 512 bits. The advanced versions of SHA (SHA-2 and SHA-3) are usually considered to be much more secure than MD5.

Syntax: **The password is 12345**

SHA-1:

567c552b6b559eb6373ce55a43326ba3db92dcbf

SHA-256:

5da923a6598f034d91f375f73143b2b2f58be8a1c9417886d5966968b7f79674

SHA-384:

929f4c12885cb73d05b90dc825f70c2de64ea721e15587deb34309991f6d57114500465243ba08a554f8fe7c8dbbca04

SHA-512:

1d967a52ceb738316e85d94439dbb112dbcb8b7277885b76c849a80905ab370dc11d2b84dcc88d61393117de483a950ee253fbaod26b5b168744b94af2958145

Physical Security Controls.

With an understanding of the secure protocols, encryption algorithms, and access lists. It is also important to have a general sense of physical security for servers and network components. Many types of physical components improve physical security, it includes mantraps, network closets, video monitoring, door access controls, proximity readers/key fobs, biometrics, keypad/ cipher locks, and an outdated security guard. This section will discuss all of these physical security components.

Mantraps

A mantrap typically consists of a two-door system that requires authentication to open each door. It is an entry path with two successive locked doors and a small space between them providing one-way entry or exit. After a person enters the first door, the second door cannot be unlocked until the first door is closed and secured. It means that if someone wants access to an environment without authentication and thinks they can hack the system, then they had better be very sure about both hacks because otherwise they will be stuck in the mantrap while the security guard and the police are on the way.

Network Closets

In small to medium-sized environments, a simple room with a lock on the door can be used to store sensitive computer and network equipment. This room might contain racks of computers, routers, switches, UPSs, and so on. Typically, there is additional physical security such as cameras or guards, and there may be more than one closet with additional equipment and connections for redundancy.

Video Monitoring

Video monitoring is a technology to enhance physical security. It has been made much easier with the development of IP cameras and closed-circuit TV systems that can be placed in key locations to find attackers and record their actions if they still proceed. It is more securable if using hidden cameras to catch the attacker.

Door Access Controls

Door access controls are generally directed by something that is in possession of someone who has the authorization to enter a locked place. That something may be a key, a badge, a key fob with a chip, or some other physical token.

Proximity readers/key fob

A proximity card and reader system are often used to allow an authenticated person to enter an enterprise or a secure area in a building. It is a fast and suitable method for the people who want security, but it can often be cheated with piggybacking techniques. The best way to prevent that type of behavior and still use the proximity reader and card is to train the people to use the card properly and enforce the fact that piggybacking is not allowed.

Biometrics

Biometric access is the best way to build physical security by using a unique physical characteristic of a person to allow access to a controlled IT resource. These physical characteristics include fingerprints, handprints, voice recognition, retina scans, and so on. This biometric is stored in the database to implement any security measures that the vendor recommends protecting the integrity of the metrics and the associated database.

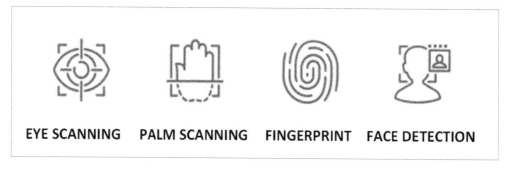

EYE SCANNING   PALM SCANNING   FINGERPRINT   FACE DETECTION

Figure 3-05: Biometric Authentication

Keypad/cipher locks

Keypads and cipher locks are often used to control access to secure areas. The most secure types of keypads scramble the number locations on the pad each time they are used, so no one can follow the code that a person is entering while they enter it. A cipher lock is a door unlocking system that uses a door handle, a latch, and a sequence of mechanical push buttons. When the buttons are pressed in the correct order, the door unlocks, and the door operates.

Security Guard

Security guards are great as they are responsible for protecting assets, building access, secure individual room, and office access, and perform facility patrols. The guard station can serve as a central control of security systems such as video surveillance and key

control. Like all humans, security guards are subject to attacks such as social engineering, but for flexibility, common sense, and a way to take the edge off of high security, professional security cannot be beaten.

Firewall Basics

Firewalls are devices or software that protect an internal network from unauthorized access by acting as a filter. Firewalls are essential tools in the fight against malicious programs on the Internet. The most basic job of the firewall is to investigate each packet and decide based on a set of rules whether to block or allow the traffic. This traffic can be either inbound traffic or outbound traffic.

This section will discuss different types of firewalls, how to use it, and how to configure on the system.

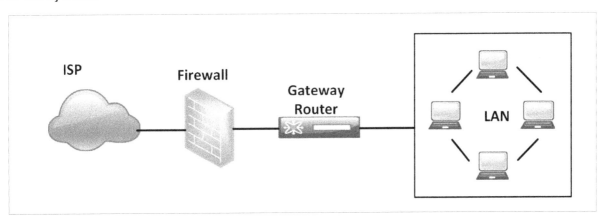

Figure 3.06: A Network Gateway

Types of firewalls

Firewalls have changed tremendously over the past ten years as technologies have grown. There are different types of firewalls categorized by functionality, two broad categories of firewalls are host based and network based.

Host-based

A host-based firewall is a set of firewall software that runs on an individual computer or other devices connected to a network. These types of firewalls are a granular way to protect the individual hosts from viruses and malware, and to control the spread of these harmful infections throughout the network. A great example of this type of firewall is the Windows Firewall.

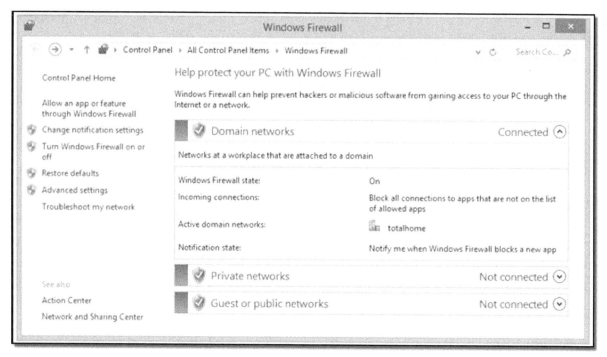

Figure 3.07: Windows Firewall in Windows 8.1

Network-based

The network-based firewall is often implemented in some sort of hardware appliance or is built into the router that is installed between the LAN and the wilds of the Internet. These firewalls form the first line of defense, protecting the whole network. Although they do a great job of protecting whole networks, they can't provide any help if the malicious traffic is originating from inside the network itself.

Software vs. Hardware

Software firewalls are generally part of an operating system or are a third-party application that installs onto the operating system and can be configurable for a single host and are therefore flexible for configuration for that host alone.

Hardware firewalls are specialized machines that are built to filter packets between networks. The main purpose of a hardware firewall is used to protect a computer or an entire network from unauthorized access from the Internet. Firewalls can be programmed to control the flow of data and filter the packets to and from multiple networks within the same organization based on the information contained in the packets.

Application-aware/Context-aware

Application-aware firewalls have developed to deal with today's application-centric threats. Application- and context-aware firewalls filtering the data traffic by using specific protocol or port. They can inspect the data that is going through the firewall.

Small office, home office firewall

Most small office/home office users depend on two different types of firewalls: software firewall and hardware firewall. Software firewalls include those in the operating systems, such as the Windows Firewall Service, and those in other security packages such as their anti-virus software. These firewalls are generally only allowing normal traffic in and out by default. Hardware firewalls provided by the LAN/WAN router that use to connect to the Internet. It can generally be controlled through the software provided by the vendor.

Stateful vs. stateless Firewall

The difference between a stateful firewall and a stateless firewall is the intelligence with which the firewall examines the packets. A stateless firewall is configured to recognize only static attributes in each packet, such as the source IP address, destination IP address, and protocol. It does not concern a stream of data that would be normal for a protocol. In compare, a stateful firewall can hold in memory the major attributes of each connection. These attributes may include IP addresses, ports, and sequence numbers involved in the connection. The stateful firewall makes the filtering more efficient and more accurate for most communication sessions. Stateful firewalls were the first step in the technical evolution toward IDSs, IPSs, and application-aware firewalls.

Unified Threat Management (UTM)

A Unified Threat Management (UTM) system performs a function of a traditional firewall. It also provides many security solutions in one component. UTM can perform many functions such as Network firewalling, Network intrusion prevention, Gateway antivirus, Gateway anti-spam, VPN Content Filtering, Load balancing, Data leak prevention, On-appliance reporting. It is commonly installed as a single physical, rack-mountable appliance.

Settings/Techniques

Firewall settings and techniques assist in determining the types of packets will be allowed or blocked through the firewall and which techniques will be used to investing a packet either IP, port or data. This all things covered in this section.

Access Control List (ACL)

Firewalls generally contain access control lists (ACLs) that allow or deny packets based on specified criteria such as IP addresses, ports, or the data they contain. The firewall generally processes from top to bottom when the traffic meets the criteria then the related action of authority or deny is applied. Usually, there is an implicit deny statement at the end of the firewall ACL that will deny any packets that have not been allowed before they reach that point. Sometimes that statement is not implicit but is listed as the default statement at the end of the list.

Virtual wire vs. routed

BASIS FOR COMPARISION	Virtual Wire Firewall	Routed Firewall
Definition	A firewall connected to a virtual machine operates on a host computer. The virtual machine must pass through the firewall before it is routed inside and outside the network.	Firewalls are mostly hardware or software-based systems to which traffic is routed and must pass through to go any farther.
Advantage	•Visibility into network traffic • Simple to install and configure, no configuration changes required to surrounding network devices •Easy to implement for proof of concept testing •The device can take action on the traffic, such as allow, block or perform QoS	Full firewall functionality, such as • Traffic visibility • Blocking traffic •Rate limiting traffic •NAT •Routing including support for common routing protocols
Disadvantage	•Cannot perform layer 3 functionality on the device, such as routing •Cannot perform any switching on the device	•Inserting device into the network will require IP configuration changes on adjacent devices

Table 3-02: Virtual wire vs. routed

DMZ

Generally, three zones are related with firewalls: Internal, External, and Demilitarized (DMZ). The internal zone is the zone inside of all firewalls, and it is considered to be the protected area where most critical servers, such as domain controllers those controlling sensitive information, are placed. The external zone is the area outside the firewall that represents the network against inside protection such as the internet. The DMZ is placed where the network has more than one firewall. It is a zone that is between two firewalls. It is created using a device that has at least three network connections, sometimes

referred to as a three-pronged firewall. In DMZ, place the servers that are used by hosts on both the internal network and the external network that may include web, VPN, and FTP servers.

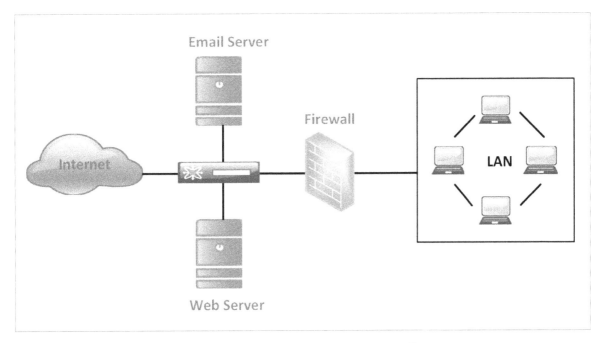

Figure 3-08: DMZ using One Firewall

Implicit Deny

The 'implicit deny' one of the best types of firewall setting treats everything not given specific and selective permission as suspicious. Network boundaries that follow an implicit deny concept only allow specific IP addresses and/or service ports while blocking all others.

Block/allow

Block and allow outbound or inbound traffic is the rule set on the firewall to give access to only desire traffic comes in a network either it is generating from inside the network or outside the network. It is based on the protocol, IP address source, IP address destination, MAC address, or even content of the message. This rule makes the firewall more efficient and intelligent.

Firewall Placement

Typically, a firewall placement is based on the perimeter of a network that controls the traffic monitoring and filtering. This type of firewall is sometimes referred to as an external firewall. On the other hand, some firewalls protect resources that are farther inside the organization's perimeter, perhaps in a more secure zone. These firewalls can be referred to as internal firewalls.

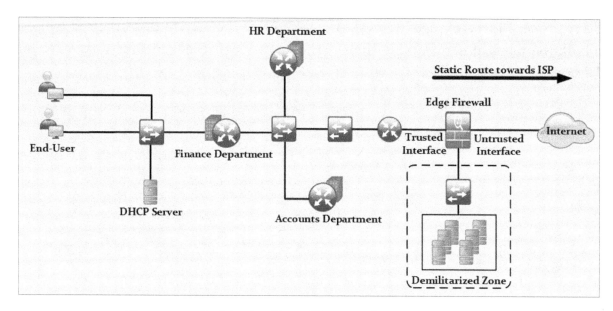

Figure 3-09: Positioning Firewall in a production environment

The previous figure shows a typical scenario of SOHO and mid-sized corporate environment where whole network infrastructure is supported by a couple of routers and switches. If the edge firewall is supposed to be the focal point of security implementation, then any slighter misconfiguration may result in high scale attacks. In general, a layered security approach is followed, and packet passes through multiple security checks before hitting the intended destination.

The position of firewall varies in different design variants. In some designs, it is placed on the perimeter router of the corporation while in some designs it is placed at the edge of the network as shown in the last figure. Irrelevant to the position, it is a good practice to implement the layered security in which some of the features like unicast reverse path forwarding, access-lists, etc. are enabled on perimeter router. Features like deep packet inspection, digital signatures are matched on the firewall. If everything looks good, the packet is allowed to hit the intended destination address.

Network layer firewalls permit or drop IP traffic based on Layer 3 and 4 information. A router with access-list configured on its interfaces is a common example of network layer firewall. Although very fast in operation and, network layer firewalls do not perform deep packet inspection techniques and detect any malicious activity.

Purpose of Various Network Access Control Methods

There are many devices and methods used to secure networks. But choosing those methods among the varieties of methods that make the network vulnerability free. This section will discuss the various methods of intrusion detection and prevention with

vulnerability scanners and also discuss more advanced and proactive methods used to decoy, trap, and catch would-be attackers.

802.1x

802.1x is a standard developed by the Institute of Electrical and Electronics Engineers (IEEE) defines a method for access control by authentication. This authentication will get when client computer requests access to a network through a device such as a network appliance or an authenticator (WAP), this authenticator passes the request to the authentication server. The authentication based on the decision of authentication server either accept or reject by following the databases. The authentication server plays an important role while authenticator just follows the authentication server instructions.

Posture assessment

Besides user authentication, authorization in NAC can be based upon compliance checking. This posture assessment is the evaluation of system security based on the applications and settings that a particular system is using. Posture assessment includes checking the type and version of anti-malware, level of QoS, type/version of operating system, and so on.

Guest Network

A guest network is a way of providing visitors access to a wireless internet connection while at the same time enhancing network security. It is a feature of wireless router that is configured for the specific purpose of providing Internet connectivity for users to browse the Web and check their email on the company's computers instead of the visitor's device. This assures that the visitors cannot connect to any internal resources of the organization and prevents the spread of malware that might have been spread if the visitor's device were allowed to connect to the network.

Persistent vs. Non-persistent Agents

An agent is someone that performs a task on behalf of someone else. In networking, when implementing access control, the agent is the software component that checks the strength of the system. A persistent agent is a software that exists on the client side responsible for making the connection, performs auto-remediation functions during a connection and will also monitor the device throughout a session to fix things that may change.

The Non-persistent agent is software running on the browser of the client. It performs the same tasks as Persistent agents do like connection, auto-remediation actions, checking, monitoring, etc. Non-persistent agents are not installed or stay with the client.

Quarantine Network

A quarantine network is a restricted IP network that can be used to contain a computer that is infected with a virus or other malware until it can be properly remediated. It provides access to only the network connections which will allow patches to be applied but not to other connections that would allow it to infect other computers. This is generally done by VLAN assignment and by manipulating Address Resolution Protocol (ARP) requests and replies.

Edge vs. Access Control

Access control list use in large networks to identify not just the source and destination address of packets but as well as protocol, port and so on. This allows controlling the access to packets to any portion of the network that leads to the destination and helps to keep traffic off of lower-bandwidth.

Edge control list is the basic control list use in small networks to identify only the source address of the packet and making all the decisions by source address only. This type of access list is generally placed on the edge that leads to the destination of the allowed traffic. It blocks the unwanted traffic while allowing the desired traffic to enter the traffic.

Summarize Basic Forensic Concepts

Computer forensics is the knowledge of gathering, preserving, and presenting computerized data. Operators are often first responders or supporters of first responders to a security incident and should follow good forensic practices.

First Responder

First responders are the people or group of people who are the first on the scene after the attack. They decide whether some event on the network qualifies as an incident then they should address, ignore, or escalate. They evaluate the scope and cause of the issue to prevent further disruption. Most incidents are resolved at the initial level. While some vast incident cannot stop, contain, or remediate by them and disaster recovery comes into play.

Secure the Area

If the attack continues then the first responder secure the area first. It is might needed to escalate the attack and get additional support to mitigate the threat. It depends upon the type of attack and the affected object. This might include securing computers and networking equipment or establishing a perimeter around an entire building.

Document the Scene

After securing the area, the next step is to document the scene to preserve the state of the equipment and anything that might need to inspect forensically. The proper documentation helps to catch the attacker by using the clues that the attacker has left behind.

eDiscovery

Electronic Discovery (eDiscovery) is the process of preserving, collecting, and processing computer data after an attack. This process is requesting that data and providing it legally. This section will briefly discuss elements of eDiscovery such as data collection, a chain of custody, data transport, forensic reports, and legal hold.

Evidence/Data Collection

This actually begins with preserving the collected data by identifying the data is potentially relevant and assuring that no changes are made to the data. Some large organizations that are going through with these events more frequently may have software and even collaborate channels to make sure this step is done properly.

Chain of Custody

This is a legal term refers to the chronological documentation that shows the seizure, control, transfer, analysis, and disposition of physical or electronic evidence. This evidence is used in a court of law or other legal procedure as a legal requirement.

Data Transport

To maintain the chain of custody, every transport of the data should be completely documented to assure that the data was not changed in transit. At the same time as with physical objects, there must be clear chronological documentation to follow.

Forensics Report

The forensic report consists of gathering information about the previous record that can be used in a legal proceeding. Therefore, a forensic report is a detailed document that provides a chronological sequence of events for the data interrogation from initial collection to eventual termination.

Legal Hold

Legal hold is a process that use to preserve all forms of relevant information when organization anticipates a legal proceeding relating to the information. It is generally coordinated between the organization and their lawyer to maintain a chain of custody of the data so that it is acceptable in a court of law.

Mind Map:

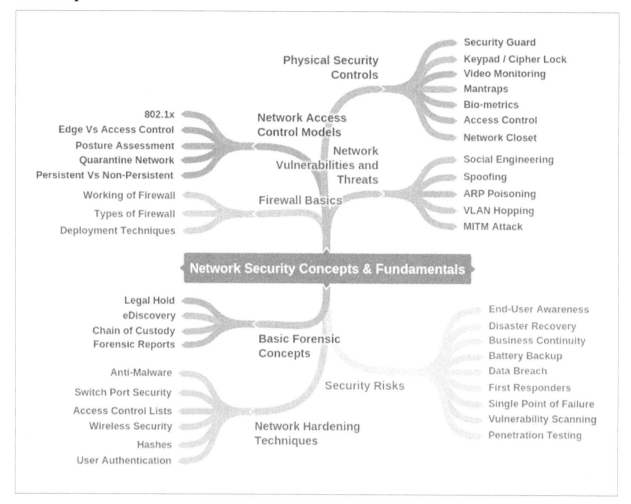

Chapter 4: Troubleshooting

Network Troubleshooting Methodology

The methodology of network troubleshooting evaluates the performance of a network and how long it continues to work and also determine the different causes of problems. These problems can be distinguished by troubleshooting methods, there are a lot of troubleshooting methodologies in networking, but this section will describe the basic troubleshooting methodologies.

Identify the problem

Let's walk through a typical scenario that might occur on your network and see how using a troubleshooting methodology will help you get to the root of the problem faster. I think you will see how having some plan is much better than having no plan at all in this scenario.

- Gather information
- Duplicate the problem, if possible
- Question users
- Identify symptoms
- Determine if anything has changed
- Approach multiple problems individually

Establishing a theory of probable cause

Once you have diagnosed the problem after gathering information about the issue, figure out a possible cause which results in this problem. You should have a theory of probable cause. This theory may not be fact, but later, you can establish a revised theory.

Top-to-Bottom / Bottom-to-Top OSI Model

Top-to-Bottom or Bottom-to-Top OSI layered Approach helps to establish a theory of probable cause by figuring out layers of OSI model in either Top-to-Bottom or Bottom-to-Top approach.

#	OSI Layer	Theory
7	Application Layer	Problem with the API results in unavailability of services to end user.
6	Presentation Layer	Incorrect encryption algorithm
5	Session Layer	Authentication failure, Issue with establishing a session, etc.

4	Transport Layer	Issues related to transport protocols such as heavy traffic flow causing a delay in receiving acknowledgment packets.
3	Network Layer	Incorrect IP address / Subnet of the machine, Missing routes, etc.
2	Data-Link Layer	The MAC address of the machine might be blacklisted, VLAN assignment issue or another layer 2 issues might be a probable cause.
1	Physical Layer	A disconnected/bad cable, bad Connector, dead NIC can make for a bad day.

Table 4-01: Establishing Theory with OSI Layers

Sometimes, starting layer approach from layer 1 founds helpful such as a scenario where equipment and devices are newly deployed. However, you can use both approaches.

Divide and Conquer

Another approach is Divide and Conquer approach. After gathering enough information about the problem, you will be focused on an appropriate OSI layer from where the issue arises. You can proceed to test the probable causes of that particular OSI layer. If you found your theory correct, further troubleshooting steps can be followed. If the theory does not seem to fit the issue, you can proceed to upper or lower layer.

Test the theory to determine the cause

In the third phase "Test the theory to Determine the cause," you have to evaluate the theory to diagnose the root cause of the problem. To understand this phase, consider a scenario where a printer is connected to the Local network. The issue arises that no one could access the printer to print. According to step 1 "Identify the Problem," you should explore the issue and gather information like troubleshooting network connectivity of users to the printer. Theory of probable cause could be disconnected or bad cabling. Now, testing the theory phase includes testing of network cables, connectors, ensuring that printer is powered on or not. If the printer is not powered on, or cable is disconnected, you can proceed to next step. If you find everything fine with layer 1, you can proceed to test layer 2 and so on.

Establishing an action plan

Once you found a possible reason for the problem, you will now establish an action plan to resolve the issue. For example, installation of new Ethernet cables, installation of new power cables, or re-installation of connectors could be an action plan to resolve the issue.

Implementation of Solutions

Implementation of solution phase is the action phase where several action plans can be enforced to eliminate the problem. Upon successful implementation, the issue must be resolved.

Verification of functionality and Implementation of Preventative measures

Verification of functionality is a phase where the resolution of an issue is verified by testing the process. For example, sending commands to print a test page from the user's machine will help to verify the functionality. Implementation of preventative measures could be preparing a policy for maintenance of cables and connectors, giving responsibility to ensure the powering of the devices could be preventative measures.

Document Findings and Outcomes

Documentation of all findings and outcomes helps to report the issue to higher administration. These documentations could be used for the legal purpose if you found any unauthorized intrusion to your devices. Furthermore, these documentations could also be used in future when a similar issue is reported.

Network Troubleshooting Tools

This scenario belongs to the network administrator of a company who troubleshoots the network issues. In this scenario, there are a great many software tools and utilities to choose from that will assist them in troubleshooting connectivity issues. In fact, many troubleshooting utilities are built into the most common operating systems.

Command Line Tools

Most of the utilities are based on the command line and are not obvious to the end user. For the network administrator, knowledge about these tools and their application regarding troubleshooting will help them to set apart of peers.

Ipconfig and Ifconfig

When troubleshooting a system connected to the network, the basic thing they will most likely want to find out is whether the system has an IP address. The following commands can be used to determine the IP settings on the system.

Ipconfig: The ipconfig command is used in Windows to display the IP address information of the system. The following is a list of popular ipconfig commands:

- **ipconfig /all**   Displays all TCP/IP settings and the MAC address
- **ipconfig /displaydns**   Displays the DNS resolver cache

- **ipconfig /flushdns**   Clears out the DNS resolver cache
- **ipconfig /renew**   Releases and renew the IP address of an adapter
- **ipconfig /release**   Releases an IP address that was obtained automatically

but does not renew an address.

Ifconfig: The ifconfig tool is used in Unix and Linux operating systems to configure interfaces and view information about configured interfaces. Remember that the syntax of the ifconfig tool is different from the syntax of ipconfig.

The following is a list of popular ifconfig commands:

- **ifconfig**   Displays the network card and IP settings
- **ifconfig etho up**   Enables the first Ethernet card
- **ifconfig etho down**   Disables the Ethernet card

Netstat

The netstat command use in all operating systems that enables a network administrator to examine network statistics about a system. These statistics include information such as the ports listening on the system and any connections that have been established. This is the output from the netstat command:

```
C:\Users\User>netstat

Active Connections

  Proto  Local Address          Foreign Address        State
  TCP    192.168.0.36:57098     xiva-daria:https       ESTABLISHED
  TCP    192.168.0.36:57112     13.94.24.143:https     ESTABLISHED
  TCP    192.168.0.36:57115     52.230.84.217:https    ESTABLISHED
  TCP    192.168.0.36:57116     sc-in-f188:5228        ESTABLISHED
  TCP    192.168.0.36:57133     fjr02s04-in-f3:https   ESTABLISHED
  TCP    192.168.0.36:57134     172.217.194.94:https   ESTABLISHED
  TCP    192.168.0.36:57136     151.101.9.132:https    ESTABLISHED
  TCP    192.168.0.36:57137     192.168.1.255:1688     SYN_SENT
```

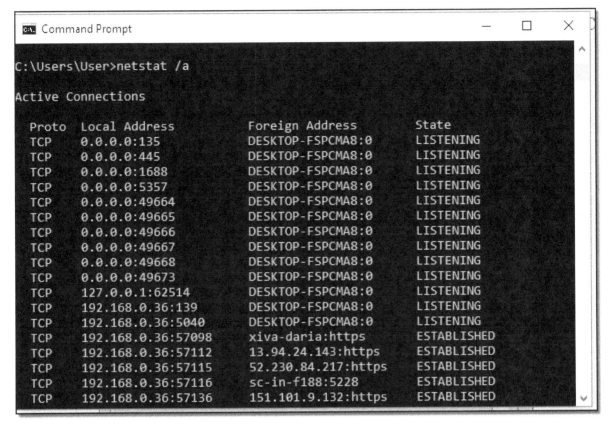

Figure 4-01: Common netstat Tool

Ping/Ping6

The ping utility generally uses in all operating systems to tests connections between two nodes. Sit has done it at one of the systems and type in ping followed by the hostname or IP address of the other node. The ping utility uses Internet Control Message Protocol (ICMP) to send an ICMP Echo Request to determine whether the other node can receive the test packet and reply to it. A node that can be reached will respond, and the ping utility will report success. Ping6 utility used in IPv6 protocol.

```
Command Prompt                                              —    □    ×

C:\Users\User>ping /?

Usage: ping [-t] [-a] [-n count] [-l size] [-f] [-i TTL] [-v TOS]
            [-r count] [-s count] [[-j host-list] | [-k host-list]]
            [-w timeout] [-R] [-S srcaddr] [-c compartment] [-p]
            [-4] [-6] target_name

Options:
    -t              Ping the specified host until stopped.
                    To see statistics and continue - type Control-Break;
                    To stop - type Control-C.
    -a              Resolve addresses to hostnames.
    -n count        Number of echo requests to send.
    -l size         Send buffer size.
    -f              Set Don't Fragment flag in packet (IPv4-only).
    -i TTL          Time To Live.
    -v TOS          Type Of Service (IPv4-only. This setting has been deprecat
ed
                    and has no effect on the type of service field in the IP
                    Header).
    -r count        Record route for count hops (IPv4-only).
    -s count        Timestamp for count hops (IPv4-only).
    -j host-list    Loose source route along host-list (IPv4-only).
```

Figure 4-02: The Ping Tool

Tracert/ Traceroute

The tracert command traces the route between two hosts. Traceroute tool or tracert tool is a network utility that uses ICMP to create a list of routers through which a packet is transmitted. Using the traceroute tool, you can determine not only the path followed by the router to reach the packet to the specified destination but also give details how long each packet will take to reach the destination.

You initiate the tracert tool on a Microsoft client by typing tracert at the command prompt followed by a space and then the IP address or hostname of the computer to which you want to test connectivity. You can find a complete list of tracert commands by typing tracert /?

Fig 4.3 shows the connection between the windows client and Google

```
Command Prompt                                          —    □    ×

C:\Users\User>tracert googl.com

Tracing route to googl.com [216.58.205.132]
over a maximum of 30 hops:

  1      1 ms     <1 ms     <1 ms   192.168.0.1
  2      *         *          *     Request timed out.
  3     10 ms      3 ms       2 ms  110.37.216.157
  4      3 ms      3 ms       3 ms  58.27.182.149
  5      5 ms      4 ms       7 ms  58.27.209.54
  6      2 ms      2 ms       5 ms  58.27.183.230
  7     18 ms     10 ms      23 ms  tw129-static213.tw1.com [119.63.129.213]
  8      5 ms     12 ms       5 ms  110.93.253.117
  9     53 ms     31 ms      28 ms  72.14.204.14
 10     20 ms     25 ms      27 ms  108.170.240.51
 11    118 ms    119 ms     120 ms  216.239.56.13
 12    119 ms    116 ms     120 ms  108.170.245.81
 13    119 ms    115 ms     122 ms  216.239.42.13
 14    126 ms    126 ms     183 ms  mil04s27-in-f132.1e100.net [216.58.205.132]

Trace complete.
```

Figure 4-03: The Tracert Tool

Nbtstat

The nbtstat (NetBIOS over TCP/IP statistics) utility that displays protocol statistics and current TCP/IP connections using NBT (NetBIOS over TCP/IP), which allows the user to troubleshoot NetBIOS name resolution issues. Normally, name resolution is made when NetBIOS over TCP/IP is functioning correctly. It does this through local cache lookup, WINS or DNS server query or Hosts lookup.

```
Command Prompt                                              —    □    ×

C:\Users\User>nbtstat

Displays protocol statistics and current TCP/IP connections using NBT
(NetBIOS over TCP/IP).

NBTSTAT [ [-a RemoteName] [-A IP address] [-c] [-n]
        [-r] [-R] [-RR] [-s] [-S] [interval] ]

  -a   (adapter status) Lists the remote machine's name table given its name
  -A   (Adapter status) Lists the remote machine's name table given its
                        IP address.
  -c   (cache)          Lists NBT's cache of remote [machine] names and their
 IP addresses
  -n   (names)          Lists local NetBIOS names.
  -r   (resolved)       Lists names resolved by broadcast and via WINS
  -R   (Reload)         Purges and reloads the remote cache name table
  -S   (Sessions)       Lists sessions table with the destination IP addresse
s
  -s   (sessions)       Lists sessions table converting destination IP
                        addresses to computer NETBIOS names.
  -RR  (ReleaseRefresh) Sends Name Release packets to WINS and then, starts R
efresh
```

Figure 4-04: The nbtstat Tool

Here are some nbtstat options with their functions:

nbtstat –n   Displays name registered locally by the system

nbtstat –c   Displays the NetBIOS name cache entries

nbtstat –a   Displays the names registered by a remote system

Figure 4-05 shows the output of nbtstat -n

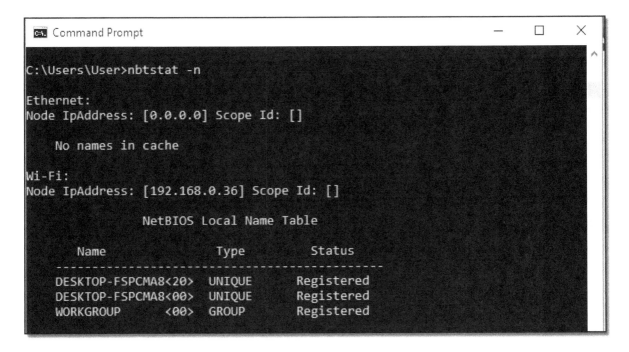

Figure 4-05: Output of nbtstat –n

Nslookup

The nslookup utility allows you to troubleshoot problems related to DNS. You can use nslookup to research information about a DNS server or to set a DNS configuration on the server. You can use nslookup in either non-interactive or interactive mode.

If you use the command in non-interactive mode, simply type nslookup in command prompt and press enter then type "?" to see the list of all commands that you want to execute and then type exit to close the session. Using commands in interactive mode are the same as those in non-interactive mode, except that you don't have to type nslookup before each command.

Figure 4-06 shows the output of nslookup in interactive mode

```
Command Prompt - nslookup                              —    □    ✕

C:\Users\User>nslookup
Default Server:   UnKnown
Address:   192.168.0.1

> server
Server:   UnKnown
Address:   192.168.0.1

*** UnKnown can't find server: Non-existent domain
> www.yahoo.com
Server:   UnKnown
Address:   192.168.0.1

Non-authoritative answer:
Name:      atsv2-fp.wg1.b.yahoo.com
Addresses:  2001:4998:44:41d::4
            2001:4998:c:1023::5
            2001:4998:44:41d::3
            2001:4998:c:1023::4
            98.137.246.7
            98.137.246.8
Aliases:   www.yahoo.com

> exit
```

Figure 4-06: The nslookup tool in interactive mode

ARP

The arp utility usually found in all operating systems helps to diagnose the problems associated with the Address Resolution Protocol (ARP). ARP is a service that operates in the background and resolves IP addresses to MAC addresses so that packets can be delivered to their destination. As you may know, each computer keeps an arp cache of entries that have been recently resolved probably within the past 10 minutes. Primarily the computer checks the arp cache; then, if the entry is not in the cache, arp will be used to broadcast into the local network and request that the computer with a specific IP address responds with its MAC address so that the packet can be addressed and delivered.

```
Command Prompt                                        —    □    ✕

C:\Users\User>arp -a

Interface: 192.168.0.102 --- 0x3
  Internet Address        Physical Address       Type
  192.168.0.1             70-4f-57-77-4a-f4      dynamic
  192.168.0.255           ff-ff-ff-ff-ff-ff      static
  224.0.0.22              01-00-5e-00-00-16      static
  224.0.0.252             01-00-5e-00-00-fc      static
  239.255.255.250         01-00-5e-7f-ff-fa      static
  255.255.255.255         ff-ff-ff-ff-ff-ff      static
```

Figure 4.07: The arp Tool

MAC address lookup table

A MAC address lookup table is a listing of MAC addresses and the connected ports on which a switch observed them. It first creates the switch from the source addresses of frames that are entering the switch's interfaces. After creating, it is then used by the switch to make frame-forwarding decisions on the frames that follow.

Pathping

Pathping is the combination of ping and tracert utility that performs the function of the connectivity test of ping with the path discovery of traceroute into one command. Pathping displays the connectivity statistics and the specific path that follow the packets. The only disadvantage to pathping is that it can be slow to run.

```
Select Command Prompt                                    —    □    ×

C:\Users\User>pathping

Usage: pathping [-g host-list] [-h maximum_hops] [-i address] [-n]
                [-p period] [-q num_queries] [-w timeout]
                [-4] [-6] target_name

Options:
    -g host-list      Loose source route along host-list.
    -h maximum_hops   Maximum number of hops to search for target.
    -i address        Use the specified source address.
    -n                Do not resolve addresses to hostnames.
    -p period         Wait period milliseconds between pings.
    -q num_queries    Number of queries per hop.
    -w timeout        Wait timeout milliseconds for each reply.
    -4                Force using IPv4.
    -6                Force using IPv6.
```

Figure 4-08: shows pathping in action

Line testers

Line testers are relatively simple devices usually used to check the reliability of twisted pair cable. Using a line tester to check a twisted pair line either it is good, dead, reverse wired, or if there is AC voltage on the line.

Certifiers

Cable certifier certifies the cable after installation and properly connected with their respective connectors. It certifies that the installed cables perform properly and ready to provide the result as per their characteristics. Many cable certifiers available for all cable types and even for wireless networks.

Multimeter

A multimeter is a device that provides with a digital readout of numerous tests including continuity, resistance, voltage, current, and so on. By simply set the multi-meter for what you want to measure. Some troubleshooting might require taking two measurements, one having good connectivity and the other one is what you are troubleshooting, and then comparing the two measurements. For example; in case of resistance, a good cable will have zero resistance (0 ohms) while the faulty or broken cable will show a higher-than-normal resistance—anything above a few ohms to infinity.

Cable tester

A cable tester is a device that is used to test the strength and connectivity of a particular type of cable or other wired assemblies. There are some different types of cable testers, each able to test a specific type of cable or wire. A cable tester can test whether a cable or wire is set up properly, connected correctly, and the communication strength between the source and destination is adequate for transmitting data.

Light meter

The light meter measures the amount of light. In computer networks, it is used to measure the strength of fiber-optic cables. The light meter system uses a high-powered source of light at one end of a run and a calibrated detector at the other end. This measures the amount of light that reaches the detector.

Toner probe

Toner probe uses to test the connectivity of wires that run through walls and other obstructions. This tool works in a pair of devices, one device produces a signal or tone on one end, and another device determines that signal can still be heard on the other end. The device that produces the signal is called the tone generator. The other device that locates the generated signal is called the tone locator. These devices not only verify connectivity, but it also traces the wire connections from the wall outlet to the patch panel.

Speed test sites

A simple way to test your network speed is to use a speed test site, such as www.speedtest.net or www.speakeasy.net. These sites are providing marketing services and attract people by providing a free speed test that gives the digital results on a meter. People should trust only the first test after they connect to the site because after that cached information might tend to make your results look better than actual. These tests are helpful in troubleshooting the speed because it can be counted as reliable.

Looking glass sites

Looking glass sites are publicly available sites on which you can test your connectivity to the Internet backbone routers. Looking glass sites are remote servers available with a browser that contain common collections of diagnostic tools such as ping and traceroute, with some Border Gateway Protocol (BGP) query tools. Most looking glass sites allow you to select where the diagnostic process will originate from a list of locations, as well as the target destination. You can use a site like www.us.ntt.net to make specific queries to specific backbone routers.

WiFi Analyzer

A Wi-Fi analyzer is any device that looks for and documents all existing wireless networks in the area. Wireless analyzers are handy tools that are useful for diagnosing wireless network issues and conducting site surveys. If your wireless network is experiencing interference, a Wi-Fi analyzer can help you find the source of the interference. It is available in dedicated, hand-held wireless analyzer tools or you can run site survey software on a laptop or mobile wireless device.

Protocol Analyzer

Protocol analyzers monitor the different protocols running at different layers on the network. A good protocol analyzer will provide Application, Session, Transport, Network, and Data Link layer information on every frame going through the network. A protocol analyzer tools come in both software and hardware versions, in its hardware interpretation, a protocol analyzer is a specified piece of hardware that is made to be carried around to various areas of the network and get information about the traffic in that area. In software version, the best and most useful protocol analyzer is Wireshark.

A network protocol analyzer can perform the following functions:

- Helps to troubleshoot hard-to-solve problems
- Helps you to detect and identify malicious software (malware)
- Helps to gather information such as baseline traffic patterns and network-utilization metrics
- Helps you to identify unused protocols so that you can remove them from the network
- Provide a traffic generator for penetration testing
- Possibly even work with an IDS

Troubleshooting Common Wireless Issues

Wireless networks are pretty magical when they work right, but the nature of wireless often makes them vexing things to troubleshoot when they don't. Let's consider a scenario in which you are in charge of the wireless connectivity for your network. There are many issues specific to wireless networks that can keep them from functioning properly. These include signal loss, interference, overlapping channels, wrong SSID, wrong encryption, AP placement, and so on. This section will discuss all of these wireless issues and more as going through this scenario.

Signal loss

There are many factors that might lead to signal loss of a wireless signal. If the signal is only weakened, then the user will still be able to communicate but at a lower bandwidth. If the signal is completely lost, then the user will not be able to communicate. This section will discuss various methods to prevent the wireless signal from losing.

Interference

One of the factors that can cause a signal loss is an interference. The interference is usually caused by radio frequency sources, RFI from non-Wi-Fi sources and RFI from Wi-Fi networks. Non-Wi-Fi sources of RFI include lighting and low-power RF devices such as Bluetooth, wireless phones, and microwave that are close to wireless frequency can cause a signal bleed and inhibit or even prevent wireless communications.

On the other hand, environmental factors such as the distance between the client and WAP as well as the type of construction between them can also affect the power of the intended signal and therefore make any interference from other signals more prominent. To prevent the signal from interference, you should place a WAP in such a way that no other devices in the area can cause interference. If the interference is on the client side, you can move the client away from the source of the interference.

Overlapping channels

Wireless networks operate at many different frequencies within a band of frequencies typically the 2.4 GHz or 5 GHz band. These frequencies are sometimes combined to provide greater bandwidth for the user. A combination of these frequencies that can be used by the end user is referred to as a channel. To establish communication between the WAP and the clients, they must be on the same channel. Most often, wireless networks use channel 1, 6, or 11 because the frequencies in those channels do not overlap each other. Channels except 1, 6, or 11 are overlapping and can cause interference and signal loss.

Standard	Frequency	Modulation	Speed
802.11a	5 GHz	OFDM	54 Mbps
802.11b	2.4 GHz	DSSs	11 Mbps
802.11g	2.4 GHz	OFDM , DSSS	54 Mbps
802.11n	2.4 , 5 GHz	OFDM	54 Mbps
802.16 (WiMAX)	10 - 66 GHz	OFDM	70-1000 Mbps

Bluetooth	2.4 GHz		1 – 3 Mbps

Table 4-02: Wireless Standards

Mismatched channels

Mismatched channels take place when the client is set to use a different channel other than configured on the access point. To avoid mismatching of channels, set your wireless device to auto channel selection.

Signal-to-noise ratio

The signal-to-noise ratio (SNR) compares the level of the Wi-Fi signal to the level of background noise. Sources of noise can include microwave ovens, cordless phones, Bluetooth devices, wireless video cameras, wireless game controllers, fluorescent lights, and more. A ratio of 10-15dB is the accepted minimum to establish an unreliable connection; 16-24dB (decibels) is usually considered poor; 25-40dB is good, and a ratio of 41dB or higher is considered excellent.

Device saturation / Bandwidth Saturation

Device Saturation or bandwidth Saturation is an issue in a network which should be considered during network designing. To understand Device saturation or Bandwidth saturation, consider a wireless network is having a large number of hosts connecting with the access point. If the hosts are exceeding the capacity of the access point, it will result in device saturation and low bandwidth.

Untested updates

It is very important to update your access point. These updates must be tested on a separate environment before forwarding to the live network.

Power levels

While deploying a wireless network, it is important to consider that an access point should place far enough that it could not cover the premises. For example, if you are in your office and you are facing trouble in connecting with the access point, you have to come closer to the access point because of the lower power level. Similarly, an access point with higher power level will cover more area.

Open networks

Open system authentication process requires six frame communications between client and the responder to complete the process of authentication.

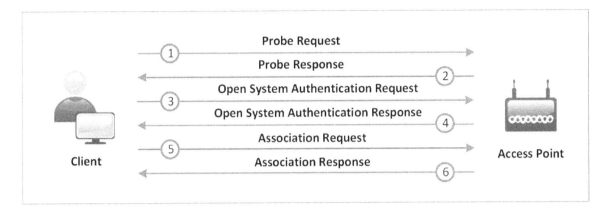

Figure 4-09: Open Authentication

- In a Wi-Fi Based LAN network, when a wireless client is attempting to connect through Wi-Fi, it initiates the process of association by sending the probe request. This probe request is to discover the 802.11 network. This probe request contains supported data rate information of the client. Association is simply a process of connecting to a wireless network.
- This probe request from the client is replied with a response containing parameters such as SSID, data rate, encryption, etc. if the access point found compatible supported data rate, encryption and another parameter with the client.
- The client sends an open authentication request (authentication frame) to the access point with the sequence 0x0001 to set authentication open.
- The Open authentication request is replied by the access point with the response having sequence 0x0002.
- After receiving open system authentication response, the client sends association request with security parameters such as chosen encryption to the access point.
- Access point responds with a request to complete the process of association and client can start sending data.

Rogue Access Point

Rogue Access point attack is a technique in which a rogue access point in a place with a legitimate wireless network with the usually the same SSID. User assumes the rogue access point as the legitimate access point and connects with. Once a user is connected with the rogue access point, all traffic will direct through it, and the attacker sniffs the packet to monitor activity.

Wrong encryption

Wireless networks are configured with the encryption algorithm to secure their communication. Different Encryption algorithms are being in use such as Wired

Equivalent Privacy (WEP), Wi-Fi Protected Access (WPA), Wi-Fi Protected Access 2 (WPA2) and Advanced Encryption Algorithm (AES). Incorrect encryption will result in failure of communication because client and server could not decrypt the communication successfully.

Bounce

Bouncing a Wireless Network is a process of spreading it into a large geographical area using repeater and reflectors. These repeaters and reflectors bounce the signal to cover a greater area. With a controlled signal bouncing, you can spread your network, but without control bounce, you will get an extraordinary bigger network. Similarly, bouncing back out of phase signal will also degrade your network performance.

AP configurations

Misconfigured access point attack include access to the legitimate access point by taking advantage of its misconfigurations. Misconfiguration may be like weak password, default password configuration, Wireless network without password protection, etc.

Environmental factors

Apart from these technical issues, before deploying a wireless network, you must consider the environment as well. If you have Concrete walls, Window film and Metal studs in your surroundings, all of them will degrade the signal strength.

Troubleshooting Common Copper Cable Issues

Shorts

Short is a scenario when one or more pin of the cable is connected to the wrong pin. Using Cable testers, you can easily check the connectivity of pins.

Opens

Faulty installation of copper cable when one or more pins of the cable could not provide connectivity. Improper installation of connector, faulty trimming of wires causes no connectivity across the pins.

Bad wiring

Bad wiring is an example where the abnormal sequence of wiring scheme is used to install a connector of a copper cable. No connection will take place in result of bad wiring. After installation of a connector, you can check the connectivity using cable testers.

Incorrect termination

Copper cables require appropriate wiring scheme on both ends of the cable. There are two standards for Ethernet cable TIA-568A and TIA-568B. Straight through cables must

be ended with either TIA-568A on both ends or TIA-568B on both ends. Similarly, Crossover cables should be ended with TIA-568A on one end while TIA-568B at the other end.

Straight-through

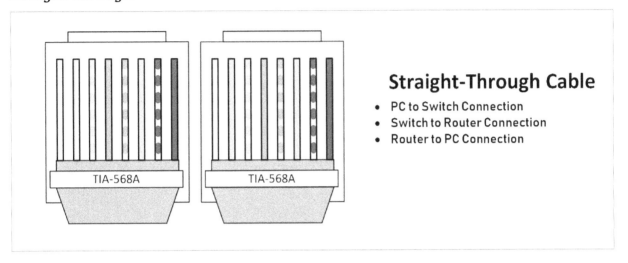

Figure 4-10: Straight-Through Cable

Crossover

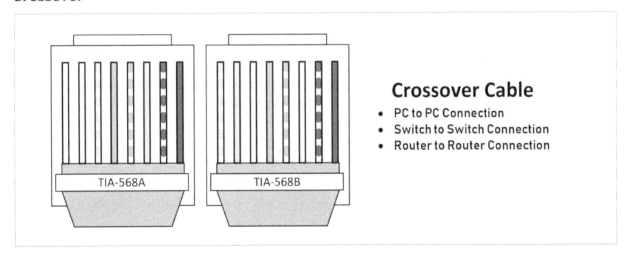

Figure 4-11: Crossover Cable

Cross-talk

Crosstalk is a scenario where signals are interfering with each other. Consider two copper wires installed closer to each other. Signals passing through one cable may interfere with the signal transmission of another cable. There are two types of Crosstalk.

1. Near-End Crosstalk (NEXT)
2. Far-End Crosstalk (FEXT)

Near-End Crosstalk (NEXT)

Near-End Crosstalk (NEXT) is an undesired condition of cabling when interference is observed in communication due to adjacent pairs of the copper cable. Usually, NEXT is observed in adjacent pairs of twisted pair cables. NEXT is usually caused by crossed or crushed wire pairs.

Far-End Crosstalk (FEXT)

Far-End Crosstalk (FEXT) is coupling between transmitting pairs. As a result, outgoing signals are coupled back into receiving signal.

EMI/RFI

Electromagnetic Interference (EMI) or Radio-Frequency Interference (RFI) is basically interference in a radio spectrum which may degrade the performance of the signal. It is an interference in a signal by an external source either by coupling, electromagnetic induction or by conductivity.

Attenuation/Db loss

Attenuation is a loss of signal strength. It is calculated in decibels (dB). During any transmission, if attenuation factor rises, transmission become more. Several factors such as Noise, Surroundings, and distance causes attenuation. To overcome attenuation, several repeaters are installed to boost the signal.

Bad connector

Connectors of the Ethernet cable must be checked after installation. Any looseness or damage to the connector will affect the communication. Improper installation of the connector will result in the unavailability of the network.

Split pairs

A split pair is a faulty wiring scenario where wires of a twisted pair are twisted with the wire of another pair. Wires of same twisted pairs are twisted to reduce or cancel interference. Hence, split pair condition creates interference.

Tx/Rx reverse

Old device's NICs do not support medium-dependant interface crossover (MDIX). Auto MDIX is a feature which can automatically detect the cable type connected to the NIC to avoid reversing the Tx/Rx signals.

Troubleshooting Common Fiber Cable Issues

SFP/GBIC Issues

SFP stands for Small Form-Factor Pluggable. SFP is a hot-pluggable transceiver module that is popularly used in telecommunication and data communication. It interfaces a network device motherboard for a switch, router, media converter, or similar device to a fiber-optic or copper networking cable. SFP issues could be poor performance, or no connectivity because of wrong cabling for the connector, wrong wiring, loops in Shielded Twisted Pair (STP), etc.

Wavelength Mismatch

Wavelength Mismatch is the scenario where transmitters at both ends of the fiber are transmitting different wavelength. The difference in wavelength causes distortion in communication.

Fiber Type Mismatch

Fiber Cable mismatch results in heavy loss of signals. Different type of Fiber cables has different parameters such as smaller or larger core diameter, higher or lower dispersion, etc. Joining different type of fibers will result in massive attenuation.

Dirty connectors

Make sure while installation of Fiber cables that both ends of each cable are clean. Presence of dirt on connectors can cause signal distortion.

Connector mismatch

Connector Mismatch includes installation of different connectors over different Fiber cables.

Bend radius limitations

As we know, Fiber Optic cables are made up of a glass of plastic. Each cable comes with precaution about bending radius by the manufactures. While installation, you must make sure that you are not exceeding the limitation. Bending the cable more than its limitation will result in leakage of light hence signal will attenuate.

Distance limitations

Each Fiber cable can support signal transmission up to several kilometers. To exceed the range, you must have to install repeaters on a suitable location to re-boost the signal.

Troubleshooting Common Network Issues

Incorrect IP configuration/default gateway

Incorrect IP configuration or wrong gateway configuration will result in the unavailability of the network. Most common problems are using static IP configuration in a dynamic host configuration environment or using incorrect static IP, subnet or gateway configuration.

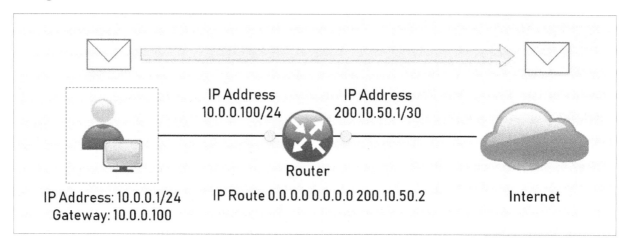

Figure 4-12: Default Routing

The figure above shows a small network connected to the internet with the correct configuration. Now consider the same scenario where host user is configured with incorrect IP address. This incorrect configuration prevents the user to access the network to which it is physically connected.

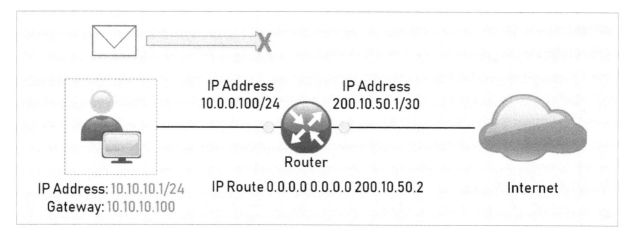

Figure 4-13: Misconfigured Default Gateway

Similarly, wrong default gateway configuration will not route the traffic destined toward the internet. The user can send traffic to the router, but the router will not forward the traffic to correct next hop because of incorrect default gateway configuration.

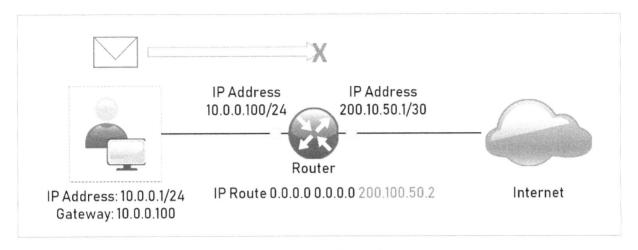

Figure 4-14: Misconfigured Route

Broadcast storms / Switching loop

A broadcast storm is a situation when one or more devices in a network start generating broadcast packets to the network. This flooding of broadcast consumes entire bandwidth and result in the unavailability of network resources. These broadcast packets can be either intentionally created to down the network, may be due to application freezing, or else. Breaking the network connectivity of suspicious device could be helpful to find the device causing trouble. You can also use packet analyzers and sniffing tools, but they might be unresponsive in the heavy broadcast storm.

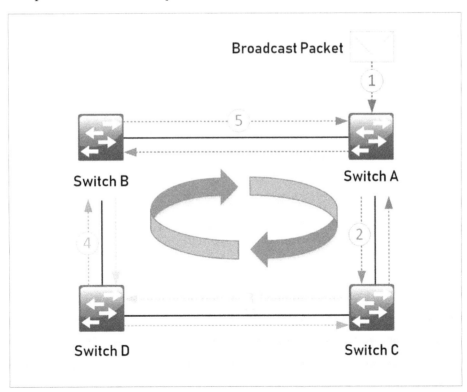

Figure 4-15: Broadcast Storm

Similarly, switching loops are created when multiple switches are connected with each other. Spanning tree protocol is the protocol configured on the switches to eliminate switching loops. To understand switching loops, consider a loop created when several switches are connected with each other for high availability. Any broadcast packet will from one switch will be forwarded again and again due to loop as shown in the above figure.

Now recall the concept defined in Spanning Tree Protocol. Spanning Tree Protocol eliminates the switching loop.

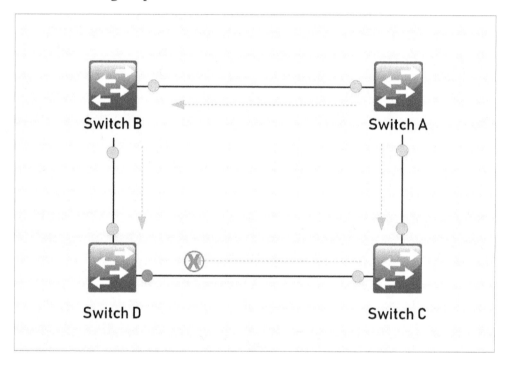

Figure 4-16: Spanning Tree Protocol Process

Duplicate IP

In Static IP addressing, there is a chance of assigning a duplicate IP address. In a network, each network device must be configured with a unique IP address to be identified. If more than one devices have the same IP address, there will a conflict of IP address.

Speed and Duplex mismatch

A different configuration of interfaces like speed and negotiation connected with each other through a link will cause Speed/ Duplex Mismatch error. The interface should be configured with either same parameters or autosensing and auto-negotiation to prevent a mismatch.

As shown in the figure next page, Switch duplex configuration is changed to full duplex. As switch detect different duplex settings, it will show CDP error message of duplex mismatch.

```
Switch-12                                          —    □    ×

Switch>
Switch>en
Switch#config t
Enter configuration commands, one per line.  End with CNTL/Z.
Switch(config)#interface ethernet 0/0
Switch(config-if)#duplex full
Switch(config-if)#ex
Switch(config)#
*May 23 07:33:15.675: %CDP-4-DUPLEX_MISMATCH: duplex mismatch discovered on
Ethernet0/0 (not half duplex), with Switch Ethernet0/0 (half duplex).
Switch(config)#
Switch#
*May 23 07:33:58.613: %SYS-5-CONFIG_I: Configured from console by console
Switch#
*May 23 07:34:12.587: %CDP-4-DUPLEX_MISMATCH: duplex mismatch discovered on
Ethernet0/0 (not half duplex), with Switch Ethernet0/0 (half duplex).
Switch#
*May 23 07:35:01.451: %CDP-4-DUPLEX_MISMATCH: duplex mismatch discovered on
Ethernet0/0 (not half duplex), with Switch Ethernet0/0 (half duplex).
Switch#
*May 23 07:35:50.900: %CDP-4-DUPLEX_MISMATCH: duplex mismatch discovered on
Ethernet0/0 (not half duplex), with Switch Ethernet0/0 (half duplex).
Switch#
```

Figure 4-17: Duplex Mismatch Error

End-to-end connectivity

End-to-End Connectivity is meant by a successful connection between to endpoints. Communication between two endpoints includes a number of intermediary devices which process or forward the packet toward the destination. End-to-End connectivity means that these intermediary devices do not alter the essential data in the packets during communication. Issues related to End-to-End connectivity are the unavailability of remote endpoint, closed ports of application server, incorrect access control list, and others

Incorrect VLAN assignment

As we know, VLANs provide Layer 2 segmentation. If a computer is in the same VLAN, it will communicate no matter located next to the source computer or located anywhere on the network. To communicate different VLANs, we require Inter-VLAN routing.

Issues related to incorrect VLAN assignment, it may result into unavailability of network resources, higher or limited security permissions, etc. To prevent incorrect assignment of

VLANs, the Network administrator must document the arrangement or division of VLANs. When any device is moved, make sure it is properly assigned to correct VLAN.

Apart from this static assignment, Dynamic VLAN assignment automate the process of VLAN assignment. When a PC connects to the network, Its MAC address is checked into the database, and its configured VLAN is assigned to the port. Similarly, you can configure a guest VLAN for new MAC addresses.

Misconfigured DHCP

Misconfigured DHCP server, DHCP Relay or DHCP Client can disconnect the client from the network. If a DHCP Client is configured to use a static IP addressing, it will not accept by the network. You must have to configure the NIC to obtain the IP address automatically if DHCP is configured. Misconfigured Relay or DHCP server cause unavailability of DHCP server, hence DHCP request will not be replied. Network Pool, Lease time, Helper Address and other parameters should be configured correctly to prevent any problem.

Misconfigured DNS

When a DNS is misconfigured, DNS queries will not resolve. The user can ping the destination by its IP address but not by its name. Misconfigured DNS settings on a client will stop name resolution, and network appears to be down.

Incorrect interface/interface misconfiguration

The interface configuration is also very important. Misconfiguration of an interface may include incorrect assignment of inside and outside interfaces while configuring NAT, Incorrect direction of an access control list (ACL) on an interface, duplex mismatches, and interface shutdown, etc. These misconfigurations can stop communication from the particular interface.

Interface errors

Interface errors include installation of bad connector, bad wiring, incorrect termination, standard mismatch, etc.

Simultaneous Wired / Wireless connections

The wired and Wireless connection cannot be used simultaneously, you have to configure the priority for the NIC to be used on preference.

Configuring network connection priority in Windows 10

1. Press the **Windows Key + X** and select **Network Connections** from the menu.

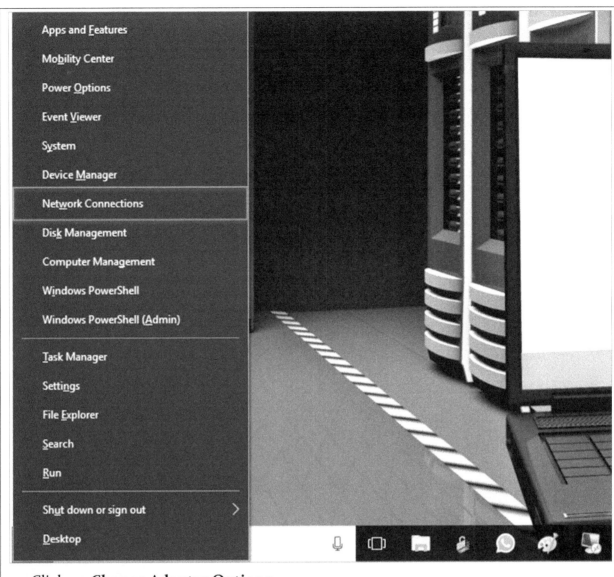

2. Click on **Change Adapter Options.**

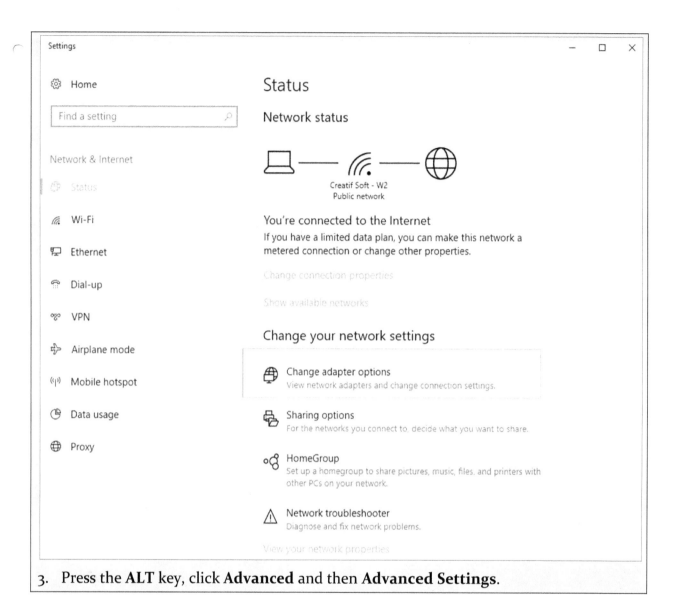

3. Press the **ALT** key, click **Advanced** and then **Advanced Settings**.

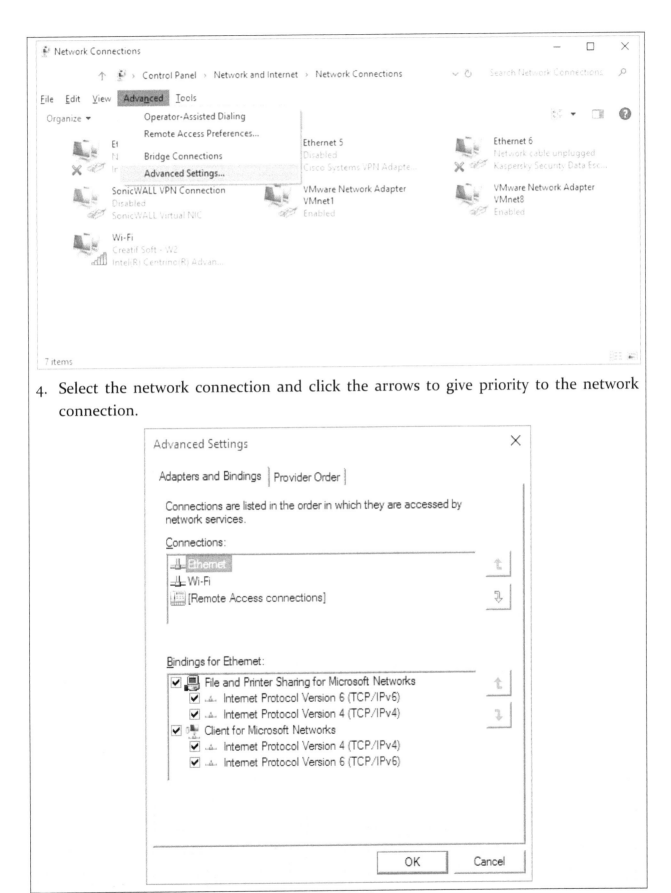

4. Select the network connection and click the arrows to give priority to the network connection.

Power failure / Power anomalies

Failure of power supply or power anomalies, such as dips and surges affect the network connectivity, performance, and hardware. These power related issues can make a network device unreachable. To fix these power issues, manage the power of the network devices through an uninterruptible power supply (UPS).

MTU/MTU black hole

MTU stands for Maximum Transmission Unit (MTU). It is the maximum possible configured value of transmission. Largest Ethernet packet MTU is 1500 bytes, but when you deal with different technologies such as DSL, a conflict may arise of fragmentation that is known as MTU Mismatch.

Path MTU Discovery (PMTU) is a method to identify the MTU value automatically. PMTU operates using Don't Fragment (DF) bit and sent series of ICMP packets to identify the MTU. MTU-Black hole is a scenario where firewall blocks the ICMP packets. As PMTU functions over ICMP packet, it will create a terrible network condition.

Runts	Giants	Baby Giant Frames
These are Ethernet frames that are less than 64 bytes and may be caused by excessive collisions. Of course, these frames have become rarer as networks have become nearly collision-free.	**Jumbo Frames (Giants)**: Today many technologies are enhancing networks by adding information to Ethernet frames. This results in **Jumbo Frames (Giants)**. This often indicates frames of 9216 bytes for Gigabit Ethernet, but technically can refer to anything over the standard IP MTU (Maximum Transmission Unit) of 1500 bytes.	What if your Ethernet frame is just a little larger than the standard MTU of 1500 bytes? Specifically, what if your frame is 1600 bytes in size? You have what networkers term **a Baby Giant**.

Table 4-03:

Missing IP routes

Missing IP routes can interrupt the traffic flow. In order to send the packet towards the destination, a route is required to be configured on intermediary devices connecting the target host to the source host. In case of missing IP route, the packet will not forward

toward next hop. Similarly, incorrect Access Control List (ACL) can block legitimate traffic and allow undesired traffic causing unavailability of resources for actual users.

NIC teaming misconfiguration

Link aggregation or NIC teaming is a method to increase the bandwidth. Configuring multiple physical interfaces to create an aggregated link requires the configuration to create a logical port. Link aggregation can be done by using vendor-neutral IEEE 802.3ad specification Link Aggregation Control Protocol (LACP) and the Cisco-proprietary Port Aggregation Protocol (PAgP).

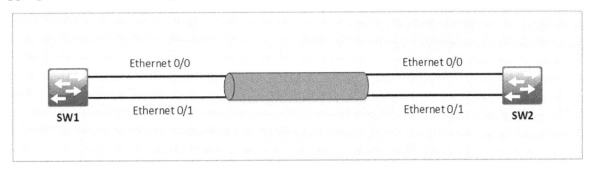

Figure 4-18: Link Aggregation

Modes of Ether Channel

- PAgP (Port Aggregation Protocol)
- LACP (Link Aggregation Control Protocol)
- On (Manual)

Standards-based negotiation protocol, known as IEEE 802.1ax Link Aggregation Control Protocol, is simply a way to build an EtherChannel dynamically. Essentially, the "active" end of the LACP group sends out special frames advertising the ability and desire to form an EtherChannel. It is possible and quite common that both ends are set to an "active" state (versus a passive state). Once these frames are exchanged, and if the ports on both sides agree that they support the requirements, LACP will form an Ether Channel.

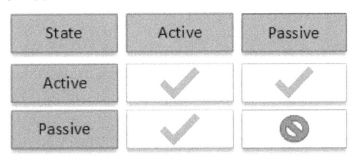

Figure 4-19: LACP Mode Compatibility

PAgP is a Cisco's proprietary negotiation protocol before LACP is introduced and endorsed by IEEE. EtherChannel technology was invented in the early 1990s. Cisco Systems later acquired them in 1994. In 2000 the IEEE passed 802.3ad (LACP), which is an open standard version of EtherChannel.

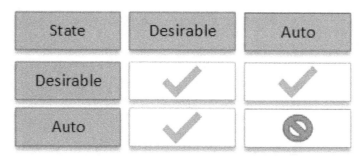

Figure 4-20: PAgp Mode Compatibility

Compatibility of Manual Setting

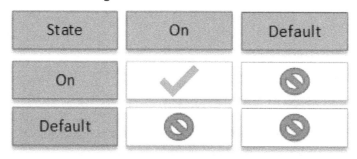

Figure 4-21: Manual Mode Compatibility

Active-active vs. active-passive

To configure an EtherChannel using LACP negotiation, each side must be set to either active or passive; only interfaces configured in active mode will attempt to negotiate an EtherChannel. Passive interfaces merely respond to LACP requests. PAgP behaves the same, but its two modes are referred to as desirable and auto.

Troubleshooting Common Security Issues

Misconfigured Firewall

Firewall are deployed in networks for security reasons in order to protect the private network from public or external threats. It is very important to configure a firewall and verify to rely on it correctly. A misconfigured firewall can cause trouble for internal network either by blocking some or all legitimate traffic or by allowing unwanted traffic to access internal resources without filtering.

While configuring a hardware firewall, the most common issue that arises is "implicit deny," which blocks all traffic by default. Similarly, improper placement of "Permit Any" can result in allowing all the traffic.

Firewalls divide the network into different portions. One portion is considered as a trusted portion of internal LAN. Public internet and interfaces connected to are considered as an untrusted portion. Similarly, servers accessed by untrusted entities are placed in a special segment known as a demilitarized zone (DMZ). By allowing only specific access to these servers, like port 90 of the web server, firewall hide the functionality of network device which makes it difficult for an attacker to understand the physical topology of the network.

Firewall Best Practice

The primary function of a firewall is to protect network infrastructure in a more elegant way than a traditional layer3/2 device. Depending on different vendors and their implementation techniques, many features need to be configured for a firewall to work properly. Some of these features may include Network Address Translation (NAT), Access-Lists(ACL), AAA base policies and so on. Misconfiguration of any of these features may result in leakage of digital assets which may have a financial impact on business. In short, complex devices like firewall also requires deep insight knowledge of equipment along with the general approach to deployment.

- Configure policies with minimum privileges
- Run required services only
- Block all unnecessary ports at the firewall and host.
- Harden weak, default configuration settings.
- Always log security outputs
- Harden the firewall and other devices to restrict the responses to footprinting and banner grabbing requests

Malware Analysis

Malware Analysis is the process of identification of a malware till its verification that malware is completely removed, including observing the behavior of malware, scoping the potential threat to a system and finding other measures.

Malware Analyses process start with Preparing the Testbed for analysis. Security Professional get ready a Virtual machine as a host operating system where dynamic malware analysis will be performed by executing the malware over the guest operating system. This host operating system is isolated from another network to observe the behavior of malware by quarantine the malware from the network.

After executing a malware in a Testbed, Static and Dynamic Malware analysis are performed. Network connection is also setup later to observe the behavior using Process monitoring tools and Packet monitoring tools and debugging tools like OllyDbg and ProcDump.

Types of Malware Analysis

Malware analysis is classified into two basic types:

Static Analysis

Static Analysis or Code Analysis is performed by fragmenting the resources of the binary file without executing it and study each component. Disassembler such as IDA is used to disassemble the binary file.

Dynamic Analysis

Dynamic Analysis or Behavioural Analysis is performed by executing the malware on a host and observing the behavior of the malware. These behavioral analyses are performed in a Sandbox environment.

Goals of Malware Analysis

Malware analysis goals are defined below: -

- Diagnostics of threat severity or level of attack.
- Diagnostics of the type of Malware.
- Scope the attack
- Built defense to secure organization's network and systems.
- Finding a root cause.
- Built Incident response actions.
- Develop Anti-malware to eliminate.

DoS

There are several ways to detect and prevent DoS/DDoS attacks. The following are common security techniques:

Activity Profiling

Activity profiling means monitoring the activities running on a system or network. By monitoring the traffic flow, DoS/DDoS attacks can be observed by the analysis of packet's header information for TCP Sync, UDP, ICMP and Netflow traffic. Activity profiling is measured by comparing it from average traffic rate of a network.

Wavelet Analysis

Wavelet-based Signal Analysis is an automated process of detecting DoS/DDoS attacks by analysis of input signals. This automated detection is used to detect volume-based

anomalies. Wavelet analysis evaluates the traffic and filter on a certain scale whereas Adaptive threshold techniques are used to detect DoS attacks.

Sequential Change-Point Detection

Change-Point detection is an algorithm which is used to detect denial of Service (DoS) attacks. This Detection technique uses non-parametric Cumulative Sum (CUSUM) algorithm to detect traffic patterns. Change-Point detection requires very low computational overheads hence efficient and immune to attacks resulting in high accuracy.

DDoS Attack Countermeasures

- Protect secondary victims
- Detect and neutralize handlers
- Enabling ingress and egress filtering
- Deflect attacks by diverting it to honeypots
- Mitigate attacks by load balancing
- Mitigate attacks disabling unnecessary services
- Using Anti-malware
- Enabling Router Throttling
- Using a Reverse Proxy
- Absorbing the Attack
- Intrusion Detection Systems

Open / Closed Ports

Open and Closed ports disclose the running services on a target system. Using Port Scanning, the attacker finds the open and closed ports to discover running services on a target system to exploit. Port Scanning is the examination procedure that is mostly used by the attackers to identify the open port. However, it may also be used by the legitimate users. Port scanning it does not always lead to an attack as it used by both of them. However, it is a network reconnaissance that can be used before an attack to collect information. In this scenario, special packets are forwarded to a particular host, whose response is examined by the attacker to get information regarding open ports.

ICMP-Related Issues

ICMP Flood Attack

Internet Control Message Protocol (ICMP) is the type of attack in which attacker attacks using ICMP request. ICMP is a supporting protocol used by network devices to operation information, errors and indications. These requests and their responses consume

resources of the network device. Thus, by flooding ICMP request without waiting for response overwhelm the resources of the device.

Bypassing through ICMP Tunneling Method

ICMP tunneling is a technique of injecting arbitrary data in the payload of echo packet and forwarded to target host. ICMP tunneling functions on ICMP echo requests and reply packets. Basically using this ICMP tunneling, TCP communication is tunneled over ping request and replies because payload field of ICMP packets are not examined by most of the firewalls, whereas some network administrators allow ICMP because of troubleshooting purpose.

Ping of Death

TCP State-Exhaustion attacks results in exhausting their finite number of concurrent connections the target device can support. The most common state-exhaustion attack is "*Ping of death.*" Ping of death is a type of DoS attaches in which attacker deliberately sends IP packets of larger than 65,536 bytes. Packet fragmentation breaks these packets into the smaller segment to proceed. In early days, it was a bug that many operating systems do not know about how to deal with these oversize packets. Hence they crash or freeze. Now patches are available to deal with a ping of death. Networks are configured to block ICMP Ping packets at the firewall to prevent DoS attack.

Unreachable Default Gateway

A man-in-the-middle attack can also be performed by using Forged ICMP packet and ARP spoofing techniques. Forged ICMP packets such as Destination unavailable or high latency message are sent to fool the victim.

A ping response of "**Destination Host Unreachable**" may also receive due to the misconfiguration issue or connectivity issue between source and destination.

The possible fix for the ICMP error message "**Destination Host Unreachable**":

- Ensure localhost configuration.
- Ensure Destination host is up.
- Disable the Firewall and check for the issue.
- Perform a trace of the route.

Unpatched Firmware / Oss

Unpatched Operating System allows malicious activities or could not completely block malicious traffic into a system. Successful intrusion can impact severely in the form of compromising sensitive information, data loss and disruption of regular operation.

Similarly, in software exploitation attack and bugs in software, the attacker tries to exploit the vulnerabilities in software. This vulnerability might be a mistake by the developer

while developing the program code. Attackers can discover these mistakes, use them to gain access to the system.

Malicious Users

Malicious Users are those users who consciously access and steal the sensitive information, damage the resources and perform other malicious activities. These malicious users either just leaking information or may attempt to escalate their privileges to access sensitive information.

Trusted / Untrusted users

An insider attack is the type of attack that is performed on a system, within a corporate network, by a trusted person. Trusted User is termed as Insider because Insider has privileges and it is authorized to access the network resources.

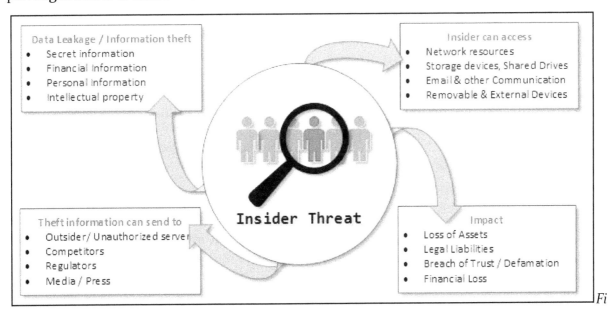

gure 4-22: Insider Threat

Similarly, it may be an insider, an employee of your organization having privileges or not, spying on your organization for malicious intentions. An insider attack is those attacks which are conducted by these insiders. These insiders may be supported by the competitor of an organization. A competitor may support a person in your organization for revealing sensitive information's and secrets.

Disgruntled Employee

Other than spying, Insider may have the intention of taking revenge. A disgruntled person in an organization may compromise the confidential and sensitive information to take revenge. An employee may be a disgruntled person when he not satisfied with the

management, trouble facing him from the organization, demotion or going to be terminated.

Packet Sniffing

Passive Sniffing

Passive Sniffing is the sniffing type in which there is no need of sending additional packets or interfering the device such as Hub to receive packets. As we know, Hub broadcast every packet to its ports, which helps the attacker to monitor all traffic passing through hub without any effort.

Active Sniffing

Active Sniffing is the sniffing type in which attacker has to send additional packets to the connected device such as Switch to start receiving packets. As we know, a unicast packet from the switch is transmitted to a specific port only. The attacker uses certain techniques such as MAC Flooding, DHCP Attacks, DNS poisoning, Switch Port Stealing, ARP Poisoning, and Spoofing to monitor traffic passing through the switch. These techniques are defined in detail later in this chapter.

Hardware Protocol Analyzer

Protocol Analyzers, either Hardware or Software analyzer are used to analyze the captured packets and signals over the transmission channel. Hardware Protocol Analyzers are the physical equipment which is used to capture without interfering the network traffic. A major advantage offered by these hardware protocol analyzers are mobility, flexibility, and throughput. Using these hardware analyzers, an attacker can: -

- Monitor Network Usage
- Identify Traffic from hacking software
- Decrypt the packets
- Extract the information
- Size of Packet

KEYSIGHT Technologies offers various products. To get updates and information, visit the website www.keysight.com. There is also another Hardware protocol analyzer product available in the market by different vendors like RADCOM and Fluke.

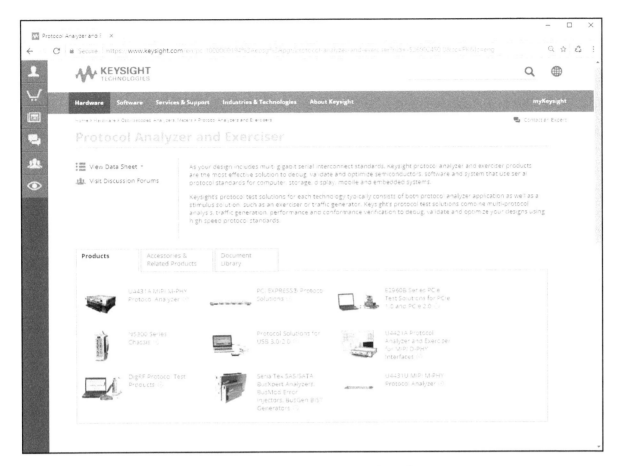

Figure 4-23: Hardware Protocol Analyzer

Defending Against Sniffing

Best practice against Sniffing includes the following approaches to protect the network traffic.

- Using HTTPS instead of HTTP
- Using SFTP instead of FTP
- Use Switch instead of Hub
- Configure Port Security
- Configure DHCP Snooping
- Configure Dynamic ARP Inspection
- Configure Source guard
- Use Sniffing Detection tool to detect NIC functioning in a promiscuous mode
- Use Strong Encryption protocols

Sniffer Detection Technique

1. Ping Method

Ping technique is used to detect sniffer. A ping request is sent to the suspect IP address with spoofed MAC address. If the NIC is not running in promiscuous mode, it will not respond to the packet. In case, if the suspect is running a sniffer, it responds the packet. This is an older technique and not reliable.

2. ARP Method

Using ARP, Sniffers can be detected with the help of ARP Cache. By sending a non-broadcast ARP packet to the suspect, MAC address will be cached if the NIC is running in promiscuous mode. Next step is to send a broadcast ping with spoofed MAC address. If the machine is running promiscuous mode, it will be able to reply the packet only as it has already learned the Actual MAC from the sniffed Non-broadcast ARP packet.

3. Promiscuous Detection Tool

Promiscuous Detection tools such as *PromqryUI* or *Nmap* can also be used for detection of Network Interface Card running in Promiscuous Mode. These tools are GUI based application software.

Authentication Issues

TACACS/RADIUS Misconfigurations

Implementation of AAA on a network device and configuring an AAA Server brings a lot of challenges for the network administrator. There are many issues related to misconfiguration of RADIUS or TACACS server which is as follows:

- Improper configuration is preventing legitimate authentication.
- Improper configuration is allowing illegal authentication sessions.
- Failing to authorize users.
- Failing to account logs.
- Failing to enforce a policy on the remote device.

Default Passwords / Settings

In a corporate network while installation of new devices, the administrator must have to change the default configurations. If devices are left upon default configuration, using default credentials, any user who does not have privileges to access the device but has connectivity can access the device. It is not a big deal for an intruder to access such type of device because default configuration has common, weak passwords and there are no security policies are enabled on devices by default.

Improper Access / Backdoor Access

When attackers successfully gain access to some system, they want to make future access as easy as possible. A backdoor application will be installed by using different techniques defined above to store confidential information which would be retrieved by the attacker when required.

ARP Issues

In ARP spoofing, the attacker sends forged ARP packets over Local Area Network (LAN). In the case, Switch will update the attacker's MAC Address with the IP address of a legitimate user or server. Once the attacker's MAC address is learned with the IP address of a legitimate user, the switch will start forwarding the packets to attacker intending that it is the MAC of the user. Using ARP Spoofing attack, an attacker can steal information by extracting from the packet received intended for a user over LAN. Apart from stealing information, ARP spoofing can be used for: -

- Session Hijacking
- Denial-of-Service Attack
- Man-in-the-Middle Attack
- Packet Sniffing
- Data Interception
- Connection Hijacking
- VoIP tapping
- Connection Resetting
- Stealing Password

Dynamic ARP Inspection (DAI)

DAI is used with DHCP snooping, IP-to-MAC bindings can be a track from DHCP transactions to protect against ARP poisoning (which is an attacker trying to get your traffic instead of to your destination). DHCP snooping is required in order to build the MAC-to-IP bindings for DAI validation.

Troubleshooting Common WAN Issues

Loss of Internet Connectivity

Loss of internet connectivity is basically a symptom which is a result of networking issue. Connector issues, wiring issue, power issue, and configuration issue may lead to disconnection of the internet. There are several parameters which are required such as IP address, Subnet, default gateway, and DNS configuration to run internet on a device. To

check internet connection status, navigate to **Control Panel > Network and Internet > Internet and Sharing.**

Figure 4-24: Troubleshooting Internet Connectivity

Another way to check the connection is using the command line. Go to command line and type "**ipconfig**" command.

```
Command Prompt                                          —    □    ×

Microsoft Windows [Version 10.0.16299.309]
(c) 2017 Microsoft Corporation. All rights reserved.

C:\Users\IPSpecialist>ipconfig

Windows IP Configuration


Ethernet adapter Ethernet:

   Media State . . . . . . . . . . . : Media disconnected
   Connection-specific DNS Suffix  . :

Wireless LAN adapter Local Area Connection* 2:

   Media State . . . . . . . . . . . : Media disconnected
   Connection-specific DNS Suffix  . :

Ethernet adapter VMware Network Adapter VMnet1:

   Connection-specific DNS Suffix  . :
   Link-local IPv6 Address . . . . . : fe80::14d7:2418:555a:7180%23
   IPv4 Address. . . . . . . . . . . : 192.168.11.1
   Subnet Mask . . . . . . . . . . . : 255.255.255.0
   Default Gateway . . . . . . . . . :

Ethernet adapter VMware Network Adapter VMnet8:

   Connection-specific DNS Suffix  . :
   Link-local IPv6 Address . . . . . : fe80::4d9b:4d6d:6329:47fe%21
   IPv4 Address. . . . . . . . . . . : 192.168.188.1
   Subnet Mask . . . . . . . . . . . : 255.255.255.0
   Default Gateway . . . . . . . . . :

Ethernet adapter Ethernet 6:

   Media State . . . . . . . . . . . : Media disconnected
   Connection-specific DNS Suffix  . :

Wireless LAN adapter Wi-Fi:

   Connection-specific DNS Suffix  . :
   Link-local IPv6 Address . . . . . : fe80::a889:6589:5b66:4523%16
   IPv4 Address. . . . . . . . . . . : 192.168.0.14
   Subnet Mask . . . . . . . . . . . : 255.255.255.0
   Default Gateway . . . . . . . . . : fe80::d66e:eff:feb3:882e%16
                                       192.168.0.1
```

Figure 4-25: Verifying IP Configuration

If you are troubleshooting the router, switch or modem devices, make sure the device is plugged in and power on successfully, then check "Green" led light of the device is blinking. Mostly all devices use a green led for connectivity status. If it is not green, power-cycle your device to re-establish the connection.

Interface Errors

Another common problem is Interface error. Usually, at the user end, Cable modem, Router, or Customer Premises Equipment (CPE) devices are deployed to provide internet connectivity. As these devices provide connectivity to the internet, it means that these devices must have at least two interfaces. One interface is facing internal Local Area Network (LAN) while the other one is facing Wide Area Network (WAN). Install the LAN connection on LAN interface and WAN connection WAN interfaces.

Similarly, Network Interface Card (NIC) may also cause trouble. Using the utility from the Operating System can verify and diagnose the issues.

Split Horizon

Consider a distance vector routing protocol scenario, as shown in the figure below, Node A and B calculate the cost they are directly connected with each other. Similarly, Node B and Node C calculate the cost of their link. Node B sends an update of Node A to Node C; Node C will calculate the path cost (i.e., 2 Hops + 4 Hop); Next Hop is Node B into its table.

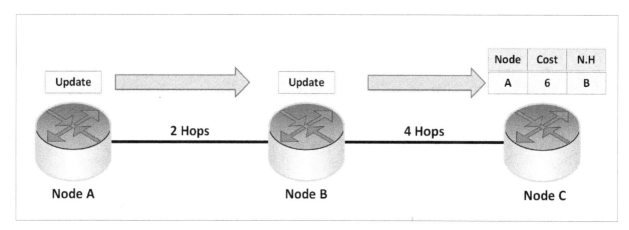

Figure 4-26: Distance Vector Protocol Periodic Update Process

When Node A is disconnected due to failure, Node B will update its table that Node A is not available. Coming periodic update from Node C towards Node B shows Node A is 6 Hops way though Node C, hence Node B will update its table after calculating the cost to reach Node A. It will continue till Cost to reach the destination reach to the maximum.

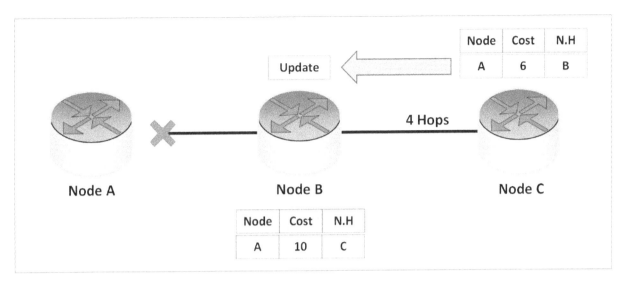

Figure 4-27: Distance Vector Protocol Periodic Update Process

Split Horizon is prevention technique to avoid routing loops in distance vector routing protocol. In short, split horizon is a technique which restricts the router to re-advertise a route back onto the interface from which it was learned. If a router re-advertises on the same interface, it will create a routing loop.

Poison Reverse is a method to prevent route poisoning in distance vector protocols. Node broadcast about the unavailability of another node connected through it.

DNS Issues

Almost every ISP provide its own DNS server however you can configure publically available DNS Servers as well. Domain Name Servers (DNS) provide Name to IP translation. DNS Issues will result in unsuccessful translations of addresses.

You can check details about your DNS Server using Nslookup command as shown below:

Figure 4-28: Nslookup Command

You will observe the following result when DNS configuration is not correct while browsing.

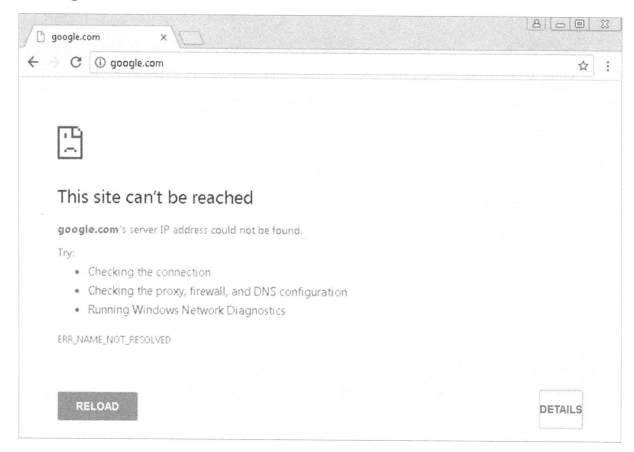

Figure 4-29: Name Resolution failed

Router Configurations

Router configuration issues are very common. Network administrators have to be careful while configuring routing, access control list, and NATing. Any misconfiguration will result in unavailability. Incorrect access control list, as defined earlier could block entire traffic, legitimate traffic and create even more trouble by allowing unwanted traffic. Similarly, misconfigured routes will drop outbound packets.

Company Security Policy

Company Security Policies are those policies which are enforced by an organization for security reasons and control the communication. The security policy may be about authenticating the access to authorized users, or prevention policy to secure data theft. If an organization is facing trouble with its internet speed, and after troubleshooting they found that guest network is consuming a lot of bandwidth. Different policies can be enforced in this scenario.

Throttling

Enforcing a throttling policy will restrict the guest network to consume a pre-defined volume. For example, 1 Gb of the volume is allowed for guest network.

Blocking

Enforcing a blocking policy will block all type of communication, or that particular type of communication when limits are exceeded. Similarly, blocking policies can be enforced when any certain violation is observed.

Fair Access Policy / Utilization Limits

After configuration, the third step is to create a fair access policy to inform all employees regarding their utilization limits.

Chapter 5: Industry Standards, Practices and Network Theory

Open Standard Interconnection (OSI) Layers

The Open Standards Interconnection (OSI) model was developed by the International Organization for Standardization (ISO) in the 1980s. The purpose of the model was to allow developers to focus on only the layers that applied to them and only on the protocols at those layers. Today, OSI model use to communicate about networking. OSI provides a means of relating the components and their functions to each other and a way of standardizing components and protocols.

The seven layers and their function in the OSI model are as follows:

Layer 1 – Physical

The Physical layer (Layer-1) controls the signaling and transferring of raw bits onto the physical medium. The Physical layer is closely related to the Data-link layer, as many technologies such as Ethernet contain both data- link and physical functions. The Physical layer provides specifications for a variety of hardware:

- Cabling
- Connectors and transceivers
- Network interface cards (NICs)
- Hubs

Layer 2 – Data Link

The Data-Link layer (Layer-2) is responsible for transporting data within a network. The Data-Link layer consists of two sublayers:

Logical Link Control (LLC) sublayer: The LLC sublayer serves as the midway between the physical link and all higher layer protocols. It ensures that protocols like IP can function irrespective of what type of physical technology is being used. Additionally, the LLC sublayer can perform flow-control and error- checking.

Media Access Control (MAC) sublayer: The MAC sublayer controls access to the physical medium, serving as a mediator if multiple devices are challenging for the same physical link. Data- link layer technologies have various methods of doing this, Ethernet uses Carrier Sense Multiple Access with Collision Detection (CSMA/CD), and Token Ring utilizes a token.

The Data-link layer packages the higher-layer data into frames so that the data can be put onto the physical layer. This packaging process is referred to as framing or encapsulation. The encapsulation type will vary depending on the fundamental technology.

Common Data-link layer technologies include following:

- Ethernet – the most common LAN data-link technology
- Token Ring – almost entirely deprecated
- FDDI (Fiber Distributed Data Interface)
- 802.11 Wireless
- Frame-Relay
- ATM (Asynchronous Transfer Mode)

Layer 3 – Network

The Network layer (Layer-3) controls the internetworking of communication and has the two key responsibilities:

Logical addressing: provides a unique address that identifies both the host, and the network that host exists on.

Routing: determines the best path to a particular destination network and then routes data accordingly.

Two of the most common Network layer protocols are:

- Internet Protocol (IP)
- Novell's Internetwork Packet Exchange (IPX).

Layer 4 – Transport

The Transport layer (Layer-4) is responsible for the reliable transfer of data, by ensuring that data arrives at its destination error-free and in order.

Transport layer communication falls into two categories:

Connection-Oriented: requires a connection establishment with specific collaborated parameters before sending data.

Connectionless: requires no connection before data is sent.

Connection-oriented protocols provide several important services:

- **Segmentation and sequencing** – data is segmented into smaller parts for transport. Each segment is assigned a sequence number so that the receiving device can reassemble the data on arrival.
- **Connection establishment** – connections are established, maintained, and ultimately terminated between devices.

- **Acknowledgments** – receipt of data is confirmed through the use of acknowledgments. Otherwise, data is retransmitted.
- **Flow control (or windowing)** – data transfer rate is exchanged to prevent congestion.

The TCP/IP protocol suite incorporates two Transport layer protocols:

- Transmission Control Protocol (TCP) – connection-oriented
- User Datagram Protocol (UDP) - connectionless

Layer 5 – Session

The Session layer (Layer-5) is responsible for establishing, maintaining, and ultimately terminating sessions between devices. If a session is broken, this layer can attempt to recover the session.

Sessions communication falls under one of three categories:

- **Full-Duplex** – simultaneous two-way communication
- **Half-Duplex** – two-way communication, but not simultaneous
- **Simplex** – one-way communication

Many modern protocol suites, such as TCP/IP, do not implement Session layer protocols. Connection management is often controlled by lower layers, such as the Transport layer.

Layer 6 – Presentation

The Presentation layer (Layer-6) controls the formatting and syntax of user data for the application layer. This ensures that data from the sending application can be known by the receiving application.

Standards have been developed for the formatting of data types, such as text, images, audio, and video.

Examples of Presentation layer formats include:

- **Text** - RTF, ASCII, EBCDIC
- **Images** - GIF, JPG, TIF • Audio - MIDI, MP3, WAV
- **Movies** - MPEG, AVI, MOV

If two devices do not support the same format or syntax, the Presentation layer can provide conversion or translation services to assist communication.

Moreover, the Presentation layer can perform encryption and compression of data, as required.

Layer 7 – Application

The Application layer (Layer-7) provides the interface between the user application and the network. A web browser and an email client are examples of user applications. The user application itself does not present at the Application layer, but the protocol does. The user interacts with the application through application layer protocol.

Examples of Application layer protocols include:

- **FTP** by an FTP client
- **HTTP** by a web browser
- **POP3 and SMTP** by an email client
- **Telnet**

The Application layer provides a variety of functions:

- Identifies communication partners
- Determines resource availability
- Synchronizes communication

Basics of Network Theory and Concepts

Networks are made to share data from one computer to another computer, so the transmission of data from one computer to another can be done by transmission media like wires. The transmission media carries data after applied some techniques. This section will discuss the modulation techniques, encapsulation/ de-encapsulation methods, numbering systems for addressing, broadband vs. baseband, and many other related techniques.

Encapsulation/De-encapsulation

As data is passed from the host device to destination device by following the OSI model,

Before transmission the data each layer adds a header or sometimes trailer containing protocol information specific to that layer. These headers are called Protocol Data Units (PDUs), and the process is of adding these headers is called Encapsulation.

When the receiving device receives the data off the wire, reading and interpreting the header information, this is referred to as De-encapsulation.

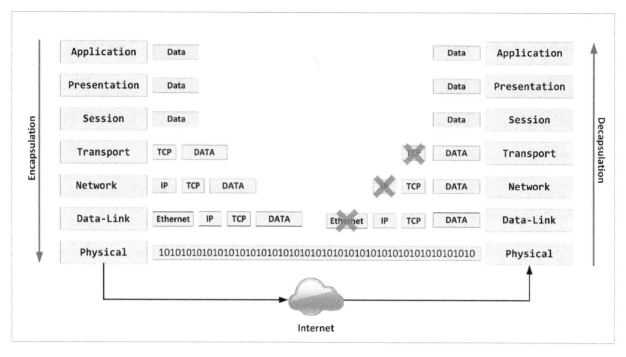

Figure 5-01: Encapsulation/De-encapsulation

During encapsulation on the sending host:

- Data from the user application is handed off to the Transport layer.
- The Transport layer adds a header containing protocol-specific information, and then hand over the segment to the Network layer.
- The Network layer adds a header containing source and destination logical addressing, and then hand over the packet to the Data-Link layer.
- The Data-Link layer adds a header containing source and destination physical addressing and other hardware-specific information.
- The Data-Link frame is then handed over to the Physical layer to be transmitted on the network medium as bits.

During de-encapsulation on the receiving host, the reverse process occurs:

- The frame is received from the physical medium.
- The Data-Link layer processes its header, strips it off, and then hands it off to the Network layer.
- The Network layer processes its header, strips it off, and then hands it off to the Transport layer.
- The Transport layer processes its header, strips it off, and then hands the data to the user application.

Modulation Techniques

In networks, modulation is the process of varying one or more properties of a waveform, called the carrier signal, with a transmitted signal that typically contains information.

Modulation of a waveform transforms a baseband message signal into a passband signal. In recent networks, modulation takes a digital or analog signal and puts it in another signal that can be physically transmitted.

The purpose of digital modulation is to transfer a digital bit stream over an analog bandpass channel. The purpose of analog modulation is to transfer an analog baseband (or lowpass) signal over an analog bandpass channel at a different frequency

The digital baseband modulation methods found in our Ethernet networks, and also known as line coding, are used to transfer a digital bit stream over a baseband channel. Baseband means that the signal being modulated used the complete available bandwidth.

Multiplexing

Multiplexing is the process in which multiple Data Streams, coming from different Sources, are combined and Transmitted over a Single Data Channel.

In networking, the two basic forms of Multiplexing are Time Division Multiplexing (TDM) and Frequency Division Multiplexing (FDM).

In Time Division Multiplexing, Transmission Time on a Single Channel is divided into non-overlapped Time Slots. Data Streams from different Sources are divided into Parts with the same size and interleaved successively into the Time Slots.

In Frequency Division Multiplexing, Data Streams are carried simultaneously on the same Transmission medium by allocating to each of them a different Frequency Band within the Bandwidth of the Single Channel.

De-multiplexing

De-multiplexing is the reverse process of multiplexing that performs at the receiving end. The multiplexed signal is separated by a device called De-multiplexer (DEMUX).

Numbering systems

As the computer understands the binary value (1s and 0s), it might be confusing that most addressing schemes such as MAC address has 0-9 value and A-F character. Well, here's a news flash: all the other addressing mechanisms are for people, not computers or network devices! That's right, in the end, all the computers and network devices can detect are the 1s and 0s; however, we make things easier on ourselves by communicating addresses in other forms such as hexadecimal or sometimes even octal addressing. So, the numbering systems are the technique to represent numbers in the computer system

architecture, every value that is saving into a computer or getting from computer memory has a defined number system.

Computer architecture supports following number systems.

- Binary number system
- Decimal number system
- Hexadecimal (hex) number system
- Octal number system

Binary

A Binary number system has only two digits that are 0 and 1. Every number represents between 0 and 1 in this number system. The base of the binary number system is 2, because it has only two digits.

Decimal

Decimal number system has only ten (10) digits from 0 to 9. Every number represents with 0,1,2,3,4,5,6, 7,8 and 9 in this number system. The base of the decimal number system is 10 because it has only 10 digits.

Octal

Octal number system has only eight (8) digits from 0 to 7. Every number represents with 0,1,2,3,4,5,6 and 7 in this number system. The base of the octal number system is 8, because it has only 8 digits.

Hexadecimal

A Hexadecimal number system has sixteen (16) alphanumeric values from 0 to 9 and A to F. Every number represents with 0,1,2,3,4,5,6, 7,8,9, A, B, C, D, E and F in this number system. The base of the hexadecimal number system is 16 because it has 16 alphanumeric values. Here A is 10, B is 11, C is 12, D is 13, E is 14 and F is 15.

Broadband/baseband

The baseband and broadband are the types of signalling techniques. These terms were developed to categorize different types of signals depending on the particular type of signal representation or modulation technique.

The main difference between baseband transmission and broadband transmission is that in the baseband transmission the whole bandwidth of the cable is consumed by a single signal. On the other hand, in the broadband transmission, multiple signals are sent on multiple frequencies simultaneously using a single channel.

Basis For comparison	Baseband	Broadband
Type of signaling	Digital	Analog
Signal range	Signals can be traveled over short distances	Signals can be traveled over long distances without being attenuated
Encoding Technique	Manchester and Differential Manchester encoding	PSK encoding
Transmission	Bidirectional	Unidirectional
Application	Best used in a bus topology	Used with a bus as well as tree topology

Table 5-01: Baseband Vs. Broadband

Bit Rates vs. Baud Rates

Bit rate and Baud rate are the two terms are often used in data communication. Bitrate is simply the number of bits (i.e., 0's and 1's) transmitted in per unit time. While Baud rate is the number of signal units transmitted per unit time that is required to represent those bits.

Basis For Comparison	Bit Rate	Baud Rate
Basic	Bit rate is the count of bits per second	Baud rate is the count of signal units per second
Bandwidth	Cannot determine the bandwidth	It can determine how much bandwidth is required to send the signal
Commonly Used	Emphasis is on computer efficiency	Transmission over the channel is more concerned
Equation	Bitrate = baud rate x the count of bits per signal unit	Baud rate = bit rate / the number of bits per signal unit

Table 5-02: Bit Rate Vs. Baud Rate

Sampling size

At its core, computers work one step at a time by turning a succession of switches on or off at very high speed. For a computer to convert analog audio signals to digital signals in a discrete step, the analog waveform is mathematically described as a sequence of discrete

amplitude values. When converting to analog, the computer captures a series of samples in specified sizes, which known as the sampling size. Each data stream sample contains items like dynamic range, frequency content, and more. The measured amplitude level in each sample is quantized by being given a value of the nearest measured increment. A computer will reproduce these values and perform them back in the same order and at the same rate at which they were captured, producing a copy of the original waveform. This is called the sample rate or sample size.

CSMA/CD

In the past, networks had contained devices called hubs. These hubs created a shared network, means that meant each computer connected to the network had equal access to the same electrical paths as the others. Since the paths were baseband and therefore could carry only one communication at a time, the computers had to take turns accessing the wire. A protocol called Carrier Sense Multiple Access with Collision Detection (CSMA/CD) was developed to sense the wire that determines whether current is fluctuating and therefore whether some other computer is using it. If another computer has the wire, then the first computer must wait until the wire is not in use before it can send its data. Once the collision is detected by the protocol, each computer will be given a set time to go again based on a back-off algorithm created by the protocol. In this way, the computers will be kept from creating subsequent collisions.

CSMA/CA

While using wireless communication between computers and devices, using a Carrier Sense Multiple Access with Collision Avoidance instead of Collision Detection.

The main purpose of this protocol is to guarantee that the data to be transmitted can be transmitted and received successfully between the two devices. It does this by first listening and then using additional frames to negotiate the network access.

Wavelength

A wavelength is a measure of distance between two successive crests (high points) or troughs (low points) in a wave. Wavelength is a repeating pattern of traveling energy like light or sound. The distance between repetitions in the waves indicates the type of wavelength on the electromagnetic radiation spectrum, which includes radio waves in the audio range and waves in the visible light range. Wavelengths are measured in kilometers, meters, millimeters, micrometers. While, radio waves have much longer wavelengths, typically measured in meters.

TCP/IP suite

The TCP/IP suite is a set of protocols used on today's computer networks specifically on the Internet. It provides end-to-end connectivity by specifying the data should be

packetized, addressed, transmitted, routed and received on a TCP/IP network. This functionality is arranged into four consideration layers, and each protocol in the suite operates in a particular layer. This section will focus only on three protocols ICMP, TCP, and UDP.

Internet Control Message Protocol (ICMP)

ICMP works at the Network layer of the OSI model and the Internet layer of the TCP/IP suite. ICMP provides error checking and reporting functionality. Additionally, ICMP provides many functions; the most commonly known is its ping utility. The ping utility is most often used for troubleshooting. In a typical ping scenario, an administrator uses a host's command line and the ping utility to send a stream of packets called an echo request to another host. When the destination host receives the packets, ICMP sends back a stream of packets referred to as an echo reply. This confirms that the connection between the two hosts is configured properly and that TCP/IP is operational.

User Datagram Protocol (UDP)

UDP also operates at the Transport layer of the OSI model and uses IP as its transport protocol, but it is a connectionless protocol means it does not guarantee the delivery of packets because UDP does not establish a session. However, UDP is quite demanding instead of TCP because the advantage of UDP is its low overhead regarding bandwidth and processing effort. Whereas a TCP header has 11 fields of information that have to be processed, a UDP header has only 4 fields. Applications that can handle their own acknowledgments and that do not require the additional features of TCP might use UDP to take advantage of the lower overhead. Services such as the Domain Name System (DNS) service also take advantage of the lower overhead provided by UDP.

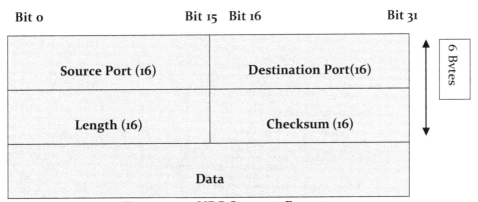

Figure 5-02: UDP Segment Format

TCP

TCP is a connection-oriented protocol that works at the Transport layer of the OSI model. It uses IP as its transport protocol and assists IP by providing a guaranteed mechanism for delivery. TCP requires establishing a session first between two computers before communicating. Additionally, TCP also includes features such as flow control, sequencing, and error detection and correction. TCP works by a process referred to as a three-way handshake.

The TCP three-way handshake works as follows:

1. TCP sends a short message called an SYN to the target host.
2. The target hosts open a connection for the request and send back an acknowledgment message called an SYN ACK.
3. The host that originated the request sends back another acknowledgment called an ACK, confirming that it has received the SYN ACK message and that the session is ready to be used to transfer data.

A similar process is used to close the session when the data exchange is complete. If a packet is not acknowledged within the timeout period, the packet is resent automatically by TCP. The only disadvantage of a connection-oriented protocol is that the large overhead associated with the acknowledgments inclines to slow it down.

Bit 0	Bit 15	Bit 16	Bit 31
Source Port (16)		Destination Port(16)	
Sequence Number (32)			
Acknowledgment Number (32)			
Header Length (4)	Reserved (6)	Code Bits (6)	Window (16)
Checksum (16)		Urgent (16)	
Options (0 or 32 if any)			
Data (varies)			

24 Bytes

Figure 5-03: TCP Segment Format

Collision

A collision is the result of two devices on the same Ethernet network attempting to transmit data at exactly the same time (milliseconds). The network detects the "**collision**" of the two transmitted packets and discards them both.

Common Wireless Standards

This section will discuss the most common wireless standards used in today's networks.

802.11 a/b/g/n/ac Standards

802.11 is the wireless standards specified by IEEE used for wireless LAN technology. It operates over-the-air interface between a wireless client and a base station or between two wireless clients. The IEEE specification accepted in 1997. The original 802.11 standard used a frequency-hopping spread spectrum (FHSS) radio signal. There have been gone through many versions since the beginning. The following are the major 802.11 standards in use today:

802.11a

802.11a uses orthogonal frequency division multiplexing (OFDM) to increase bandwidth. This standard uses the 5 GHz radio band and can transmit at up to 54 Mbps. It is not commonly used today.

802.11b

802.11b Uses direct sequence spread spectrum (DSSS) modulation technique that operates in the 2.4 GHz wireless band. This standard can transmit at up to 11 Mbps with fallback rates of 5.5 Mbps, 2 Mbps, and 1 Mbps. It has been updated by the newer and faster standards.

802.11g

802.11g Uses dual modulation techniques DSSS and OFDM and operates at 2.4 GHz wireless band. This standard enhances the 802.11b standard and can transmit at speeds up to 54 Mbps. It is backward compatible with 802.11b, since both can use DSSS and the 2.4 GHz band.

802.11n

802.11n also uses DSSS and OFDM at the 2.4 GHz and the 5 GHz bands. This standard enhances the 802.11g standard and can transmit at speeds up to 600 Mbps, although most

devices support speeds only up to about 300 Mbps. This standard is backward compatible with 802.11g and 802.11b and 802.11a.

802.11ac

802.11ac Uses the 5 GHz band and Multiple Input Multiple Output (MIMO) technologies This standard enhances the 802.11n standard and can transmit at speeds up to 1 Gbps, although most devices in use today support speeds only up to about 500 Mbps. Devices that support 802.11n standard also support 802.11ac.

Common Wired Connectivity Standard

Today's businesses depend on many types of wired connections to provide for the transfer of data throughout their networks. The following section will discuss the main types of wired connections and the standards associated with them. These will include Ethernet, wiring, and broadband standards.

Ethernet standards

In the early 1980s, the Institute of Electrical and Electronics Engineers (IEEE), that defines industry-wide standards in the fields of electronics and computing, adopted the DIX Ethernet standard as a general standard for networking. The IEEE working group (or committee) responsible for general networking standards known as the 802 committees, and Ethernet became IEEE 802.3 standard.

Ethernet Standardization are as follows:

10BaseT

The term 10BaseT describes an Ethernet cabling system generally use in a star bus topology. 10BaseT follow the naming convention used for earlier Ethernet cabling systems. In 10BaseT 10 refers to the speed: 10 Mbps, Base refers to the Baseband modulation, and T refers to the cable type: Twisted-pair cable. As per assumption, the maximum distance permitted between a node and a switch is 100 meters.

100BaseT

100BaseT follows the same terminologies as 10BaseT. 100BaseT is also known as Fast Ethernet that operates at 100 Mbps over twisted-pair cabling.

1000BaseT

1000BaseT (IEEE 802.3ab) Gigabit Ethernet over four pairs of wires in CAT 5e or better UTP cabling.

1000BaseTX

1000BaseTX belongs to category 5 cabling. It contains two-pair UTP wiring up to 100 meters long. Not used today and has been replaced by Category 6 cabling.

10GBaseT

10GBaseT is a standard created by the IEEE 802.3an committee to provide 10Gbps connections over conventional UTP cables (Category 5e, 6, or 7 cables). 10GBaseT supports RJ-45 used for Ethernet LANs. It can support signal transmission at the full 100-meter distance specified for LAN wiring. If you need to implement a 10Gbps link, this is the most economical way.

100BaseFX

100BaseFX (IEEE 802.3u) Uses 62.5/125-micron multimode fiber cabling, support up to 412 meters long and point-to-point topology. It uses ST and SC connectors, which are media-interface connectors.

10Base2

10Base2 is also known as thinnet and can support up to 30 workstations on a single segment. It uses 10Mbps of baseband technology, coax up to 185 meters in length, and a physical and logical bus with Attachment Unit Interface (AUI) connectors. In 10Base2 10 means, 10Mbps and Base mean baseband technology, and the 2 means almost 200 meters. 10Base2 Ethernet cards use BNC (Bayonet Neill-Concelman) and T-connectors to connect to a network.

10GBaseSR

An application of 10 Gigabit Ethernet that uses short-wavelength lasers at 850 nm over multimode fiber. It has a maximum transmission distance between 2 and 300 meters, depending on the size and quality of the fiber.

10GBaseER

An application of 10 Gigabit Ethernet running over single-mode fiber that uses extra-long-wavelength lasers at 1,550 nm. It has the longest transmission distances possible of all the 10 Gigabit technologies: anywhere from 2 meters up to 40 km, also depending on the size and quality of the fiber used.

10GBaseSW

10GBaseSW defined by IEEE as 802.3ae is a mode of 10GBaseS for Multimode Fiber (MMF) with an 850 nm laser transceiver and a bandwidth of 10Gbps. It can support up to 300 meters of cable length. This media type is designed to connect to SONET equipment.

IEEE 1905.1-2013

IEEE 1905.1-2013 is an IEEE standard that defines a convergent digital home network for both wireless and wired technologies. The IEEE 1905.1 Standard Working Group is sponsored by the IEEE Power Line Communication Standards Committee (PLCSC). The idea behind the 1905.1 technology standards is a simple setup, configuration, and operation of home networking devices using both wired and wireless technologies. This will take advantage of the performance, coverage, and mobility benefits of multiple interfaces (Ethernet, Wi-Fi, Powerline, and MoCA), which enables better coverage and throughput in every room for both wireless and fixed devices.

Ethernet over HDMI

HDMI Ethernet Channel technology combines video, audio, and data streams into a single HDMI cable, combining the signal quality of HDMI connectivity with the power and flexibility of home entertainment networking. It incorporates a dedicated data channel into the HDMI link, enabling high-speed, bi-directional networking at up to 100Mbps.

Ethernet over power line

The IEEE Standard 1901-2011 is a standard for high speed up to 500 Mbit/s at the physical layer of communication devices through electric power lines, often called broadband over power lines (BPL). BPL will allow just to plug a computer into a wall power socket and have more than 500Mbps for up to 1,500 meters. It can also be used to deliver Internet access to the home users.

Wiring standards

As we know, UTP cables and connectors come with associated color codes and wiring schemes. Each wire inside a UTP cable must connect to the proper pin on the connector at each end of the cable. The wires are color-coded to help in properly matching the ends. Two industry organizations, the Telecommunications Industry Association (TIA) and the Electronic Industries Alliance (EIA), developed a variety of standard color coding schemes to facilitate installation. EIA disbanded in 2011 and moved the standards to TIA, but the term TIA/EIA or EIA/TIA still discussed by the technicians.

EIA/TIA 568A/568B

Two major wiring standards, T568A and T568B, determine the order of the wires placed in the RJ45 connector. Using an established color-code scheme ensures that the wires match up correctly at each end of the cable. This regularity makes troubleshooting and repair easier.

The T568A wiring standard has the wires in the order white/green, green, white/orange, blue, white/blue, orange, white/brown, and finally brown. The only difference between

the two standards is that the orange and green pairs of wires are interchanged regarding their pin assignment. The most common wiring standard in use today is T568B standard.

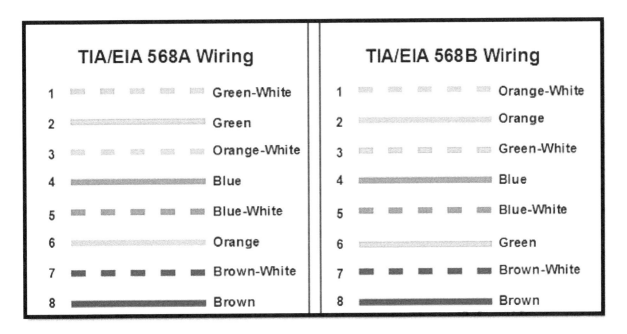

Figure 5-04: EIA/TIA 568A/568B

Broadband standards

In this section, standards of the broadband system are described. The main standard of broadband is DOCSIS. Although it has many versions of this standards, but all of these are beyond of this discussion.

DOCSIS

Data over Cable Service Interface Specifications (DOCSIS) This specification provides the interface requirements for a data-over-cable system, including that of high-bandwidth data transfer to an existing cable TV system. All cable modems and similar devices have to measure up to this standard.

Implementation of Appropriate Policies or Procedures

In a scenario in which you are in charge of implementing the policies and procedures in your organization, you should know the following information. As a general rule, policies and procedures should be clearly outlined in writing in your organization. These rules and procedures are written and authorized by the management. These policies may

include Security Policies, Network Policies, Acceptable policy use, and standard business documents.

Security Policies

Security policies should be designed and acceptable by the concerned authority members. While designing security policies it should be kept in mind, the authorized person will have permission to enter the organization and uses assets while unauthorized guys will have not permission to do this. Security policies can be done by locks, cameras, timers, guards, dogs, and so on.

Network Policies

A good network security policy should be setting a standard of security by establishing access of users to resources with the least privilege that each user of the network needs to do their job, and that includes the administrators. It will establish local controls and logging mechanisms that can be used in the event of a breach. It will also establish security checks on access to the network from a remote location.

Acceptable use policy

An Acceptable Use Policy (AUP) is a simple set of rules that define how the computer equipment and network can be used. It is generally a very small document that a new employee can read and understand quickly, so they know what they are signing. It may refer to other documents such as the larger security policy, but it should be concise and easy to understand. It should clearly define the expected code of conduct, what should be considered inappropriate or even illegal, and the concerns of violating the policy.

Standard Business Documents

Standard Business Documents does not relate to the security policies but instead related to the business. These documents should be easy to understand for the customer that makes the business viable.

The business-related documents that you should understand are the following:

SLA

A Service-Level Agreement (SLA) is the part of a service contract between a service provider and the customer that fully defines what services are expected and how they are to be accomplished. It might include a contracted delivery time for initial services and then an expectation of mean time between failures (MTBF) and mean time to repair (MTTR) when a failure occurs. It might also identify a specified quality of service that could be measured by data rates, throughput, and so on.

MOU

A Memorandum of Understanding (MOU) is a formal interpretation of a gentleman's agreement or handshake. It establishes expectation levels of both parties, so as to prevent future arguments, but it holds no enforceable power and implies no legal commitment on behalf of either party. The main reason an MOU is sometimes used is that the two parties are in different countries, establishes an MOU agreement to avoid time wasting documents and legal fees. MOUs are also sometimes used internally to an organization to establish the specific responsibilities of various departments regarding a project.

MLA

A Master License Agreement (MLA) is a document created by a software company that defines how their product can be used. It defines the proper use of the software and the liabilities associated with its improper use. It may also define how the software may be modified and who should benefit or be compensated for any profits related to its use. MLAs are commonly used by large software vendors with their large customers.

SOW

A Statement of Work (SOW) is a formal document that defines the work activities, what is to be delivered, and the timeline associated with its delivery. It usually includes pricing information and payment terms as well. Also, it may include compensation terms to the customer if the work is not done on time or in a satisfactory manner. A SOW is generally drawn up by an attorney and is a legally enforceable document.

Summarize Safety Practices

Everyone has a worth taking and has its value, so management should always maintain safety standards that minimize the chance of danger to employees and damage to network equipment and servers. This might include electrical safety measures for people and devices, emergency procedures, fire-suppression systems, and so on.

Electrical safety

IT administrator spend a lot of time in dealing with electrical devices. Therefore, electrical safety should be anxious in all procedures. In this section, we'll look at key issues involved with electrical safety, relevant to preventing injuries and for preventing damage to network equipment.

Grounding

Grounding is the electrical term for providing a path for an electrical charge to follow for returning to earth. When working with electric devices, it should be assured that the devices are grounded. It provides safety from harm and damaging electrical goods.

Electrostatic discharge (ESD)

Electrostatic discharge (ESD) is a sudden spark of electricity that sometimes happens when two materials are moved close to each other and have an opposite charge. ESD can be generated easily by walking across a carpeted floor.

To prevent ESD damage, always use mats, wearing a wrist strap, using antistatic bags, spray, and so on when working on electrical equipment.

Static

When ESD is created, it's a form of static energy. When computers are used in the area where extremely dry conditions make the problem of static electricity worse. This is why the humidity of the area must be controlled so that it's not too humid; which causes corrosion of electrical connections, and not too dry; which causes static buildup and potential for damage.

Installation safety

During preventing electrical damage, the safety against installation is very important. So here are the broad categorize regard safety installation.

Lifting equipment

When lifting heavy equipment, don't be a hero. Lift with your legs and not your back. If there is any question as to whether it's too heavy, get some help. Use tools such as a hand truck to lower the load and make it safer.

Rack installation

Follow the vendor recommendations when installing and securing the racks. The main thing that you want is for a rack to fall over while you are loading it up with very expensive equipment. Follow your organizational guideline for the correct installation of your server racks.

Placement

The main factor to consider in the placement of a rack is that it should be secure and stable. Some racks stand on the floor and are sometimes attached to the floor. Others are made to stand next to a wall and take their stability from wall mounts as well. Racks should be placed in such a way that you can easily reach the front and back of it to control the cables.

Tool safety

Using the right tools for the right job in an appropriate manner for achieving safety reasons.

Material Safety Data Sheet (MSDS)

A Material Safety Data Sheet (MSDS) is a document or web page that prescribes the correct way to use a product that could be dangerous if handled improperly. In this document describe the safety instruction, room temperature, humidity, potential health risk and so on. An MSDS also describes what damage could be caused and how to treat the injury. MSDS can get while purchasing the product and it also is available on company's website.

Emergency procedures

Every organization should be prepared for emergencies of all types. If possible, this planning should start with the design of the facility and its layout. This section will go through some of the components of a well-planned emergency system along with some guidelines for maintaining safety on a regular basis.

Building layout

Planning for emergencies can start with the layout of the building.

Here are some key considerations:

- All walls should have at least two-hour fire rating.
- Doors must be a peaceful entry.
- The location and type of fire suppression systems should be known.
- Flooring in server rooms and wiring closets should be raised to help mitigate flooding damage.
- Separate AC units must be dedicated to the information processing facilities.
- Backup and alternate power sources should exist.

Fire escape plan

The organization should develop such plan that identifies the escape route in the event of a fire. They should create a facility map showing the escape route for each section of the building, keeping in mind that it's better to use multiple exits to move people out quickly. These diagrams should be paste in all areas.

Safety/emergency exits

All escape routes on the map should have the following characteristics:

- Clearly marked and well ignited

- Wide enough to accommodate the expected number of people
- Clear of obstacles

Fail open/fail close

Door systems that have electronic locks may lose power during a fire. When they do, they may lock automatically or fail to close and unlock automatically or fail open. While a fail close setting may enhance security during an electrical outage, it should be considering the effect of the departure and take steps to ensure that everyone can get out of the building when needed.

Emergency alert system

All areas of the building should be equipped with a system to alert all employees when a fire or any other type of emergency occurs. It might be advisable to connect the facility to the Emergency Alert System (EAS).

Fire suppression systems

Fire extinguishers are important and should be placed throughout a facility when large numbers of electronic devices are present; it is worth the money to protect them with a fire-suppression system. Fire suppression systems generally come in two flavors: water sprinkler systems and gaseous agents. The gaseous agent is the best for your network equipment and servers. In gaseous agent, an inert gas is used that takes the oxygen away from the fire and puts it out. But before any agents are released into an enclosed area, an alarm will generally sound that tells when to leave the area.

Heating, ventilation, and air conditioning (HVAC)

The heating and air-conditioning systems must support the huge amounts of electronic equipment deployed by most enterprises. Computing equipment and networking devices like routers and switches do not like the following conditions: Excessive heat, High humidity, Low humidity, which can damage equipment.

Installation and Configuration of Equipment in the Appropriate Location using Best Practices

When infrastructure equipment is purchased and deployed, the ultimate success of the deployment can depend on selecting the proper equipment, determining its proper location in the facility, and installing it correctly. Let's look at some common data center or server room equipment and a few best practices for managing these facilities.

Intermediate Distribution Frame

An intermediate distribution frame (IDF) serves as a distribution point for cables from the main distribution frame (MDF) to individual cables connected to equipment in areas distant from these frames. It is connected to the MDF and is used to provide greater flexibility regarding the distribution of the communications lines to the building. It is typically a sturdy metal rack that is designed to hold the bulk of cables that are coming from all over the building.

Main distribution frame

The main distribution frame connects equipment to cables and subscriber carrier equipment. It also terminates cables that run to intermediate distribution frames distributed throughout the facility. It often has protection devices for lightning or other electrical spikes. It is also used as a central testing point.

Cable management

There are a large number of cables coming from the distribution frames, to managing these cables is important both to protect the integrity of the cables and to prevent overheating of the networking devices caused by masses of disruptive cabling.

Patch panels

A patch panel is generally a rack or wall-mounted structure that arrange cable connections. A patch cable generally plugs into the front side, while the back holds the punched-down connection of a permanent cable. The purpose of the patch panel is to offer the administrator way to change the path of a signal quickly when needed. For example, if a cable inside a wall becomes damaged or fails, a network administrator can patch around that cable by simply changing the connection on two patch panels.

Power management

Electronic devices of all types always need clean and uninterrupted power. Network infrastructure provides such power management system that will not be fluctuated and never facing power loss. Here are some power management devices that will become a part of your power management system.

Power converters/ Inverters

As we know, regular electricity is not suitable for network devices or servers. Before supply electricity to these devices, the current must pass through such converters that convert the AC power to DC power referred to as power Convertors.

There is also a special device that converts DC power to AC power. It produces no power and must be connected to a DC source referred to as power Inverters.

UPSs and Circuits

There are two main circuits to provide for power when the power company is not providing it anymore, namely inline UPS and offline UPS. In the case of an offline circuit, which is not commonly used in today's networks. It has a very fast switch transfers power to the secondary source as soon as it senses that the primary power source is down. Due to its fast switching, it is rarely used in today's network. On the other hand, in the inline circuit, the components are already running on power that is going through the battery system, which is constantly recharged by the power company. In the event that the power from the power company fails, the batteries continue to supply the power that the devices need, and often then a diesel or natural gas engine kicks in and turns on a generator that recharges the batteries.

Power redundancy

Some large organizations whose role is to host computers and network of the other organization and ensure that they will be operational at 24/7. These types of organization have a whole other power company or at least another power grid. It might also be used by utility companies, government installations, and so on. The idea is that even if one grid goes down, the other will stay up.

Device placement

The device should be placed in such a way that heavy device place at the bottom and lightweight devices place on the top of the heavy device. Therefore, switches go at the top, followed by routers, servers, and finally the UPS at the bottom of the rack. This is because the UPS generally has very heavy batteries in it and you don't want to make the rack top heavy.

Air Flow

Most networking devices and servers produce heat as a side effect of just being powered on. Airflow around the equipment is critically important to keep devices in operation. When hot air is not removed from the area and replaced with cooler air, the devices overheat and start doing things like rebooting unexpectedly, and maybe the high heat will shorten the life of the costly equipment.

The air flow between racks must be controlled to remove the heat. Some organizations use thermal dividers to create hot and cold zones that they can work with individually. Sometimes heat is removed from the top of a hot zone by forcing the cooler air from the cold zone into the hot zone air. The hotter air will then rise to the top and be collected and cooled or eliminated from the place.

Cable trays

Cable trays are metal trays used to organize the cabling neatly and keep it away from the heating areas. Cable trays are often used in today's networks to support insulated cables used for communication and power. They provide a physical management system that protects the cables but also leaves them accessible for inspection and any necessary changes. Also, additional cables can be easily added to a tray by just dropping in another cable instead of having to pull it through a duct.

Rack systems

Rack systems are used to hold and arrange the servers, routers, switches, firewalls, and other rack-ready equipment. Rack system provides a cleaner appearance and easier management, better airflow, redundant power supplies, and so on. These racks can place switches, routers, UPSs, and other equipment as well. They are typically 19 inches wide to accommodate all of the equipment that is specifically made to fit that width. Devices that are made to fit these are referred to as rack-mounted devices. The height of the devices is measured in rack units that are each called a U, and a standard rack stands 42 U tall. A U is approximately 1¾ inches. Rack systems provide a great amount of flexibility in their design.

Server rail racks

Server rail racks are used to hold servers in one of the types of racks (Two-post racks or Four-post racks). They are designed to hold the server while allowing the server to be slid out from the rack for maintenance.

Two-Post Racks

Two-post racks provide just two vertical posts to which devices can be attached from the front and back. They are especially good for telecommunications installations of equipment that is generally lighter and requires less maintenance.

Four-Post Racks

Four-post racks have four vertical posts that allow for the installation of rails and the support of heavier devices such as servers, switches, routers, and so on. They are generally more expensive than two-post racks.

Free-standing racks

A freestanding rack is one that does not reach the ceiling and stands on its own.

Labeling

In a data center, server room, or wiring closet, correct and updated labeling of ports, systems, circuits, and patch panels help a lot in troubleshooting and configuration updates. In this section, some types of labeling discuss below.

Port Labeling

Ports on switches, routers, patch panels, and another system should be properly labeled and resemble with the wall outlets to which they lead. Port labeling has been done by considering an agreement with the naming convention which is used because all technicians are operating from the same point of reference. They also should be updated in any case where changes are made that directive an update.

System labeling

Other systems that are installed in racks, such as servers, firewall appliances, and redundant power supplies, should also be labeled with IP addresses and DNS names that the devices hold.

Circuit labeling

Circuits arriving at the facility should also be labeled. Circuit label can be done over electrical receptacles, circuit breaker panels, and power distribution units by circuit information, voltage and amperage, the type of electrical receptacle, and wherein the data center the duct terminates.

Naming conventions

A naming convention guides and manages to label and ensures regularity. No matter what name or numbering system you use, be regular.

Patch panel labeling

The significant issue when labeling patch panels are to ensure that they're correct. Also, you need to make sure that the wall outlet they're connected to is the same.

Rack monitoring

Racks should contain monitoring devices that can be operated remotely. These devices can be used to monitor the following issues:

- Temperature
- Humidity
- Physical Security
- Water Leaks
- Vibration
- Smoke

Rack security

Rack devices should be secured from the robbery. There are several locking systems that can be used to facilitate this.

These locks are typically implemented in the doors on the front of a rack cabinet:

- Swing handle/wing knob locks with common key
- Swing handle/wing knob locks with unique key
- Swing handle with the number and key lock
- Electronic locks
- Radio-frequency identification (RFID) card locks

Explain the Basics of Change Management Procedures

As we know, documentation always needed when we make configuration changes in future. So, these documents should be changed with the system changes. In this section, we will discuss documenting the reason for the change, change requests, approval processes, maintenance windows, notification, and final documentation of the change.

Document reason for a change

Every change in a network should be properly documented. Although it is not an easy task to update the document concerning any changes occurs in the network. For this, many organizations hire people to perform this responsibility and some uses software to update the track.

Change request

A change should start its process as a change request. This request will move through various stages of the approval process and should include certain parts of information that will guide those tasked with approving or denying it.

Configuration procedures

The particular steps required to implement the change and the particular devices involved should be detailed. Complete documentation should be produced and submitted with a formal report to the change management board.

Rollback process

Changes always carry a risk. Before any changes are implemented, plans for reversing the changes and recovering from any opposing effects from the change should be known. Those making the changes should be completely briefed in these rollback process, and they should show a clear understanding of them before to implementing the changes.

Potential impact

One of the benefits of performing this process is that it can identify systems that may need to be more closely monitored for their reaction to the change as the change is being implemented.

Notification

When all systems that may be affected by the change are identified, system owners should be notified of all changes that could potentially affect them.

Approval process

The actual approval process will depend on the organization. Some organizations may approve by with a verbal statement of the change, while others may require documentation. The main factor is that the change should reflect the overall goals of the company regarding network connectivity, disaster recovery, fault tolerance, security, and so on.

Maintenance window

A maintenance window is an amount of time a system will be down or unavailable during the implementation of changes. Before this window of time is specified, all affected systems should be examined with respect to their criticality in supporting mission-critical operations.

Authorized downtime

When the time required to make the change has been compared to the maximum allowable downtime, a system can suffer and the optimum time for the change is identified, and the authorized downtime can be specified. These amounts help reach a final decision on when the change will be made.

Notification of change

When the change has been completed and a sufficient amount of time has passed for issues to manifest themselves, all affected members should be notified that the change is complete. At that time, these affected members can continue to monitor the situation for any residual problems.

Documentation

The process isn't complete until the paperwork is complete. In this case, the following should be updated to reflect the changed state of the network:

- Network configurations
- Additions to network

- Physical location changes

Compare and Contrast the following Ports and Protocols

There are many protocols run on the different layers of the OSI model and that protocols are identified by their port numbers. This section will discuss the importance of protocols and ports associated with them.

80 HTTP

Hypertext Transfer Protocol (HTTP) is the protocol that users utilize to browse the World Wide Web. HTTP clients use a browser to make special requests from an HTTP server that contains the files they required. The files on the HTTP server are formatted in web languages such as Hypertext Markup Language (HTML) and are located using a Uniform Resource Locator (URL). The URL contains the type of request being generated (http://, for example), the DNS name of the server to which the request is being processed, and optionally the path to the file on the server.

443 HTTPS

Hypertext Transfer Protocol Secure (HTTPS) provides a more secure solution that uses a Secure Sockets Layer (SSL) to encrypt information that is sent between the client and the server. For HTTPS to operate, both the client and the server must support it. While browsing through HTTPS

you need to fill out forms, sign in, authenticate; and encrypt an HTTP message when you make a reservation or buy something online.

137-139 NetBIOS

NetBIOS is a legacy protocol that was used by computers running Microsoft operating systems as a name-resolution tool. It has been superseded now by DNS. There is still an implementation of NetBIOS over TCP/IP on newer operating systems, if a legacy application requires it.

110 POP

Post Office Protocol (POP) gives us a storage facility for incoming mail, and the latest version is called POP3. POP3 is one of the protocols that is used to retrieve email from SMTP servers. Using POP3, clients connect to the server, authenticate, and then download their email. Once they have downloaded their email, they can read it.

Normally, the email is then deleted from the server, although some systems hold a copy of the email for a period of time specified by an administrator. One of the drawbacks of POP3 authentication is that it is generally performed in clear text. This means that an attacker could sniff your POP3 password from the network as you enter it.

143 IMAP

Internet Message Access Protocol (IMAP)v4 is another protocol that is used to retrieve email from SMTP servers, but IMAPv4 offers some advantages over POP3. IMAPv4 provides a more flexible method of handling email. You can read your email on the email server and then determine to want to download this email to your own PC. Since the email can stay in the mailbox on the server, you can retrieve it from any computer that you want to use, provided that the computer has the software installed to allow you to access the server. Google Gmail is a good example of an IMAPv4 type of service. You can access your Gmail account from any browser. You can then read, answer, and forward email without downloading the messages to the computer that you are using. This can be very useful for the traveling users.

25   SMTP

Simple Mail Transfer Protocol (SMTP) defines the process of email transferring between the hosts on a network. SMTP works at the Application layer of the OSI model and uses TCP to guarantee error-free delivery of messages to hosts.

5060/5061 SIP

Session Initiation Protocol (SIP) is an incredibly popular signalling protocol used to build up and break down multimedia communication sessions for many things like voice and video calls, video conferencing, streaming multimedia distribution, instant messaging, presence information, and online games over the Internet. It also enables IP telephony networks to utilize advanced call features such as SS7.

2427/2727 MGCP

Media Gateway Control Protocol (MGCP) is a standard protocol for handling the signalling and session management necessary during a multimedia conference. The protocol defines a means of communication between a media gateway, which converts data from the required format for a circuit-switched network to that required format for a packet-switched network. MGCP can be used to set up, maintain, and terminate calls between multiple endpoints.

5004/5005 RTP

RTP defines a standardized packet format for delivering audio and video over the Internet. It is frequently used in streaming, video conferencing, and push-to-talk applications.

1720   H.323

H.323 is a protocol that provides a standard for video on an IP network that defines how real-time audio, video, and data information is transmitted. This standard provides signalling, multimedia, and bandwidth control solution. H.323 uses the RTP standard for communication. H.323 is also used for multimedia communications on mobile phones and other portable devices.

69   TFTP

Trivial File Transfer Protocol (TFTP) has similar functionality as FTP that both allows the transfer of files within a network. Although FTP allows for the browsing of files and folders on a server, but TFTP requires to know the exact name of the file you want to transfer and the exact location where to find the file. Also, whereas FTP uses the connection-oriented TCP, TFTP uses the connectionless UDP. TFTP is most often used for simple downloads such as transferring firmware to a network device, for example, a router or a switch.

445 SMB

Server Message Block (SMB) is a legacy protocol that is used to provide shared access to files, folders, printers, and so on over a computer network. It has been substituted by other more efficient and more secure protocols.

3389 RDP

Remote Desktop Protocol (RDP) is a proprietary protocol used by computers running the MS operating systems, although clients exist that allow Linux and Unix systems to connect to MS computers using RDP. It can be used to connect to a computer and take control of the system remotely. Every MS client since Windows XP has RDP software built-in. For security means, it is not initially enabled. To connect to a computer remotely, you must enable the software and configure the appropriate authentication.

Mind Map:

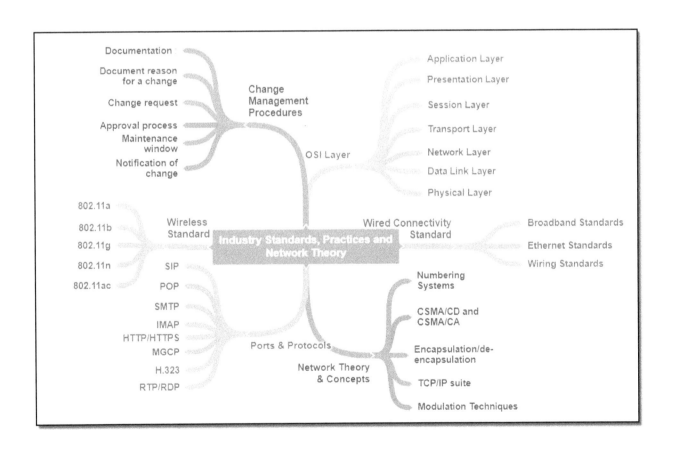

References

https://www.cengage.com/resource_uploads/downloads/1111138214_259146.pdf

http://nvlpubs.nist.gov/nistpubs/SpecialPublications/NIST.SP.800-12r1.pdf

http://bok.ahima.org/doc?oid=300244#.WkzPTN-WaM8

http://www.iaps.com/security-overview.html

http://www.brighthub.com/computing/smb-security/articles/31234.aspx

https://www.kaspersky.com/resource-center/threats/top-seven-mobile-security-threats-smart-phones-tablets-and-mobile-internet-devices-what-the-future-has-in-store

https://us.norton.com/internetsecurity-malware-what-is-a-botnet.html

https://www.safaribooksonline.com/library/view/improving-web-application/9780735651128/ch02s07.html

https://msdn.microsoft.com/en-us/library/ff648641.aspx

https://www.cisco.com/c/en/us/td/docs/ios/12_2/security/configuration/guide/fsecur_c/scfdenl.html

https://www.ietf.org/rfc/rfc3704.txt

Note from the Author:

Reviews are gold to authors! If you have enjoyed this book and helped you along certification, would you consider rating it and reviewing it?

Link to Product Page: